THE TIMES THAT TRY MEN'S SOULS

ALSO BY JOYCE LEE MALCOLM

Peter's War: A New England Slave Boy and the American Revolution

Guns and Violence: The English Experience

The Struggle for Sovereignty: Seventeenth-Century English Political Tracts, 2 vols.

To Keep and Bear Arms: The Origins of an Anglo-American Right

Caesar's Due: Loyalty and King Charles, 1642-1646

The Scene of the Battle, 1775

The Tragedy of Benedict Arnold

THE TIMES THAT TRY MEN'S SOULS

The Adams, the Quincys, and the Battle
for Loyalty in the American Revolution

JOYCE LEE MALCOLM

PEGASUS BOOKS
NEW YORK LONDON

THE TIMES THAT TRY MEN'S SOULS

Pegasus Books, Ltd.
148 West 37th Street, 13th Floor
New York, NY 10018

First Pegasus Books cloth edition December 2023

Interior design by Maria Fernandez

Library of Congress Cataloging-in-Publication Data is available.

ISBN: 978-1-63936-475-6

10 9 8 7 6 5 4 3 2 1

Printed in the United States of America
Distributed by Simon & Schuster
www.pegasusbooks.com

To my husband Michael

with love

Contents

Preface

Posterity! You will never know, how much it cost the present Generation,
to preserve your Freedom! I hope you will make a good Use of it. If you do
not, I shall repent in Heaven, that I ever took half the Pains to preserve it.
—John Adams to Abigail Adams, April 26, 1777[1]

We all live surrounded by great events in the larger world. Most of these don't touch our daily lives, though they give us food for conversation. Others, like large economic fluctuations, epidemics, dramatic weather, or political disruptions and wars, yank us from our ordinary activities as the larger world thrusts itself into our smaller one.

All wars are dangerous and painful. Foreign wars pull men from home to fight and perhaps die abroad and bring changes at home. But the very worst war, that can sever family relationships and bonds of friendship, that touches even those of no fixed opinion, is a civil war. The American Revolution was one such war.

Growing intolerance of differences, leading to intimidation and violence, required oaths of allegiance, intransigence on the part of both colonial leaders and royal officials, lost opportunities for reconciliation, and forced individuals to choose sides. Those opposed to British policies took charge of local and colonial governments. Those loyal to the royal government, its officials and sympathizers, fled into exile and were eventually banished or stayed home to support and join the British troops or play the spy and provide them with intelligence. Many, perhaps most people, were cautiously neutral, keeping their heads down trying to get on with ordinary life in extraordinary times.

The wrenching pain of families who split along party lines, with husbands divided from wives, fathers from children, siblings and close friends from each other, is the central topic of this book. It is also about loyalists who fled to England, confident Britain would win promptly. Their lives as exiles eventually brought the realization that they did not fit into English society and were, in fact, Americans longing for home, wondering whether there would, or could, be reconciliation.

The sadness of the separation and its permanence is an important and often ignored part of the Revolutionary War story. Those who risked their lives battling the great British Empire and those who left home loyal to the British government were all caught in the times that tried their souls.

Introduction

God knows what is for the best, but I fear our perpetual banishment from America is written in the book of fate; nothing but the hopes of once more revisiting my native soil, enjoying my old friends within my own little domain, has hitherto supported my drooping courage; but that prop taken away leaves me in a condition too distressing to think of.
—Samuel Curwen, exiled from Salem, Massachusetts, judge, 1777[1]

I t was September 1778, the third year of the Revolutionary War, when Massachusetts passed the Banishment Act that sealed the fate of the exiles. The act was a bill of attainder, now unconstitutional. The 300 persons listed were simply pronounced guilty of having left the state and either "joined the enemies thereof," or at least having left when "they ought to have afforded their utmost aid . . . against the invasions of a cruel enemy."

Those banished included wealthy gentlemen, judges, former office-holders, tradesmen, merchants, blacksmiths, mariners, yeomen, and laborers. Nearly all had left family members behind, fathers and mothers, brothers and sisters, wives and children. Samuel Quincy, only surviving son of Josiah Quincy, was one of these exiles. His wife opposed his politics and refused to accompany him to England. She and their three children abandoned their grand Boston mansion and moved into her brother's home in Cambridge to await whatever happened. Samuel would never return. John Adams's best friend, Jonathan Sewell, sailed to England with his wife and children after being attacked and threatened by a violent mob. His wife's dear sister Dorothy was married to the prominent patriot John Hancock. James Otis, great champion of American rights, brother of the historian Mercy Otis Warren, was married to Ruth Cunningham, whom he loved dearly although he described her as a "High Tory." They had two daughters; Elizabeth, who married Captain Brown of the British army, and Mary, who married Benjamin Lincoln, son of a major general in Washington's army. Benjamin Franklin's son William did not flee but remained the loyalist governor of New Jersey. He was captured and paroled on his promise to take no further part in the conflict but continued to sabotage the patriot cause. Few families, famous or less known, escaped painful divisions.

Samuel Curwen, a judge from Salem, Massachusetts, became so upset as the tempers of his neighbors became "more and more soured and malevolent against all moderate men, whom they see fit to reproach as enemies of their country," including him, that by spring of 1775 he felt it the "duty I owe myself to withdraw for a while from the storm which to my foreboding mind is approaching." He sailed that autumn for England in search of security.[2] Samuel's wife stayed behind, preferring their hostile neighbors to a hazardous sea voyage. By January 1777, less than two years later, with his purse "nearly empty," Curwen regretted his decision: "For what now appears to me a chimera, I abandoned my dwelling, friends and means of life . . . on the comparative trifling condition of insults, reproaches, and perhaps a dress of tar and feathers; an alternative I now see much to be preferred to the distresses of mind I am daily suffering."[3]

Like Samuel Curwen, Thomas Hutchinson, former governor of Massachusetts, wrote from exile of his "deepest wish to return" home. Hutchinson had become so bitterly unpopular, attacked by mobs and ineffective, that the king recalled him. Yet in exile, Hutchinson discovered "upon the whole I am more of a New England man than ever, and I will not despair of seeing my country and friends again, though I fear the time for it is farther off than I imagined when I left." Hutchinson was never able to return to his beloved farm in Massachusetts.

Many families whose desperate pleas that their loyalist relatives stay and help support and defend them and their country had been ignored. It was hard for them not to feel offended and dismayed that personal safety had driven loved ones to flee and abandon them.

The new Massachusetts law decreed that any banished individual who returned was to be forcibly transported to some British possession. If he returned a second time without permission, he was to "suffer the pains of death without benefit of clergy." The absentees had assumed their panicky flights to England for safety would involve just a short stay. They would return home when the conflict was over. But now, their exile was made permanent.

Massachusetts and other states were not done with the absentees, however. A year after the Banishment Act came the Confiscation Act, authorizing the confiscation of "the estates of certain persons commonly called absentees." Families that had remained behind were stripped of the family property. The estates of those accused of adhering "to the said king of Great Britain," or merely having "withdrawn, without the permission of the legislative or executive authority," could now be confiscated, auctioned off, and sold.

Twenty years earlier, friends and family could debate the issues of taxes and regulations in a civil manner without risking mob violence or legal punishment. As today, when friends and family gathered, political differences could be tactfully sidestepped. All were loyal, it was just a matter of approach. The controversy over the Stamp Act of 1765 changed that.

With the outrage over the Stamp Act came the creation of local committees of observation to report neighbors with improper views, and the establishment of the Sons of Liberty, who could resort to mob violence. Many of the 300 banished individuals had been ostracized by neighbors and terrorized by mobs, sometimes brutally, and their homes vandalized. By 1774, a year before the first battle, and 1775, a year before the Declaration of Independence, when negotiation seemed desirable and likely, many on the banishment list began to leave. By 1776, Congress recommended that residents who refused to take an oath to oppose the British government be forcibly disarmed and, if necessary, arrested.

As disagreements and fears over the loss of rights rose in the years after the Stamp Act, the cost of political and philosophical divisions sharpened. This book deals with the personal impact of the looming political crisis. Where did loyalty lie? What was life like, living through the deepening anxieties and desperate choices splitting friends and family? How did those facing war with the world's most powerful naval empire feel? What would happen if they lost? Benjamin Franklin, touring the country after the battle at Lexington, didn't find anyone wanting independence. Why did it take a year after the first battle and much bloodshed before independence was declared? Samuel Eliot Morison, in his classic history of the American people, explains why:

> Loyalties were being torn apart. Americans were members of the greatest empire since Rome. Independence meant sailing forth on an uncharted sea. America was not like Ireland, Poland, or other states which cherished romantic traditions of an independent past. All the mystic chords of memory which (as Abraham Lincoln said) make a people one, responded to English names and events—the Magna Carta, Queen Elizabeth, the Glorious Revolution, the Bill of Rights, Drake, Marlborough, Wolfe. Dared one break with all English memories and glories?
>
> It was a hard choice for a man who read and thought. . . . If one looked into the Bible for guidance, there was St. Peter in his First Epistle urging his flock, 'Submit yourselves to every ordinance of man for the Lord's sake.' As freemen, said he, you are not to use 'your liberty for a cloke of maliciousness; but as the servants of God. Honour all men: Love the brotherhood: Fear God; Honour the king.' What could be more explicit? Were not some of the Sons of Liberty using 'liberty for a cloke of maliciousness?'" [4]

"There is even a touch of nostalgia," Morison adds, "in Jefferson's draft of the Declaration of Independence where he wrote: 'We might have been a free and a great people together.'"

Unlike our customary focus on key individuals, political events, and battles, this book looks at how individuals coped with the growing emergency and, with it, family turmoil. What happened on the home front as men and women faced the uncertainties and privations of a civil war and revolution? How did those who stayed at home to defend their state and their rights feel about those who fled? And what of the absentees? Unlike loyalists who joined with the British army, they were not fighting against their countrymen, but simply safely away from the dangers of conflict. But safety came at a high cost. They were refugees not knowing how long they would be absent from home, not certain how to occupy their resources and time, unsure of their welcome in England or America.

These are the stories of Americans, notably the Quincy family and their friends, at home or in exile, whose souls were tried during the American Revolutionary era in a war without an enemy. When the war was over and the peace treaty had been signed, could the exiles return home? Would families be able to forgive, forget, and reunite?

In the centuries since the Revolutionary War, the American and British people have come to enjoy and treasure a special relationship. How many, during the Revolutionary era, wished we "might have been a free and great people together?"

ONE

Over the Sea: The Family Divided

What a scene has opened upon us . . . Such a scene as we never before Experienced, and could scarcely form an idea of. If we look back we are amazed at what is past, if we look forward we must shudder at the view. . . . All our worldly comforts are now at stake—our nearest and dearest connections are hazarding their lives and properties. . . . Colln. Quincys family have several Times been obliged to flee from their house and scatter themselves about.

—Abigail Adams to Mercy Otis Warren,
Braintree, Mass., May 2, 1775[1]

On May 13, 1775, less than a month after the first shots were fired at Lexington and Concord, Samuel Quincy prepared to sail to England, leaving the only home he had ever known, abandoning his wife, his children, his father, and his country.

"I am going, my dear friend," he wrote to his brother-in-law, "to quit the habitation where I have been so long encircled with the dearest connections. I am going to hazard the unstable element,

and for a while to change the scene . . . My political character
with you may be suspicious; but be assured, if I cannot serve my
country, which I shall with the upmost of my power, I will never
betray it. The kind care of my family you have so generously
offered penetrates me with the deepest gratitude. . . . Would
to God we may again enjoy the harmonious intercourse I have
been favored with since my union with your family. . . . God
preserve you in health and every earthly enjoyment, until you
again receive the salutation of

Your friend and brother,
Samuel Quincy

Samuel was a Crown official in a fiercely anti-British family. Now on
the eve of his departure his sister, Hannah, wrote, pleading with him to
stay. She was the third of Josiah Senior's four grown children. Two of her
three brothers had died. Her older brother Edmund, ill with a pulmonary
disease, died at sea in 1768. Her younger brother Josiah Junior had died of
the same ailment just seventeen days before, shortly after that first Revolutionary War battle. Apart from three young stepsisters, just Hannah and
Samuel remained to comfort their father. By month's end there would be
only Hannah.

There were hopes Samuel might still choose the patriot side.[2] Hannah
had slipped her note to Samuel into her father's farewell letter to his only
surviving son. She started off gently, hoping to persuade her brother to put
politics aside and remain:

I have not forgotten that you are my *only* brother . . . I fear I
shall never see him again. Our two departed brothers died upon
the seas. . . . I have not time to enlarge upon the complicated
distresses of our country, of families, or of individuals, but shall
briefly say that our connections have experienced such a series
of melancholy events as are not to be paralleled. We, my
brother, I hope, can sympathize in sorrowing for the loss of

a brother, whose character was, as far as any man's of his age ever was, unimpeachable.

With the mention of their younger brother, however, Hannah lost her temper:

> Let it not be told in America, and let it not be published in Great Britain, that a brother of such brothers fled from his country—the wife of his youth—the children of his affection—and from his aged sire, already bowed down with the loss of two sons, and by that of many more dear, though not so near connections, to secure himself from the reproaches of his injured countrymen, and to cover such a retreat, obliged to enlist as a sycophant under an obnoxious Hutchinson [former governor], who is a tool under a cruel North, and by them to be veered about, and at last to be blown aside with a cool 'to-morrow, sir.'

Neither pleading nor anger deterred Samuel. He sailed to London hoping for a business opportunity, expecting that some reconciliation could be found to stop the impending war, and promising to return quite soon to his wife and family.

This bitter parting, shared by other families caught in the public calamity, was encircled for the Quincys by a cluster of very private family sorrows. As Josiah Junior, Samuel's ailing younger brother, neared home from a secret and fruitless mission to England for the Continental Congress, his two little children, Josiah and Abigail, lay ill. On April 13, while their father was close to the end of his homeward journey, his baby daughter died.[3] She would be buried in the Boston Granary Burial Ground, a small stone marking her resting place. Many little children died in those years, and parents could console themselves that there would be other children. But in this case, her husband lay dying. There would be no other babies. Baby Abigail's mother had little time to mourn her death. Within the week, ,shooting started at Lexington and Concord. British soldiers, besieged by thousands of local militia, fought their way back to the safety of Boston. Abigail snatched her little son and fled with her sisters to the safety of Connecticut. She was there on April 26, when Josiah's health failed just as his ship was approaching Gloucester harbor and home. He never knew about the battle that his secret mission to England had hoped to prevent, or his little daughter's death. Among the effects his wife later retrieved was a ring for his father inscribed, OH, SAVE MY COUNTRY![4]

Terrified families packed what belongings they could and fled from the Boston area, away from the coast, while thousands of local men, rifles in hand, raced to besiege the city and prevent the regulars from marching out to take revenge for the battle. The attempt failed, and before Samuel's ship docked in England, where he hoped to find promising professional opportunities and remain faithful to his oath as a British official, the Battle of Bunker Hill took place. It was far more deadly than the running battle at Lexington and Concord. More than 1,000 British soldiers and 450 Americans were killed or injured, and the nearby town of Charlestown set ablaze. Worse, beyond the human casualties, the chance of a peaceful resolution of grievances between the colonists and the Mother Country was slipping away, and with it the hoped-for reconciliation and reunion of families torn apart by the conflict.

How would they fare: the feisty Quincy patriarch, Colonel Josiah Senior, bereft of the support of sons and responsible for widows and orphans; Hannah, a recent widow, childless; all those Quincy cousins, friends, and neighbors who now faced the terrors of a war against the great British Empire? They were all traitors in the eyes of that government. And then there were "absentees," like Samuel, who fled to England to ride out the storm as refugees and exiles. There is always the assumption that a war will be short. It is usually mistaken and was again this time, at a high personal cost.

TWO

Beginnings

Massachusetts settlers were a cantankerous lot. The Quincys and their neighbors knew their rights and were determined to preserve them. It took that stubborn mindset to convince them to abandon their homes in England despite their already established opposition to the English church, cross a tumultuous Atlantic Ocean in frail wooden ships, and settle in a wild and untamed country. Over successive decades that feisty attitude toward any perceived intrusion by the royal government on their precious liberties was met with suspicion and resolve. One wonders whether the Crown ever regretted permitting such an obstinate and independent people to populate the British colonies in the first place.

Up until 1775 neither Josiah Quincy Junior nor his brother Samuel nor any of the colonists really had to choose between loyalty to the Mother Country and loyalty to their colony. You could be a good subject and a good patriot, defend your promised rights but be grateful for the English legacy and the protection of the British Empire. Samuel's great-grandfather, Edmund Quincy, and generations of his descendants thrived in such a world.

King James had sworn to harry dissenters from the English church out of Britain. Yet to lure Englishmen to the shores of North America, the royal charters he gave them stipulated that they and their descendants were to have all the rights of Englishmen as if born and abiding in England. James's son and successor, Charles I, followed his father's example, promising that the inhabitants of the Massachusetts Bay Colony and their children "shall have and enjoy all liberties and immunities of free and natural subjects . . . as if they . . . were born within the realm of England."[1] The recipients meant to hold the king to that promise.

The stubbornness and courage of the Quincys' predecessors was revealed almost at once. In 1664, the Massachusetts Bay assembly dispatched a letter of protest to their "Dread Soveraigne," then Charles II, taking issue with a royal commission that accused the New England colonies of passing laws "repugnant to the laws of England" and not paying customs.[2] The Massachusetts representatives insisted their colony had "an exemption to the payment of customs" imposed by the Navigation Acts. While the other New England colonies complied with the demand, however unhappily, the Massachusetts assembly reminded Charles II that their charter, reconfirmed by him just two years earlier, granted "unto them their heirs, assignes & associations forever, not onely the absolute use & propriety of the tract of land herein mentioned, but also full & absolute power of governing all the people of this place, by men chosen by themselves, & according to such lawes as they shall from time to time see meete to make & establish, being not repugnant to the laws of England." King Charles was reminded that they were to pay only the fifth part "of the oare of gold & silver that shall here be found for & in respect of all duties, demands, exactions, & services whatsoever."[3] They even objected to the royal commission itself: "Wee are like to be subjected to the arbitrary power of strangers, proceeding not by any established lawe, but by their owne discretions!" "If these things goe on," they warned, "your subjects here will either be forced to seeke new dwellings or sinck & faint under burdens that will be to them intolerable."[4] The Crown officials withdrew the commission, but the Massachusetts assembly refused even to answer the charges.

In 1686, Charles's successor, his brother James II, tried to bring the colonies under tight administrative control by creating the Dominion of New England, encompassing both New England and mid-Atlantic colonies, headed by a royal appointee, Governor Edmund Andros. Andros and his council levied town taxes in Massachusetts without consulting the colony's assembly.[5] The Ipswich town meeting protested that the taxes were illegal and refused to pay them. Andros arrested the leaders of the protest—the Reverend John Wise and five others—and refused them habeas corpus. When they pleaded this was in violation of the Magna Carta, Joseph Dudley, chief judge of the colony, informed Wise and the others that they must "not think the Laws of England follow [them] to the ends of the earth or whither [they] went," that the only privilege they had was "not to be sold as a slave."[6] When the colonists were found guilty by a stacked jury, the Massachusetts assembly moved their cases to the colony's Supreme Judicial Court and "empowered that court to exercise powers comparable to those in the courts at Westminster," entitling them to grant habeas corpus.[7] In 1692, with a new king and queen, the collapse of the hated Dominion, and a new royal governor for Massachusetts, the assembly passed a law similar to the English Habeas Corpus Act of 1679, and other colonies followed suit.[8]

Braintree, home to generations of Quincys, Adamses, Hancocks, and other prominent New England families, was an old town as New England towns went. It was first settled in 1625, just five years after the pilgrims landed at Plymouth, and was incorporated in 1640. Frigid ocean winds off the North Atlantic swept over the town, and thick fog frequently blanketed it, making it damp and overcast much of the time. Its residents, like other New Englanders, endured seasonal swings from freezing cold winters to warm and hot summers, more extreme conditions than were common in the Mother Country. The town was named for Braintree in England, a truly ancient city built along a Roman road. It had been a flourishing wool and textile center in the 14th and 15th centuries. The American Braintree was just ten miles south of Boston, enabling families like the Quincys to work farms in Braintree while also plying the lucrative shipping trade in Boston. Farming in Braintree was arduous. The land was stony. The stones were put to use for walls to line their fields and served as foundations for their homes. The soil was not very fertile, and constant work was required to wrest a decent yield of hay, maize, pumpkins, and apples, but the locals believed in the virtue of hard work. By 1776, when the Declaration of Independence was proclaimed, Braintree had a population of 2,871.[9]

The town was governed by a board of five selectmen elected by their neighbors, at least those neighbors qualified to vote by ownership of land and the true religion, who assembled in regular town meetings. These assemblies busied themselves with local and colonial issues of all sorts, erection and staffing of schoolhouses, requirements for the town mill, rules for land sales, levying taxes, deciding "whether the Town will grant a Premium on the heads of Birds & Squirrells," and other pressing matters.[10] Fires were a constant worry, and the town required every house to have a ladder against its chimneys to protect against sparks.[11] The Braintree town meeting efforts to prevent fire did not spare the Quincy house from burning twice during those years. In 1770 Josiah built a fine house on the estate he had inherited overlooking Boston Harbor and moved there, where he lived the rest of his life.

The town also elected representatives to sit in the colonial assembly in Boston, the Massachusetts General Court. In the 1760s and 1770s the town meeting sent the colonial legislature statements on their opinions of English taxes and policies. All these matters, large and small, local and colonial, gave the men of the community plenty of opportunity for real experience in governance.

Josiah Senior had reason to be proud. His Quincy ancestors were among the first settlers of Braintree. They arrived early and stayed. A section of Braintree that became an independent town in 1792 would later be named Quincy in their honor. Josiah might have been arrogant, but that was not the Quincy way. As the saying he knew well goes, from those to whom much is given much is expected. Josiah took that to heart.

Edmund Quincy had emigrated to Boston with John Cotton and disembarked on September 4, 1733, with his wife, his children, and six servants, and then moved a few miles south. The family home was built on land purchased in 1635 from the Indian sachem of Mos-Wechusett. This property became part of Braintree. Edmund died soon after the purchase, but his son maintained the family position and prominence. The first Braintree town meeting records, in 1640, mention an "Edmond" Quincy. Another Edmund, born in 1681, became one of the most distinguished men in the colony. He followed what was to become the traditional family career path, farming in Braintree and going into business in Boston. Edmund was a Harvard man, as his son and grandsons would be. Able and respected, he held a train of ever more important posts, serving as a town selectman, a justice of the peace, colonel of militia, and Braintree representative to the Massachusetts General Court. There he caught the attention of the governor and became a member of the governor's council. Then he served for nineteen years as a justice on the Supreme Judicial Court of Massachusetts Bay, the colony's highest court, until he was named agent for the colony at the royal court in Britain. The following year he died in London and was buried there. He left his heirs a vast fortune of over £14,000, equivalent to about $8,000,000 today. [12]

Josiah looked with satisfaction on the family past, generation after generation. The Quincys were hardworking, enterprising, prosperous, and, at least initially, lucky. Edmund Quincy's sons, Edmund and Josiah, while less distinguished for their public service than their father, followed in his footsteps. They were involved in farming their Braintree estates, engaging in commerce and active in public affairs.

Josiah Senior, father of another Edmund, Samuel, Josiah, and Hannah, was born in the house of his great-grandfather. [13] John Singleton Copley's portrait of Josiah when he was fifty captured Josiah's bright eyes and thoughtful expression, which seem to take the measure of the viewer as he looks up from the book he has been reading. He is neatly and handsomely attired, supremely confident, a man to be reckoned with.

He and his older brother Edmund attended Boston Latin School, where Benjamin Franklin was a classmate of Josiah. Edmund and Josiah went on to attend Harvard College and, in 1735, followed their father's profession and went into the merchant-shipping business. The two brothers and Edmund's brother-in-law Edward Jackson established a shipbuilding and commercial firm in Boston. In 1737 their father took Josiah on an exciting voyage to England and on to Europe to learn the business. After his father's death, Josiah continued crossing the Atlantic, seeking business opportunities, and keeping up a correspondence with contacts in Paris, Cadiz, and Amsterdam, as well as England.[14]

Venturing across the ocean was dangerous. Josiah's three sons would all die at sea. Apart from the hazards of sailing the Atlantic, however, Britain's enemies, Spain and France, were a danger for the ships of her American colonies. But Josiah and Edmund were undeterred. In 1748 they prepared to send their ship, *Bethel,* to the Mediterranean, taking the precaution of fitting her out with 14 guns and obtaining a letter of marque authorizing them to seize enemy ships as prizes. Still, with only a small crew of 37, the *Bethel* was no match for a powerful man-of-war.[15] One night out on the Atlantic, the *Bethel* encountered a large Spanish vessel, the *Jesu Maria & Joseph,* armed with 26 guns and a crew of 117 men. The captain of the *Bethel* took advantage of the dark to disguise his vessel as an English war-ship, placing lanterns in the rigging and hats and cloaks on sticks along the ship's rails. The trick worked. The Spanish captain surrendered his ship with its crew. What a prize! The Spanish ship was laden with a cargo of 161 chests of silver and 2 of gold, a windfall. Josiah resigned from his Boston business and returned to Braintree a wealthy man, settling on the family's 400-acre "Lower Farm."

Josiah's brother Edmund decided to remain in the shipping business, even-tually forming a partnership with his own sons. Unfortunately, Edmund's business suffered reverses and, in 1757, less than ten years after Josiah left, Edmund was forced to declare bankruptcy and, like Josiah, retired to his paternal estate in Braintree. Despite this reversal, which would have ruined the reputation of most men, Edmund remained well-respected and went on to become a magistrate of Suffolk County (which included Boston). He was known ever after as "Squire" or "Justice" Quincy.

Edmund and his wife Elizabeth were parents of nine children. Edmund's children, growing up, like Josiah's, in increasingly trying and divisive times, would, like Josiah's, be divided in their loyalties. Their daughter Dorothy married John Hancock, famous signer of the Declaration of Independence, while her sister Esther married Jonathan Sewell, the last British attorney general of Massachusetts. When the time came for choosing parties, Jonathan Sewell would be as staunch a loyalist as his brother-in-law John Hancock was a staunch patriot. But that was in the future.

In 1733, two years before launching his Boston shipping business, Josiah married Hannah Sturgis, a young woman from Yarmouth on Cape Cod, the first of his three wives. Having several wives or husbands was not unusual in those days since the hazards of childbirth took the lives of many women, while both men and women were susceptible to various diseases beyond their doctors' ability to cure. Hannah and Josiah were fortunate, for their marriage lasted over twenty years. They had four children. Sons Edmund and Samuel were born in Braintree before the move to Boston, and Hannah and Josiah were born in Boston. Their homestead in Boston was a large house on Summer Street with extensive gardens that backed onto those of his brother Edmund. It was a shock and deep sorrow for the little family when mother Hannah died in 1755. Josiah Junior was a boy of only eleven. Daughter Hannah, now a young woman of nineteen, would take over her mother's responsibilities in the household.

Two years later Josiah married Elizabeth Waldron, daughter of the Reverend Marsh, a Boston minister. During their brief marriage they had a daughter, also named Elizabeth, but Josiah's second wife Elizabeth died in 1759 leaving him to care for their tiny daughter. Two years after that he married once more: Ann Marsh, daughter of a Braintree minister. Ann was a close friend of Abigail Adams and intriguingly described as "a woman of uncommon excellence and animation." She gave birth to two more daughters, Nancy and Frances, and raised Josiah's three little girls. She was his companion for the rest of his life, seeing the family through all the trials and tribulations to come.[16] Josiah really had two families. He was the father of four older children, three sons and a daughter, then a second family of three young daughters.

Back in Braintree Josiah could have been content to farm and enjoy his wealth, but he had too much energy and enthusiasm and instead plunged into a variety of commercial and civic activities. He invested in promising commercial enterprises. Taking advantage of the colony's booming whale fishery, he started a spermaceti works, turning whale sperm into valuable oils. He also helped establish the first glass manufacturer in the colonies. One of the partners was Benjamin Franklin's favorite brother, John, and later John's son James. [17]

As his father and grandfather before him, Josiah was immersed in Braintree and Massachusetts Bay politics, good avenues to protecting the business and political rights of the colonists. He served on various Braintree town committees, was elected moderator of the town meeting several times, and was chosen to serve as the Braintree representative to the Massachusetts General Court. [18]

Capture of a Spanish ship may have made Josiah a rich man, but the more dangerous and persistent enemy of the American colonists was not Spain but France. Year after year the French, with their Indian allies, came streaming down from Canada to raid the New England colonies, burning, killing, looting—the Native Americans sometimes taking captives to kill or adopt. The state of Maine, then part of Massachusetts, was especially vulnerable to these attacks. The colony's militia were well armed and always on the alert for dangers on the frontiers and along their long, irregular coast. In 1755, the year of Hannah's death, Josiah was commissioned by the then governor of the colony, William Shirley, to persuade the colonies of Pennsylvania and New York to join Massachusetts in building a fortress near the French fort at Crown Point, on the great Hudson River. Helped by his friend in Pennsylvania, Benjamin Franklin, Josiah's efforts were successful, but the expedition was a failure.

The French and Indian War, what the British call the Seven Years' War, was just beginning. For the first time the British government was prepared to send a substantial number of troops to North America and join with their colonists to defeat their old French competitors. A year earlier Massachusetts had voted for 1,200 provincial soldiers to take part in an expedition against Fort Saint-Frederic and in a battle at Lake George on the New York and Vermont borders. It was a good number but fewer than what was wanted and needed. Once the British prime minister, William Pitt, the Elder, called for sending a great army from Britain, however, the Americans were much keener to do their part. The British requested thousands of provincial troops, and the New England colonies—Massachusetts, Connecticut, New Hampshire, and Rhode Island—dutifully complied. Massachusetts alone raised and sent six regiments. Unlike professional soldiers or militia, provincial soldiers were raised for a particular campaign season. They played an important role in the campaign although often manning garrisons while the British regulars did much of the fighting. The French were building a fort on the Hudson at Ticonderoga and other forts in the Ohio Valley on land claimed by British colonies and threatening their possessions. The British, with men from Massachusetts, Connecticut, and other colonies undertook an expedition to Lake George. The provincial troops that joined with the British regulars found themselves looked down on by the British officers and soldiers they now served with. In 1762 Josiah was commissioned colonel of the Suffolk Regiment of the militia, which included Boston, and from that time was known as Colonel Quincy. John Adams commented on how impressive Colonel Josiah Quincy looked in his militia officer's uniform.[19] The colonial militia, consisting of able-bodied men from sixteen to sixty were, except for emergencies, used as a home guard during the war. While Josiah served, his older sons, Edmund and Samuel, do not seem to have done so. Edmund was traveling abroad for his shipping business and Samuel, who had graduated from Harvard, was completing his legal training and, in 1758, was admitted to the bar.

Through the brilliant leadership of General James Wolfe, Britain managed to defeat the French at their nearly impregnable fortress at Quebec, the capital of New France, and won the war. It was an amazing victory and, in 1763, drove the French out of Canada and their Ohio forts, ceding the Ohio Valley to British control. It was an immense relief to New Englanders not to have French raiding parties descending on them, causing mayhem. But there were lessons that the colonists didn't see coming during their general rejoicing at the triumph. The British had brought large numbers of troops to America at great expense and didn't seem interested in removing them. Worse, the troops were left in the cities along the coast, not protecting the frontiers as one would have expected. The enormous costs of their transportation and now their upkeep would have to be paid by taxpayers on both sides of the Atlantic. The new Quebec Act passed by Parliament dashed colonial expectations of vast new land to farm. It prohibited American colonists from crossing the mountains to settle the Ohio Valley. Instead, they made that western territory part of their new province of Canada. The French-Canadian colonists and Indians were protected and benefited, not the Americans who had fought alongside the British. Then there was the resentment colonial soldiers felt at the obvious disdain in the manner the British officers treated them.

It was also a vicious war. The French and especially their Indian allies committed terrible atrocities. A particularly egregious example, long remembered in Massachusetts, was the slaughter at Fort William Henry, where some of Massachusetts's provincial soldiers were serving on garrison duty. In the summer of 1757 French attention was focused on Fort William Henry, at the southern shore of Lake George north of Albany. The fort guarded the gateway from New France south to Albany and then down the great Hudson River to New York City. British possession of Fort William Henry, commanded by Colonel George Monro, a Scots-Irish officer, was vital. The French first attacked the fort's supplies and outbuildings outside its walls. In August French general Louis-Joseph de Montcalm descended on the fort with some 7,000 troops and Indians. They encircled it and he summoned its commander to surrender. Monro called urgently for help from the commander of Fort Edward, some sixteen miles away, who had earlier promised him support, and pleaded with the governors of New York and New England to send their militias as quickly as possible. Connecticut and Massachusetts responded immediately.[20] Massachusetts mobilized four western regiments to march to New York, alerting all the colony's twenty-six militia battalions "to hold themselves in readiness to march at a minute's warning." More than 4,200 New England men were encamped outside the fort by August 12. In the emergency, with the large

French army bearing down, the commander of Fort Edward changed his mind about sending some of his troops to help Monro. After days of withering bombardment, Monro's men were exhausted from serving five nights running. Monro then discovered that relief columns would not be sent from Fort Edward. With no other reinforcements able to relieve the besieged soldiers in time, Monro agreed to negotiate surrender terms.

Montcalm's terms were generous. He promised safe passage for the entire garrison, soldiers, their families, and camp followers, to Fort Edward and to care for any wounded left behind in the fort. However, his Indian allies had been expecting plunder, were furious the terms had been signed without consulting them, and gave them nothing.

The British surrendered and evacuated the fort, moving to an encampment where they were to remain while awaiting an escort of French soldiers to accompany them to Fort Edward. After they left the fort, the Indians rushed into it, attacking the seventy sick and wounded men there, and would have scalped them all had not some French soldiers and missionaries stopped them. The Indians then moved on to the camp where the rest of the garrison waited, and spent the night plundering and terrorizing them. The next day hundreds of warriors attacked the evacuees, demanding they surrender arms, equipment, and clothing. They carried off to Canada enslaved black people, women, and children. When the French army began to escort the English garrison, the still enraged Indians seized, tomahawked, and slaughtered those unprotected at the rear of the column. Guaranteed safe passage by the French commander, men, women, and children from Fort William Henry were massacred by his Indian allies. The militia who had rushed to protect the fort arrived far too late to save the hapless colonists and soldiers. Montcalm, an honorable man, had given his word, but French honor, in the eyes of Americans, was now meaningless.

The French and Indian War left a legacy of anger, not just at the French and the Indians who allied themselves with them, but also outrage at the British Quebec Act that deprived the American colonists of lands to the west. There was also bitterness at the lack of respect from British officers, and the burden of a succession of deeply resented taxes to pay for what colonists saw as an army of occupation.

In Braintree, life went on. It was in this comfortable household that Edmund, Samuel, Hannah, and Josiah were fortunate to grow up. It was a prosperous, highly respected family, with a father politically active and enterprising. But fortune is fickle and was to turn in tragic ways. Death was to strike the young as the public danger loomed. The larger Quincy family, as well as their own, was about to become embroiled in the gathering tensions and divisions as the country slid into civil war.

THREE

Fathers and Children

Colonel Josiah Quincy's family and their friends and neighbors praised God for the grand British victory in the French and Indian War. Canada and the Ohio Valley now belonged to the British, not the French. It was a joy and relief. But within months joy turned to disappointment and anger. Five years later the same colonists would be opposing the British and anxiously defending their rights as Englishmen. Josiah's family was among the leaders of that defense, but they were dismayed by the violent American mobs making a mockery of a civil response and, on a personal level, grief-stricken at the untimely death of a loved son and brother. Everything that had been so promising seemed to have gone wrong.

How did Colonel Josiah's family fare during those more tranquil years before it all went wrong? They were fortunate to be a wealthy and respected family, surrounded by friends and relations. Josiah took pains to ensure his children were well educated. The three eldest, Edmund, Samuel, and Hannah, were close in age. Edmund was born in 1733, Samuel two years later, and Hannah the following year, 1736. Their brother Josiah Junior was born after a gap of eight years. Education was a public responsibility in Massachusetts, and every town established primary schools for its children, both boys and—parents willing—girls. Secondary schools or grammar schools were another story. They were intended for boys, particularly those

aiming to enroll in college. Joseph Marsh had a fine private school in
Braintree that prepared boys for Harvard.[1] Edmund, Samuel, and Josiah
Junior all had such training and were then enrolled in, and graduated from,
Harvard College.

Hannah had no opportunity to attend college or even a grammar or
secondary school. But in an era when many women were unable to write
their names and signed documents with an *X*, Hannah was schooled either
at home by a tutor or in a special school for wealthier young women. Her
letters reveal how articulate she was, as were her friends Abigail Adams
and Mercy Otis Warren. Although, unlike her brothers' essays that were
published in local newspapers, only family and friends had the opportunity
to read Hannah's letters.

Hannah's three brothers could not have been more different. Birth
order seems always to be important. Edmund, Josiah's eldest child, was
a promising and thoughtful young man, a son to make a father proud.
He was trained for university and sent to Harvard. He graduated at the
age of nineteen, not an unusual age for graduates in those days. Afterward he followed the typical Quincy career path and moved to Boston
to become an international merchant as his father had been. Despite the
hazards of the ongoing war against the French, Edmund sailed to England
on business in 1760 and again, at the end of the war, in 1763.[2]

Apart from Edmund's business contacts, he corresponded with distinguished intellectuals in America and Britain, among them Thomas
Hollis of London, a philosopher of liberty and a friend of America.[3] As
for his politics, in his memoir of his father Josiah Junior's life, his son
describes his uncle Edmund as a zealous Whig and a political writer.
This was obviously family tradition, as Josiah's son never met his uncle,
but knew he was a good friend of committed Whigs. Edmund was a fine
essayist but not a radical. Essay writing was to be a family tradition and
an important contribution to the colonial conflicts brewing.

Middle son Samuel was solid, sensible, and keen to make his mark
on the world. Samuel was two years younger than Edmund and followed him to Harvard. Like Edmund he was bright, talented, and

hardworking, and unlike him happily free from the pulmonary disease that had vexed and would eventually kill poor Edmund. Also unlike Edmund, Samuel veered from the traditional Quincy career path. Perhaps if he had followed his father and Edmund into business, the family's unity might have survived the coming war and everything might have turned out quite differently. But Samuel decided on a career in the law, an exciting and practical profession with plenty of possibility for advancement in the colonial government. Samuel was ambitious and keen to take advantage of that option. If he was a staunch defender of colonial rights, he was cautious in his views, careful not to offend the authorities or dim his future prospects.

Samuel and his friend and neighbor John Adams were admitted to the bar on the same day. In 1761, Samuel married Hannah Hill, daughter of Thomas Hill, a wealthy Boston distiller. It was an elegant and joyous summer wedding. The young women dressed in white muslin, embroidered with flowers, the men in fine linen coats.[4] Josiah Senior gave the young couple some 400 acres of land in Lincoln, a town wedged between Lexington and Concord, to the west of Boston. That first battle of the Revolution would pass through Lincoln.

Hannah's family were, and remained, committed patriots, as were many merchants. Samuel arranged for the great Boston artist John Singleton Copley to paint a portrait of his wife. In her portrait, Hannah appears a fine, elegant woman, not beautiful but expensively and fashionably clothed. Samuel chose what she was to wear for her portrait and was careful to have her dressed in the latest fashion, wearing the sort of "rich and sensuous" clothing he felt suitable for the wife of a prosperous professional.[5] There is no hint of Puritan austerity in her soft pink satin dress with its sumptuous lace and jewelry. Her head was adorned in a dashing hat set at a jaunty angle, sporting long white feathers.

Six years later, in his early thirties, Samuel sat for his own portrait. Copley's portrait of Samuel depicts a handsome, well-fed young man, smartly clothed now as a Crown lawyer, wearing the appropriate wig, quill pen in hand, exuding the same calm composure as his father in his portrait. The effect of Hannah's and Samuel's portraits is of a well-to-do, confident young couple with great expectations.

Law suited Samuel and he turned out to be a talented and successful barrister. He would succeed Jonathan Sewell, husband of his cousin Esther, to the important post of Crown solicitor general for Massachusetts, an excellent position for an aspiring attorney. It made him a member of the royal government in Massachusetts. Samuel, like his brothers Edmund and Josiah, was a talented writer and, in those years before the crisis, a good friend of men who would become leading American patriots. The future looked bright.

By 1759, daughter Hannah had grown into a lovely belle of twenty-two. Eligible and beautiful, from a fine family, Hannah was a flirt, with many suitors, including a shy Braintree minister as well as the future president, John Adams, vying for her hand. Adams was smitten with her. The two met toward the end of 1758 and, in early January, seated at a tea table at her father's house, had their first intimate conversation. Adams referred to Hannah as Orlinda when he wrote Richard Cranch in December 1758 to confess: "If I look upon a Law Book and labor to exert all my Attention, my Eyes tis true are on the Book, but Imagination is at a Tea Table with Orlinda, seeing That Face, those Eyes, that Shape, that familiar friendly look, and [hear]ing Sense divine come mended from her Tongue. . . . When the rest of the family are at their Devotions I am paying same Devoirs across a Tea Table to Orlinda. . . . I go to bed, and ruminate half the night, then fall asleep and dream of the same enchanting scenes till morning comes and brings Chagrin, fretfulness and Rage, in exchange for Bliss and Rest. If, as grave folks say Madness is occasioned by too long and close an Attention to one set of Ideas, I shall soon I fear grow mad for I have had no Idea, but that of Orlinda, that Billet and Disappointment in my Head since you saw me."[6] Indeed he began to propose to her, but the pair were interrupted, and the opportunity did not come again. With many promising young men to choose from, Hannah made the wrong choice, and before Adams could reiterate his proposal, she was engaged to Bela Lincoln.

Adams was bitterly disappointed and angry. He wrote Cranch, "Shall such Cruelty go unpunished. Nor may she be in less than a year from this day be tied in the everlasting Chains of Wedlock."

His curse came true; chains they turned out to be. Hannah wed Dr. Bela Lincoln of nearby Hingham, a Harvard classmate of her brother Samuel. Bela came from a Hingham family of more modest means and returned there after he finished his studies in medicine. Much family hope and support was invested in his education. His younger brother, Benjamin, did not have the advantage of a college education, because of the family's limited income and the need for his help on the farm. In the upcoming war, however, Benjamin would rise to become a major general in the Continental Army and would later serve as the first United States secretary of war. As for Bela, after practicing medicine for some time in Hingham, he traveled to Britain to continue his medical studies. He earned the degree of doctor of medicine from the University of Aberdeen, an ancient university on the cold, bleak northeast coast of Scotland. The grim Aberdeen climate would have suited Bela, whose cold and cruel disposition became all too evident soon after his marriage to Hannah. The two were married on May 1, 1760, and settled in his hometown of Hingham.

It was gossip and Bela's personal pride that apparently sealed Hannah's fate, according to John Adams. John wrote in his diary that Lincoln had told him:

> My father gave me a serious Lecture last Saturday night. He says I have waited on H.Q. two Journeys, and have called and made Visits there so often, that her Relations among others have said I am courting of her. And the Story has spread so wide now, that, if I don't marry her, she will be said to have Jockied me, or I to have Jockied her, and he says the Girl shall not suffer. A story shall be spread, that she repelled me.[7]

He took the hint and proposed. On such slights and pride are fates and unhappy marriages made, at least in this case.

John Adams tells of the terrible abuse that lovely, lively Hannah suffered from the beginning of her marriage to Bela. Adams witnessed the cruel treatment she received when visiting at her father's house. He writes that Lincoln "treated his Wife, as no drunken Cobler, or Clothier would have done, before Company. Her father never gave such Looks and Answers to one of his slaves." He continued to report Lincoln's "hoggish" and "brutally rustic" conduct toward Hannah, which made her sink "into silence and shame and Grief."[8] And there she remained as long as Bela lived.

It was Josiah Junior, youngest of Josiah's four oldest children, who would become the best known. While their father was referred to as "Colonel Quincy," the son would be known as "the Patriot." Like his older brothers, Josiah attended Harvard College, and after graduating in 1763 at nineteen, he followed his brother Samuel's example and pursued a career in the law rather than commerce. He was a pupil in the law office of Oxenbridge Thatcher, a well-respected lawyer and patriot leader. Thatcher had a large practice in Boston and, according to John Adams, was "beloved for his learning, ingenuity, every domestic and social virtue, and conscientious conduct in every relation of life." The key characteristic of this eminent attorney was his ardent patriotism, a patriotism Josiah shared.[9] In May 1763, Thatcher was also one of Boston's representatives in the colonial legislature. James Otis was a colleague of his, and together they argued the renowned case against the writs of assistance. Thatcher would be reelected to the Massachusetts legislature annually until his death in 1765, the year the Stamp Act was imposed. Adams attributes Thatcher's death in that year to his deep agitation over the Stamp Act and the British government's efforts to increase its control over the colonies. Thatcher had a profound influence turning the colonists, including Adams and Thatcher's young pupil Josiah, against the restrictions the Mother Country was imposing on their promised liberties.

It would be the Townshend Acts and the Stamp Act that drove Josiah Junior into a whirlwind of writing and publishing essays in the Boston press. He took a leading role in the formation of the Sons of Liberty. For now, however, the slim, elegant young man depicted in Copley's portrait, with his kindly expression, somber dress, hand clutching a scroll, and law books piled at his elbow, was not yet the famed patriot he would become. The political events that would thrust him into the limelight were still in the future. His calm, handsome portrait did not reveal any symptoms of the pulmonary disease that had stricken his brother Edmund and would eventually threaten his life as well.

FOUR

Men of Moderation

Born and educated in this country, I glory in the name of Britain.
—George III in his accession speech to Parliament

The year 1760 seemed to hold great promise for Britain and her American colonies as the handsome twenty-two-year-old ascended the British throne as George III, third of the Hanoverian kings. He became heir to his grandfather, George II, when his own father died suddenly at the age of forty-four. George III would be branded in America's founding documents as a "tyrant." He was many things, but a tyrant he was not. He kept within the political bounds of his office as a British monarch, whatever Americans thought of his policies, and ruled throughout with the consent of Parliament. He was the first of the Hanoverian monarchs to have been born in England. English was his mother tongue. George started life as a fragile baby, born two months early and not expected to live, but live he did and went on to reign longer than any of his predecessors.

George's mother, Augusta, saw to it that her son was given an excellent, even formidable education. His tutors instructed him in the sciences, mathematics, French and Latin, history, agriculture, and constitutional law. He was taught social graces and sports. The queen also ensured that George was strictly brought up in the Anglican faith with her own ethical behavior drilled into him. By the age of eight, family letters boasted that he was able to read and write in English and German and was, to some extent, knowledgeable about politics.

He suffered political setbacks during his reign, the worst of which would be losing the American colonies. Perhaps it was because, despite his studies in constitutional law, he was tone-deaf to the sensitivity of Americans about their rights. Their complaints clashed with his own view of his role as a monarch who demanded and expected the loyalty and lawful obedience of all his subjects, whether in Britain or overseas.

As George saw it he was asking no more than what he expected of himself. A year before he became king, he wanted to marry Lady Sarah Lennox, but his grandfather and Lord Bute, his mother's adviser, were against the match and he desisted.[1] "I am born for the happiness or misery of a great nation, and consequently must often act contrary to my passions," he wrote. On September 8, 1761, a year after his accession, George dutifully married Princess Charlotte of Mecklenburg-Strelitz, meeting her for the first time on their wedding day. Despite this prearranged match it was an unusually happy marriage until late in his life, when George suffered the disease that gave him bouts of madness. He and his queen had fifteen children, nine sons and six daughters. George was a dutiful husband and a homebody. He never left England or even ventured from the south of England, never setting foot in his kingdoms of Wales, Scotland, and Ireland.

Apart from the devastating loss of the thirteen American colonies, it would be a glorious reign. George and his kingdom enjoyed a great victory over the French in the Seven Years' War—America's French and Indian War—and an outstanding victory over Napoleon at the Battle of Waterloo in 1815. In 1807 the British Parliament banned merchants from participating in the transatlantic slave trade. The king was, when sane, a serious and meticulous monarch, poring over endless reports and keeping careful notes. His serious governance of his kingdom may have been the reason for that American failure.

Here was a new, well-educated, thoughtful king. But he saw himself in possession of a new broom, and he meant to sweep clean. George III was intent on enforcing the long-evaded restrictions on colonial trade and bringing the colonists to their just obedience and loyalty. Parliament was happy to comply. The English people were heavily burdened with taxes of one sort or another, so why shouldn't the Americans contribute their fair share? The colonies were, after all, designed to improve the financial well-being of the Mother Country and its people. The French and Indian War had been very expensive, with the government transporting an army to North America and supporting it there. Enforcing unpopular laws on a people three thousand miles away, however, was bound to be problematic. It had been attempted occasionally in the past but proved ineffective and was quietly neglected.[2] Not surprisingly, therefore, smuggling was rampant. It benefited both colonial merchants and their customers. Their black market economy was thriving. When unpopular economic restrictions such as the Navigation Acts have been long evaded, it is especially difficult to suddenly reverse course, expecting a cheerful obedience.

There was a long history of economic regulation of colonial trade. The Navigation Acts had been passed by Parliament a hundred years earlier, and over time new items, pushed by English manufacturers, were brought under controls and forbidden to be produced in the colonies. A whole series of goods could not be manufactured there. These eventually included hats, rice, naval stores, and copper, while woolen fabric could not be shipped across any colonial boundary. In 1750 the Iron Act prevented the colonies from erecting mills for rolling and slitting iron, setting up iron forges, and establishing iron-making plants. Furthermore, the English insisted on being the middlemen for colonial goods and purchases. Goods could not be shipped directly to or from Europe. Articles and materials from the colonies were to be shipped to Britain before being sent on to Europe, and European goods had to be shipped to Britain before being sent on to the colonies. The requirement that the colonists purchase sugar cane exclusively from British possessions in the Caribbean was intended to help British West Indies growers compete with the French and other West Indian producers but was often evaded by timely bribes to customs agents and other schemes. The colonists pleaded that the British West Indies alone could not produce enough molasses for their booming rum industry, to no avail. Eventually some 80 percent of molasses arriving in America had been smuggled into the colonies. Royal policies also had a serious impact on the most basic aspects of the colonial economy. Even something as essential as sufficient currency for commerce was a problem the royal government was unwilling to fix. Money was in such short supply that the colonies requested permission to print their own money. This was denied. Little wonder there was increasing frustration on the American side of the Atlantic.

To King George, his cabinet, and most members of Parliament, it seemed perfectly fair that the colonists should, at the very least, shoulder some responsibility for the benefits they enjoyed as part of a great, seaborne empire, protected by the British fleet, enjoying fair British governance, and the thicket of rights of freeborn Englishmen. Subjects in England had been burdened with an increasing variety of taxes for decades.[3] It would be unfair to tax them further while leaving the Americans basically free to ignore the mild taxes imposed upon them. Taxes on English subjects had to be approved by Parliament and were, for the most part, not direct but indirect taxes on tariff duties.[4] They were also aimed at the wealthier among them. There were ancient duties of tunnage (a levy on wine) and poundage (a tariff on all non-staple goods) exported or imported by foreigners. In 1667 Charles II passed the coal tax to help rebuild the city of London after the devastating fire of 1666. Like so many taxes put in place on an emergency basis, it lasted decades. The coal tax was not repealed until 1889. In 1692 a national land tax was imposed on rental properties that remained in force well into the 18th century. On May 1, 1707, after Scotland joined the union of England and Wales, the window tax expanded the Act of Making Good the Deficiency of the Clipped Money of 1696. It was a progressive tax, with a flat-rate tax of two shillings per house and a variable tax for the number of windows above ten, while houses with ten to twenty windows paid twice the amount, those over twenty still more. Some wealthy people, more concerned about saving money than the considerable amenity of light and an attractive view, blocked up some of their houses' windows to reduce their tax. The window tax was eventually repealed, in 1851.

In addition, there was a vast range of local dues imposed on specific items by ports and towns, which eventually totaled some 1,425 articles. These included duties on tea, coffee, cocoa and sugar, liquors, tobacco and snuff, lace, silk, playing cards, dried fruit, salt, starch, and even coffin nails. The tax on playing cards, which would be included in the hated Stamp Act of 1765, was imposed on the subjects of the United Kingdom in 1711 and lasted until 1960.

With residents of the Mother Country laboring under all these taxes, albeit approved by their representatives in Parliament, it seemed selfish for American colonists to complain that they needed a more lenient tax system. Of course, large numbers of Americans did not see it that way and argued that they had no voice in the British Parliament, which was imposing these duties on them. The theory was that everyone, subjects in Britain and colonists, even those who could not vote, were represented in person or by proxy. There were complaints by British subjects about the situation, and American activists, including the Sons of Liberty, thought their compatriots in the Mother Country would sympathize with the colonists' plight. George III and Parliament, and probably the vast majority of Englishmen, thought otherwise.

New taxes and new threats to colonial rights followed as the royal government was determined to bring the obstinate colonials to heel. The passage of the Sugar Act of 1764 not only tightened the enforcement of purchasing exclusively from British colonies but listed more foreign goods to be taxed, including sugar itself, certain wines, coffee, pimiento, cambric, and printed calico, and even regulated the export of lumber and iron. The tax on molasses caused an almost immediate decline in the rum industry in Massachusetts.

If the colonists were frustrated and upset, so was the British government. When they managed to bring smugglers to trial, colonial juries refused to find them guilty. Hundreds of defendants were charged during the 1600s and 1700s, but no more than half a dozen prosecutions were brought, and only two convictions were obtained.[5] Judges in most of the colonies served at the pleasure of the government rather than based on their good behavior, meaning that they could be removed at any time they displeased the royal administration.[6] Juries, therefore, were crucial as a means to protect rights and shelter the colonists from laws they found unfair and in violation of their rights.

A first challenge arose early in 1761 over the imposition of writs of assistance to help customs agents stop the rampant smuggling at American ports, a measure imposed a century earlier in England without undue opposition. The colonists had seemed unaware of the measures to come from the new monarch and Parliament. As the year began, Americans were still basking in the British victories over the French at Quebec and Montreal two years earlier, delighted at the approaching end of French control of Canada, and unaware of the threats to their own liberty that would follow. Without the French threat, the royal government could concentrate its attention on imposing order on, and giving orders to, their American, and soon Canadian, colonists. But the Boston trial in February 1761 over the imposition of the so-called writs of assistance, a legal measure that violated the prized right to privacy, was a foretaste of trials of all sorts to come.

FIVE

The Quincys and the First Trials

Taxation without Representation is tyranny.
—James Otis, "Rights of the British Colonies Asserted," 1764

The colonists are by the law of nature freeborn, as indeed all men are, white or black.
—James Otis, "Rights of the British Colonies Asserted," 1764

Whatever was happening in the larger world in 1761, major personal events were taking place in the smaller world of Colonel Josiah's family. It was a joyous year of weddings. Josiah Senior's second wife, Elizabeth, had died two years earlier after a short marriage, leaving the father of four grown children with an infant daughter. This new year would see him married to a local woman, Ann Marsh, a friend of Abigail Adams, intriguingly described as a "woman of uncommon excellence and animation!"

His eldest son, Edmund, barely back from one voyage across the Atlantic on business, was anticipating another. Son Samuel had broken family tradition; rather than going into business, he had trained for the law. There were few lawyers in the colony and a wide array of businesses, land transactions, and court cases to employ them. Samuel had now completed his legal training and was launching what had all the hallmarks of a very successful legal career. Samuel was soon to wed Hannah Hill, daughter of a wealthy Boston distiller. Her father, Thomas Hill, was a prominent merchant from an outspokenly patriotic family. Young Josiah Junior was studying at Harvard, as his brothers had before him, and planning to follow Samuel into the law. The only fly in this otherwise promising ointment was the fortunes of Josiah Senior's lovely daughter Hannah, who was just months into what was already a very unhappy marriage to Dr. Bela Lincoln.

Political tensions in Massachusetts heightened as the year began. In February 1761 their neighbor John Adams sat in a packed chamber of the Massachusetts Superior Court for several days to hear attorney James Otis dispute the legality of the writs of assistance. James Otis, thirty-six years old at the time, was a big, boisterous man from Cape Cod, attorney, pamphleteer, brother of that extraordinary woman, Mercy Otis Warren. He considered himself a moderate but was a firebrand. He was married to Ruth Cunningham, daughter of a merchant, an heiress. Though their political views differed—he jokingly labeled her a "High Tory"—he loved her, telling Adams that whatever her politics, she was a good wife, too good for him.[1] That may have been the case, or at least she was patient with her flamboyant husband's sudden fits of temper that would later evolve into serious mental problems.[2]

Otis surrendered his prestigious government post as advocate general of the admiralty court in order to challenge the writs. There is some disagreement about why he did so. He may have been upset when the governor failed to appoint his father chief justice of the Massachusetts Supreme Judicial Court, instead appointing Otis's longtime opponent Thomas Hutchinson to the post. On the other hand, he is usually credited with resigning this important post out of principle, to represent sixty-three Boston merchants claiming the writs violated their basic right to privacy and security. No matter, his stirring defense of this fundamental right transformed the Massachusetts attorney into a celebrated champion of the rights of the colonists. He was shortly afterward elected to the Massachusetts provincial legislature.

Although they trampled on personal rights, there was good reason for the new general warrants that permitted government officials or their appointees to burst into private homes and warehouses at will. Smuggling was rampant in the colonies, and many respectable Massachusetts merchants were among the scofflaws keen to evade port duties. Local juries were unwilling to convict their neighbors and liked the lower prices for goods. One governor of Massachusetts had complained, not without cause, that "a Customs house officer has no chance with a jury," while another grumbled, "A trial by jury here is only trying one illicit trader by his fellows, at least his well-wishers."[3] In short, the writs were needed to catch smugglers. The right to privacy, especially in the home, was keenly valued, but to help customs officials catch the local smugglers with contraband on their premises, Parliament issued writs of assistance. The writs authorized government officials to break into homes and warehouses of suspects, day or night, to search for smuggled goods. Constables and even passersby could be required to aid in the search.

Parliament had approved general writs for use in England against smugglers a century earlier, where they were used without great public outcry despite legal treatises questioning their legality. Yet when they were introduced in the American colonies a century later, they provoked outrage. The Boston suit started when James Paxton, a Massachusetts customs official, applied to the Massachusetts Superior Court for a writ. Ordinarily James Otis, the colony's advocate general, would have been expected to support Paxton. Instead, he resigned his post and agreed to represent the furious merchants.[4]

Otis's co-counsel was the highly respected Oxenbridge Thatcher, whose law office, opposite the south door of the Old State House, Josiah Junior would soon join as a student.[5] Thatcher came from a family of ministers and trained for the ministry himself but abandoned that choice because his "slender frame" and weak voice would have made him an ineffective preacher. Still, in this legal role arguing against the writs of assistance, Adams noted he argued with "the softness of manners, the ingenuity and cool reasoning, which were remarkable in his amiable character" and charged that the writ was "against the fundamental principles of English Law." Otis quoted the great English jurist Sir Edward Coke in *Dr. Bonham's Case*: "An act against the constitution is void. An act against natural equity is void."[6] Even Parliament, Coke had insisted, could not pass legislation that was against fundamental law.[7] This government intrusion into privacy, permitting government agents to burst into homes and businesses, was against fundamental law. For the benefit of the Court, Otis went into a very lengthy and detailed history of that principle, from ancient Saxon laws and the Magna Carta, that key to English rights that parliaments had confirmed no less than fifty times. Violators of the Magna Carta had been executed. "The security of these rights to life, liberty, and property," Otis reminded the Court, "had been the object of all those struggles against arbitrary power, temporal and spiritual, civil and political, military and ecclesiastical, in every age. He asserted that our ancestors, as British subjects, and we, their descendants, as British subjects, were entitled to all those rights, by the British Constitution, as well as by the law of nature and our provincial charter, as much as any inhabitant of London or Bristol, or any part of England; and were not to be cheated out of them by any phantom of 'virtual representation,' or any other fiction of law or politics, or any monkish trick of deceit and hypocrisy."[8]

The justices ruled, unsurprisingly, that they had the right to issue the writ and granted Paxton's request. But Otis's insistence that the writs were a violation of fundamental law affirmed by the Magna Carta resonated throughout the colonies.[9] This insistence on a right against unreasonable searches would be ultimately embedded in American state and federal constitutions. And the claim that an act against fundamental law is void has been the foundation of American judicial review. The British won the court challenge and battle but not the war.

More taxes were rapidly passed by Parliament, heightening the anxiety about the continuing presence of a standing army in a time of peace, a long-standing Anglo-American fear of being governed by an army. European countries had lost their liberty when policed by armies under the direction of their rulers. Sending an army to America to fight the French was helpful but expensive, as was keeping them there. The Americans had assumed the British soldiers would leave when the war ended or be stationed along the frontiers, but that was not to happen. British taxpayers were already being squeezed hard for revenue. It seemed only fair to the government that Americans, who were to benefit from the victory of those forces, should help pay the costs. A series of militia acts from 1757 through 1763 authorized British lords lieutenant or their deputies "to seize and remove the Arms, Clothes and Accoutrements" of the militia whenever the officer "shall adjudge it necessary to the Peace of the Kingdom."[10] As Britain continued to press the implementation of the long-ignored Navigation Acts, designed to benefit British merchants and search for more avenues to pry money from their colonists, Americans on the watch for intrusions on their rights and merchants upset at the impositions on their businesses grew increasingly angry.

In 1764, Parliament passed the Sugar Act in April to take effect on September 29. It was the first act specifically aimed at raising money in the colonies for the Crown. It revised the Molasses Act of 1733, which had expired in 1763. It cut the duty on foreign molasses but retained a high duty on foreign refined sugar and prohibited any importation of foreign rum. The act also increased duties on non-British goods shipped to the colonies. These included wine, coffee, and textiles and banned the shipment of several important commodities, such as lumber, directly to Europe.

Many provisions of the act dealt specifically with enforcement. Customs collectors were to personally report to their posts in the colonies rather than relying on appointees. All masters of ships had to post a bond and carry affidavits of the legality of their cargo, and these were examined by officials, assisted by the Royal Navy, at every stop in their voyage. If caught with illegal cargo, they were to be tried by a judge at a vice-admiralty court in Halifax, Nova Scotia, not a traditional common law court before a friendly jury of neighbors.

Several days after passage of the Sugar Act, the Currency Act was passed, banning colonial paper currency and requiring the Sugar Act be paid in gold and silver. Clearly Parliament was determined to control American commerce, both markets and revenues. Currency was still in short supply in the colonies, but members of Parliament feared inflation that would hurt Britain.

American merchants had begun to plan their response years before. Since the 1750s, even before the French and Indian War, Boston merchants had been meeting in the front room of Boston's British Coffee-House on King Street to discuss their complaints and opposition to government policies. Ships were being seized for contraband, their American sailors pressed, really kidnapped, by the Royal Navy, which was always short of seamen.

These regulations and harms particularly affected Boston. It was a major port and the city was crowded with merchant traders like the Quincys and Hancocks. Samuel's father-in-law-to-be, Thomas Hill, was a distiller. Massachusetts was famous for the rum it made from molasses with the sugar imported from the Caribbean. Hill would be especially anxious about the Molasses and Sugar Acts. Josiah Senior, while no longer personally involved in the shipping business, kept a wary eye on the problems faced by his son Edmund and other family members and friends. He was especially anxious about the maintenance of their rights.

In addition to their commercial interests, the Quincys took an active part in Braintree town governance. Most Braintree town meetings focused on very local concerns. One looks in vain for a reference to writs of assistance, however upset local merchants with businesses in Boston were. In May of 1761 the town meeting was concerned with the taverns and inns within the community. While acknowledging that "Licensed Houses, so far as they are conveniently situated well accommodated & under due Regulation a usefull Institution" they fretted:

That the present prevailing Depravity of Manners through the Land in General & in this Town in particular and the shamefull neglect of Religious & Civil Duties, so highly offensive in the

sight of God, & injurious to the peace & Welfare of Society are
in a great measure owing to the unnecessary license Increase of
Licensed Houses.[11]

That being the case the town meeting voted that "for the future there
be no Persons in this Town, Licens'd for retailing spiritous Liquors & that
there be three persons only approbated by the Selectmen as Inn-holders,
suitably situated, one in each Precinct."[12] Larger government questions did
not yet impinge on what seemed more relevant concerns.

Braintree and other town meetings may have been busy with local concerns, but there were informal meetings of merchants in Boston. They drew
up petitions, which were presented by them and other groups, concerned
with the constitutional impact of new royal policies. As time went on, town
meetings were increasingly called upon to instruct their colonial representatives on their grievances with current policies. In a family like the Quincys,
with a father actively engaged in public service, sons whose livelihood was
in commerce and law, keen to play a role in the disputes of the time, and
happy to publish essays on their views, there was no way Josiah Senior
and his three sons were going to quietly go about their personal business.

Edmund, Josiah's eldest son, however, was busy with his merchant-
shipping business during these years leading up to the dramatic turn in
events. Tragically Edmund's very promising career would be hindered a
few years later by illness. The young man became gravely ill with "pulmonary disease." His youngest brother, Josiah Junior, later suffered from
the same debilitating complaint. What was this pulmonary disease? To
begin with it was not consumption, or tuberculosis, which is contagious.
Rather, it was a progressive and potentially deadly ailment attacking the
lungs, making breathing increasingly difficult, causing shortness of breath
and painful coughing spells. It was a wasting disease, causing terrible
night fevers. The disease could stabilize for periods than reappear.[13] There
was, and is, no cure. We can only speculate about its cause in Edmund's
case. It may have been genetic but his father was fit and lived to a fine
old age. While his mother died in her forties, she did not suffer from it.

Edmund may have smoked a pipe, as most men did, or his home may have been excessively smoky, like other homes of the time. By his early thirties, Edmund was so ill that his planned marriage to Rebecca Lloyd in the summer of 1766 was postponed to permit him to follow his doctor's advice and sail to the West Indies in hopes of improving his health. Family and friends prayed that the journey might restore his vitality.

Son Samuel was loyal and cautious. While the tensions over British policies grew in the early 1760s, Samuel Quincy concentrated on his career. Close friends, family, and colleagues would be drawn into active opposition to the government. He was good friends with John Adams and John Hancock. Samuel was well-educated and a fine essayist, but his hopes for a post in government required cautious loyalty to the Crown. He also had a lawyer's disgust at the growing political violence against Crown officials, pulling him toward a "law-abiding" stance. It was a stance with which many, if not most, people sympathized.

Samuel and wife Hannah lived in a fine house on South Street in Boston, a fashionable neighborhood, and soon were parents of three children, sons Samuel and Thomas and daughter Hannah. Hannah was obviously a very popular name, as Samuel's little Hannah had a grandmother, an aunt, and a mother named Hannah.

Samuel was pulled in both directions, obedience or resistance, but happily there was no need for any open break. Instead, he looked forward to a distinguished career in government. He was a relative of Jonathan Sewell, British attorney general of Massachusetts, who was married to Samuel's cousin Esther Quincy. Such connections were always helpful. Samuel, like his brothers, was a talented writer, and even a poet, but does not seem to have published any essays during the growing controversies over taxes and rights. Clearly, it was prudent not to enter the fray, at least not publicly.

Josiah Junior couldn't have been more different in temperament and views from his older brother Samuel. Where his father became known as Colonel Quincy, Josiah would become known as "the Patriot." He had been frail from childhood, but the frail body held a passionate and daring disposition. He would be a son to make his father proud. Josiah had decided to become a lawyer like his brother and had the intelligence and eloquence to succeed. At Harvard, he won the freshman lecture and during his time at the college compiled a fine academic record. When he received his master of arts, he was selected to deliver the English oration. He chose as his subject, "Liberty." The speech was remembered years later for its fiery defense of patriotism. Josiah graduated in 1763, the year the French and Indian War ended, and joined the law office of one of the most distinguished attorneys in Massachusetts, Oxenbridge Thatcher. Thatcher had taken an active role alongside James Otis in the writs of assistance case. A biographer describes him as a radical patriot but demonstrating "at certain crucial moments, surprisingly cautious and restrained counsel and actions." [14] Sometimes a certain amount of caution is a virtue. In the writs case, both Otis and Thatcher were opposed by Jeremy Gridley, who had trained them both in law. Gridley, for his part, remarked he was confronted in the Court by the "two young eagles" he had reared.

Brother Edmund was busy building his shipping business, brother Samuel planning a fine career in a government post. Josiah had neither concern. He had become a student of Thatcher, the learned defender of colonial rights, and absorbed that respected attorney's patriotic fervor, although not his cautious approach. Josiah's dramatic essays on behalf of colonial rights would come later. He was still a student-lawyer learning his trade.

Even before passage of the Sugar Act, colonial leaders began to press merchants to hold more formal meetings and correspond with each other. If the problem with the government was basically economic, they could use economic weapons to combat it. The British wanted more money; the colonists would see that they got as little as possible with a boycott. A lot of social pressure was used to achieve this. But by the end of 1764, many Americans were boycotting the English products that were taxed. They began what they called a "nonimportation" movement. The movement was not precisely gentle. There was peer pressure and strenuous intimidation to ensure the boycott was honored. Merchants in Massachusetts, Rhode Island, and New York began to meet. In response to the Sugar Act and the growing restrictions on trade and basic rights, in 1764 Massachusetts leaders began to organize into committees of correspondence. These were aimed at keeping in contact with Massachusetts towns and with other colonies to encourage opposition and response to the British restrictions.

In 1764, James Otis published a pamphlet, *Rights of the British Colonies Asserted and Proved*, in which he made the claim, taken up quickly by his fellow countrymen, that their British rights asserted that taxation without representation was tyranny. Americans had not a single representative in the Westminster Parliament. [15] Otis pointed out in blunt and stirring prose that the supreme legislature cannot assume a power "of ruling by extempore arbitrary decrees" nor are "taxes . . . to be laid on the people, but by their consent in person, or by deputation." He reminded the colonists that "all the northern colonies who are without one representative in the House of Commons, should not be taxed by the British Parliament" and that "the colonists, black and white, born here, are free born British subjects, and entitled to all the essential civil rights of such." Otis opposed slavery. He was among the first to stress that while Parliament could legitimately pass taxes for those it represented, it did not represent the colonists. On the other hand, he believed, or claimed to believe, the king "has given abundant demonstrations, that in all his actions, he studies the good of his people, and the true glory of his crown, which are inseparable." The king's ministers may be misguided, members of Parliament might be wrong-headed, but the king, left to himself, was a benevolent ruler of his colonies.

Poor Otis, having staunchly defended American rights in the court-room, the assembly, and the press, suffered a mental breakdown in 1771. Otis, John Adams wrote, became "raving mad, raving against father, wife, brother, sister, friend." An opponent of Otis, Governor Thomas Hutchinson, sneered that Otis "was carried off, bound hand and foot . . . though that he had been as good as his word—set the Province in a flame and perished in the attempt." Otis struggled from bouts of mental illness the rest of his life. He retired from public life and lived in the country.

Otis was a close friend of Oxenbridge Thatcher, in whose law office Josiah was now a student. Josiah was also passionate about colonial rights and the need to protect them at whatever cost. This berth with Oxenbridge

Thatcher enhanced Josiah's dedication to the cause, much to the delight of his father.

Josiah was well-placed to play an active role in the resistance to Britain's growing demands, but having just graduated from college and begun his legal training he was not ready quite yet. It was the Stamp Act the following year, 1765, that brought everything to the fore—the foundation of the Sons of Liberty, heightened resentment spilling over into mob violence, and intimidation of government officials and loyalist neighbors. Josiah Jr. would be in the thick of it.

By 1765, the government's measures had outraged increasing numbers of residents and produced organized dissent and disorganized mob violence. There would be a raft of political associations of merchants, committees of correspondence, the Loyal Nine (a precursor of the Sons of Liberty), and the Sons of Liberty themselves, backed by complaints and declarations of opposition from town meetings, from ever more strident newspaper reports and essays, and from stirring patriotic sermons from the pulpit. Could as prominent and educated a family as the Quincys avoid being enveloped by the whirlwind blowing about them? A better question is: Would they?

SIX

The Stamp Act and the Sons of Liberty

He has heard with great pleasure the right of taxing America asserted and not disputed. If disputed and given up, he must give up the word 'colony' for that implies subordination. . . . If America looks to Great Britain for protection, she must enable her to protect her.

—Charles Townshend, MP for Harwich
during Parliament's debate on Stamp Act

When the Resolution [for the Stamp Act] was taken in the House [of Commons] to tax America, I was ill in bed: if I could have endured to have been carried in my bed, so great was the agitation of my mind for the consequences, I would have solicited some kind hand to have aided me down on this floor, to have borne my testimony against it.

—William Pitt, Earl of Chatham,
Letters of George III, December 1765, lxxxix[1]

By the great Charter [Magna Carta] . . . no Freeman shall be taken or imprisoned or be disseised of his Freehold or Liberties or Free Customs nor

passed upon nor condemned but by lawful judgment of his Peers or by the
Law of the Land.

—"Instructions to their Representative," Braintree,

Massachusetts Town Meeting

protesting the Stamp Act, 1765

P arliament's passage of the Stamp Act in the spring of 1765 culminated a year of decision for the Quincys and their neighbors and other colonists. Nearly everyone opposed the act, but the form that their opposition should take divided the population into activists ready to resort to any tactic, up to and including violence, and others, probably most Americans, who were against violence and the mob rule that would likely follow. They were ready to protest peacefully in the traditional manner, with declarations and petitions, but in the end obey the law. They understood the rule of law was essential for a peaceful society, especially one on the fringes of empire. That year saw the birth of the Sons of Liberty and exposed the split that drove moderate men into quiescence or flight and demonstrated how hard it was for the Sons of Liberty to stop a mob once it had been set going. Was violence in a popular cause acceptable? What was a loyal American, proud of his rights and a loyal subject of the British Empire to do?

Tensions that led to violence in 1765 began in 1764. Just after Parliament passed the Sugar Act, the leadership casually announced their plan to consider a stamp tax next. Its members began debating the stamp measure early in 1765. If the Sugar Act was resented, passage of the Stamp Act sparked outrage and violence. For most members of Parliament and King George as well, "An Act for granting and applying certain Stamp Duties, and other Duties, in the British Colonies and Plantations in America, towards further defraying the Expenses of defending, protecting, and securing the same" seemed sensible and fair. The royal administration had sent thousands of troops to the New World during the French and Indian War to evict the French from North America and were planning to keep

10,000 troops in the colonies. It was all tremendously costly. The British debt nearly doubled. British subjects at home were already taxed to the hilt. What could be more reasonable than those who had benefited, and were benefiting, from British protection on land and sea, and from good British government, ought to help pay for it.

This new revenue bill was novel. Rather than the customary tax on imports, it was a direct tax on activities within the colonies. Special stamped paper was to be used for all legal documents, such as deeds and diplomas, playing cards, dice, and newspapers. There was a hefty duty of £10 on every sheet of the stamped paper used for a license, appointment, or diploma. The paper for a license for retailing of wine was a duty of £3, for a pack of cards one shilling, for a pair of dice ten shillings. The tax had to be paid in British currency, which was scarce.

There was more in the act than just the tax, deeply annoying as that was. Those charged with violations of the act were no longer to be brought before American common law juries. Instead, they were to be tried in vice-admiralty courts where a judge sat without a jury. Previously admiralty courts only dealt with crimes on the high seas. While the admiralty judges were themselves colonists, they were paid by the British government and thus unlikely to be biased or even neutral in the colonists' defense. Worse, in vice-admiralty courts the accused was considered guilty until proven innocent, a sharp reversal of the most basic tenet of English law. The 1764 Currency Act passed a year earlier stipulated that the accused might even have to appear before the vice-admiralty court in distant Halifax, Nova Scotia.

The ministry allowed time for comments from those who would be subject to the tax, but in fact they only agreed to hear the comments from four colonial agents: Benjamin Franklin from Pennsylvania, Jared Ingersoll from New Haven, Richard Jackson for Connecticut, and Charles Garth for South Carolina. The last two were members of Parliament serving as colonial agents. Apart from these four men, Parliament simply ignored the flood of petitions and letters of protest submitted by the colonial legislatures and other groups.

The debate on the Stamp Act in the House of Commons spotlights the thinking of the British members there. There were, of course, no members from the colonies. George Grenville, the chancellor of the exchequer, began the debate pointing out that the new law "is founded on the great maxim that protection is due from the Governor, and support and obedience on the part of the governed." Charles Townshend, whose various government offices gave him familiarity with colonial affairs, supported the act characterizing Americans as "children planted by our care, nourished up by our indulgence until they are grown to a degree of strength & opulence, and protected by our arms," asking, "Will they grudge to contribute their mite to relieve us from the heavy weight of that burden, which we lie under?"

Townshend's characterization of the colonists outraged Colonel Isaac Barré, an Irish-born MP and soldier who had personal experience in the colonies when he fought in the French and Indian War:

> They planted by your care? No! your oppressions planted them in America. They fled from your tyranny to a then unculti-vated and unhospitable country—where they exposed them-selves to almost all the hardships to which human nature is liable, and among others to the cruelties of a savage foe. . . . And yet, actuated by the principles of true English liberty, they met all these hardships with pleasure . . .
>
> They nourished up by *your* indulgence? They grew by your neglect of them: as soon as you began to care about them, that care was exercised in sending persons to rule over them, in one department and another . . . sent to spy out their liberty, to misrepresent their actions and to prey upon them . . .
>
> They protected by *your* arms? They have nobly taken up arms in your defense, have exerted a valour amidst their constant and laborious industry for the defense of a country, whose frontier, while drenched in blood, its interior parts have yielded all its little savings to your emolument. And believe me, remember I

this day told you so, that same spirit of freedom which actuated
that people at first, will accompany them still.

Barré was not alone in these sentiments. He was one of forty-nine
members of the Commons who voted against the act. Nonetheless it was
passed overwhelmingly.

The argument that the hundreds of thousands of colonists were
not represented by a single member in the Parliament that was taxing
them was given short shrift by the majority of MPs. They accepted the
British system that the opportunity to vote was based on ownership of a
certain amount of property and antique lists of towns exclusively qualified to send two MPs, towns important in their day but often shrunk
to mere villages by the 18th century. The newer "great trading towns,"
as Grenville pointed out, were not represented at all. He added, "Not
a twentieth part of the people are actually represented." It has been
estimated that probably 75 percent of British men could not vote.[2]
The operating theory was that whether you could cast a vote or not,
everyone was represented in person or by proxy. Parliament represented
the kingdom and colonies, period. In short, the American argument for
representation fell on deaf ears.

The Stamp Act passed easily on a vote of 205 to 49. Members signed
it and the king approved it on March 22, 1765. It was to take effect in
November.

Although the Stamp Act was not to take effect until November 1, Grenville began to appoint stamp distributors shortly after it passed. Plenty of
colonists were happy to apply for the well-paid posts. If Grenville wasted
no time preparing to implement the stamp tax, the colonists wasted no
time preparing to oppose it. The Quincys, the Adams, the Hancocks, and
other friends and neighbors worked to prevent the implementation of the
act with publications, arguments, and organization. Colonel Josiah became
a member of the Sons of Liberty. Others, more cautious or uncertain, stayed
prudently silent, including Josiah's son Samuel. Probably he, like Jonathan
Sewell, one of John Adams's closest friends and husband of their cousin

Esther Quincy, disliked the act but "was careful not to commit himself publicly in the dramatic debates" over it.[3] Those loudest in opposition appeared to them simply anti-administration. Best not to be linked with them. Others, like John Adams and Josiah Senior, approved of the Sons of Liberty but not the violence their demonstrations incited. On the other hand, Samuel Adams, John's cousin, and others were prepared to achieve their aims by intimidation and rioting. Josiah Junior's mentor, the great patriot and attorney Oxenbridge Thatcher, was said to have been so upset by the act that when he died later that year, many claimed it was due to his great dismay over the imposition of the Stamp Act. Josiah Junior would take over his practice after his death.

Americans had not waited for Parliament's vote on the Stamp Act. They began to organize coordinated action in advance. A year earlier, in June 1764, Massachusetts had created a five-person Committee of Correspondence to coordinate activities against the Sugar Act, and other colonies formed similar committees. They sent protests to England by the end of the year, opposing this taxation without their consent. The Stamp Act was debated in the colonies shortly after its passage in March. In May, Samuel Adams's rhetoric alerted his fellow Americans to the dangerous precedent of the act:

> For if our Trade may be taxed why not our Lands? Why not the Produce of our Lands & every thing we possess or make use of? This we apprehend annihilates our Charter Right to govern & tax ourselves—It strikes our British Privileges, which as we have never forfeited them, we hold in common with our Fellow Subjects who are Natives of Britain. If Taxes are laid upon us . . . without our having a legal Representation where they are laid, are we not reduced from the Character of free Subjects to the miserable State of tributary Slaves.[4]

Massachusetts was not alone in protesting the impending Stamp Act. In May, the Virginia House of Burgesses met, and while many delegates left without considering the act, one of those who stayed to draw up resolutions against it was the new member, Patrick Henry. Henry's Virginia Resolves passed the House of Burgesses at the end of May. These stated that the settlers of the colony "brought with them, and transmitted to their Posterity, and all other his Majesty's subjects since inhabiting in this his Majesty's said Colony, all the Liberties, privileges, Franchises, and Immunities that have at any Time been held, enjoyed, and possess, by the People of Great Britain." These included the key constitutional tenet:

> The Taxation of the People by themselves, or by Persons chosen by themselves to represent them, who could only know what Taxes the people are able to bear, or the easiest method of raising them, and must themselves be affected by every Tax laid on the People, is the only Security against a burdensome Taxation, and the distinguishing characteristic of British Freedom, without which the ancient constitution cannot exist.[5]

In the fall of 1765, Samuel Adams, John's older and more radical cousin, invited him to his study. There Samuel admitted he "felt an ambition, which was very apt to mislead a man, and he wanted to consult a friend who might suggest some thoughts to his mind." Samuel's ambition was to devise and implement tactics to thwart the enforcement of the Stamp Act by whatever means seemed suitable. We don't know what John's advice was, but Samuel's tactics ranged from peaceful protests to public shaming of anyone who was willing to carry out or obey the law. They also included the use of rowdy mobs attacking the homes of those assigned to act as stamp officials. The Sons of Liberty were a brainchild of Samuel's. His strategy was simple—threaten and intimidate anyone willing to be a government agent for the stamps until they resigned or fled. With no one willing to enforce the act, no one willing to pay the tax, the Stamp Act would have to be withdrawn.

The plan began with a group of like-minded Boston businessmen, the Loyal Nine, who met secretly to plan public protests. While not himself a member, Sam's fingerprints were all over the group's makeup. The secretary was John Avery, a distiller, and it included another distiller, two jewelers (one a cousin of Sam Adams), a painter, a ship's captain, and most important, the printer of the *Boston Gazette*, another friend of Sam's. There was no lawyer. The group chose Ebenezer Mackintosh to organize great crowds of people, and the two distillers in their group would see the crowd was plied with food and drink. Food was no problem, drink another matter, for it was bound to excite the mob.

The employment by the Loyal Nine of Ebenezer Mackintosh was a giveaway. Upstanding families like the Quincys were ready to write essays against the Stamp Act, protest the Act in town meetings and the colonial legislature, and speak about the dangers of the new taxes to liberty. But did they approve of using mob violence to achieve their ends? Josiah Junior and other leaders of the new Sons of Liberty wanted strong protests but feared violence would demean their cause. The Loyal Nine were to find, as others orchestrating popular rage had learned, that mob outrage was easy to start, difficult to control. Nevertheless, the Loyal Nine picked Ebenezer Mackintosh, the leader of Boston's South End gang, to organize crowd protests. With Sam Adams's help, they unified the rival North End and South End gangs with Mackintosh leading both groups. Mackintosh's task was to arouse crowds to harass and defy the British government. He exceeded expectations. That August, in the heat of a Boston summer, he led a crowd of more than 3,000 people—merchants, workers, dockside toughs, and sailors—to protest the Stamp Act. Stoking mob violence was like riding the tiger's tail. Sometimes it was a danger to those who started it.

The public drama organized by the Sons of Liberty began on August 12, ostensibly to celebrate the birthday of the Prince of Wales. Some of the group began to shout "Pitt and Liberty" for William Pitt, who had opposed the Stamp Act. The demonstrators planned to return later in the week to hang Andrew Oliver in effigy. Oliver had been appointed to be the colony's stamp master. He was a wealthy merchant, father of seventeen children, with a long career of public service in Massachusetts. He was connected by marriage with Lieutenant Governor Thomas Hutchinson, later a loyal and much-hated governor. Oliver's mistake was that, while he may have been privately against the Stamp Act, he agreed to assume responsibility for administering it in the colony. The crowd was in high spirits as they returned on August 14th, and assembled at an elm tree near the Boston Common. It became the famous Liberty Tree. There, in a mock hanging, they hoisted an effigy of Oliver in the tree alongside a large boot, symbol of Lord Bute, with the head of a devil, horns and all, climbing out of it, all to much laughter. A sign was posted with the rhyme, *"A goodlier sight whoe-er did see?/A Stamp man hanging on a tree."*[6] That evening the figures were cut down, and the Sons of Liberty carried the effigies in a torchlight parade through town, deliberately marching past the building where Governor Francis Bernard and his council were meeting. The marchers were joined by a group of tradesmen and some two thousand residents. They proceeded to the building, still under construction, which they believed was meant to house the office of the new stamp master and, in high spirits, demolished it. Carrying some of the timbers they had torn off, they then marched to Oliver's house and built a bonfire in front of it. They tossed the beheaded effigies on the pile and burned the lot. Most of the crowd felt a point had been made and headed home, but a small group remained at Oliver's home, where they burned his carriage, destroyed his garden and outdoor furniture, smashed his windows, and broke into his wine cellar and drank the wine. The next day Oliver resigned.

According to Samuel Adams, the news of the mob action and Oliver's resignation was widely popular: "The people shouted and their shout was heard to the distant end of the continent."[7] But a line had been crossed. Mob violence was a far cry from peaceful protests and once begun did indeed become difficult to control. The more moderate residents of Massachusetts and other colonies, who may have opposed the Stamp Act, were readier to condemn than shout their pleasure at the rampage.[8] Indeed Mercy Otis Warren, who witnessed these events, disagreed with Samuel's claim: "So universal was the resentment and discontent of the people, that the more judicious and discreet characters were exceedingly apprehensive that the general clamor might terminate in the extremes of anarchy."[9]

The riots continued a few nights later, this time attacking the home of Lieutenant Governor Hutchinson. He opposed the Stamp Act but as chief justice he felt, and was, obliged to uphold the law. The mob besieged his house on Garden Court Street calling on him to explain his views. Hutchinson barred the doors and windows but was saved when a neighbor told the mob Hutchinson had gone to his country house in Milton.

Governor Bernard retreated to Castle Island in Boston Harbor. But the rioting was not over. Twelve days later there was more mob violence. It began that night, targeting the customs house and admiralty office. It started with a bonfire at dusk on August 26.[10] A fire warden who tried to put it out was struck by one of the mob and fled. The customs house was ransacked and the admiralty records set on fire. The crowd, armed with clubs and staves, marched to the house and office of the register of the admiralty, broke into the building, and burned his official and private papers. They moved on to the house of the controller of customs, where they destroyed his fence, smashed his windows and furniture, stole his money, and drank his wine.

Thomas Hutchinson, the lieutenant governor, descended from an established and distinguished Massachusetts family and a popular individual, was not at first a target. But after the mob finished its destruction of the customs house and admiralty, it marched to Hutchinson's home. He was warned the mob was coming. "I directed my children to fly to a secure place and [I] shut up my house as I had done before," he later wrote. He and his daughter fled to a neighbor's house just seconds ahead of the mob. His son, still in the house, also just managed to escape, as the mob hacked open the door and rampaged through the rooms. He and his family escaped just in time. With the crowd giving chase Hutchinson fled "through the yards and gardens to a house more remote," where he remained until four in the morning, "by which time one of the best finished houses in the province had nothing remaining but the bare walls and floors."[11] The mob took vengeance on his grand house, breaking the doors with axes, destroying or stealing everything inside, tearing down the woodwork. They were furious and thorough. In a frenzy, they hacked down partition walls and the cupola, stripped the slates and boards from the roof, "and all my trees . . . broke down to the ground. Such ruin was never seen in America." Samuel Adams's biographer tries to distance his man from the brutal lawlessness. He argues that the mob was not assembled by the Sons of Liberty but consisted of dock workers and other laborers who had suffered from economic decline, a plague of smallpox, and other problems, and generally were enraged at the government.[12] Whatever the truth of who called out and directed the mob, the damage had been done to the credibility and honor of American intentions. It was a warning to all.

Josiah Jr. privately deplored the wild mob violence, deploring that despite "the Fury of Revenge against those who they thought had disclaimed the Name of Sons for that of Inslavers and oppressive Taxmasters of their *native* Country, they committed Acts totally unjustifiable." He felt the "best asylum, that Glorious Medium, the BRITISH CONSTITUTION."[13]

The Boston authorities held a town meeting the next day and unanimously denounced the rioters, some of those present quietly voting against themselves. Those arrested and to be tried for the devastation were released by a crowd of friends who forced the jailer to hand over the keys.[14] When the authorities learned that the Customs House, which held a large sum of money, was scheduled to be attacked the following night, a guard of soldiers was summoned to protect it. The troops confronted the mob, who refused to leave until the soldiers were ordered to take aim. Apart from various further demonstrations, calm was restored.

If the more cautious members of the Sons of Liberty in Massachusetts did not organize or approve the rampage that achieved their aims, they seemed unable to stop the increasing viciousness and were likely to be implicated in it. When mob action was again being planned, by Sam Adams in January 1770, Josiah would argue that crowd intimidation was illegal and imprudent.[15] But he was outvoted. The initiative had been taken out of their hands, and their methods were quickly adopted in other colonies.

Nearby Rhode Island copied the Massachusetts pattern. On August 27 a crowd led by three merchants built a gallows near the Town House in Newport, where they brought effigies of the three officials named as stamp distributors, Augustus Johnson, Dr. Thomas Moffat, and Martin Howard, a lawyer. Having stirred up the populace to protest in the Massachusetts manner, the merchants, like those in that colony, lost control. That night the crowd returned, led by John Weber, a poor man, and attacked the homes of two of the stamp appointees. As in Massachusetts they ransacked the houses, destroying the walls, fences, furniture, and art, and enjoying the owner's wine. The colony's Sons of Liberty at first opposed violence, and when Weber was arrested, they refused to support him. But when the mob threatened to destroy their own homes, they agreed to help Weber and he was released. Martin Howard publicly supported the Stamp Act in a pamphlet, *A Colonist's Defence of Taxation*, but felt obliged to flee the colony for his safety.

Four days after the attack on Hutchinson's house, James McEvers, New York's stamp distributor, resigned his appointment. When the stamps for several of the northern colonies arrived in New York's harbor in October, placards posted in the city warned that "the first man that either distributes or makes use of stamped paper let him take care of his house, person and effects."[16] New York merchants agreed not to sell any English products until the Stamp Act had been repealed. Here too the Sons of Liberty were unable to control the crowds, as protests continued until the end of the year. Threats of violence did the rest to quiet any public opposition.

Maryland was spared the problem of violence when a court of magistrates found the Stamp Act illegal and in November ordered that businesses and colonial officials carry on business without them.

Opposition to the Stamp Act continued sporadically in Massachusetts, but in a more customary manner. Town meetings issued resolutions of protest. In September the Braintree town meeting put aside its focus on taverns and other local matters for the moment, and formed a committee to instruct their representative to the colonial legislature "on this important & alarming occasion."[17] John Adams and Norton Quincy were among its members. They drew up a draft for their representative and presented it to the meeting. It began politely:

> Stamp Duty impleaded: Sir, In all the Calamities that have ever befallen this Country, we have never felt so great a Concern nor so many alarming apprehensions as at this time. Such is our Loyalty to the King, such our veneration for both Houses of Parliament, and such our Friendship to all our fellow subjects in Britain that measures which seem to discover any unkindness toward us in that country are the more sensibly & intimately felt. And we can no longer forbear Complaining that many of the measures of the late ministry and some of the late Acts of Parliament have a Tendency in our apprehension to divest us of some of our most Essential Rights and Liberties.

They then focused on the Stamp Act, a tax they described as "very burthensome and in our opinion unconstitutional" subjecting them to "enormous Penalties which are to be prosecuted, and for & recovered at the option of an Informer at a Court of Admiralty without a Jury." This they labeled "the most Grevous of all . . . the alarming extension of the Powers of Court of Admiralty." They claimed the tax would drain the colony of cash and worse, "strip multitudes of poorer people of all their property and Reduce them to absolute beggary." The draft was approved and sent to their representative in the colonial legislature.

That October, after weeks of protests and violence, representatives from nine colonies met in New York City to take joint action against the act. Virginia, North Carolina, and Georgia sent no representatives because their governors refused to convene assemblies to elect delegates, and New Hampshire later signed the Declaration. James Otis, Samuel Adams, Oliver Partridge, and Timothy Ruggles (a brigadier in the militia) were the Massachusetts representatives. The delegates passed a Declaration of Rights and Grievances insisting on their rights as British subjects, stressing that they not be taxed by Parliament where they had no representation, but solely

by their own assemblies, and that they were entitled to trial by jury.
Ruggles refused to sign it, and when the war started ten years later, he
would become a loyalist. This was the beginning of his downfall, and
along with other so-called Tories he would eventually face virulent
attacks. One of the earliest denunciations came in the form of a censure
from the Massachusetts assembly, where he had sat for many years as
a representative. Its censure was led by James Otis Jr., for Ruggles's
refusal to approve the actions of the Stamp Act Congress, although
Ruggles was president of the group. Despite the censure of Ruggles,
the militia brigadier would continue to be elected as the representative
from conservative Hardwick, and was reelected to the General Court
as late as 1770. There were still enough moderates cautious about open
opposition to the government to keep him there.

Within a year Parliament repealed the Stamp Act due to the difficulty
of finding men to distribute the stamped paper or anyone to enforce the
act. Further protests and political pressures were brought by the English
merchant class, which was experiencing large losses due to the colonial
boycotts. In their joy at the removal of the hated tax, Americans generally
failed to notice that as Parliament withdrew the Stamp Act, it passed the
Declaration of Right, asserting its right to tax the Americans in all cases
whatsoever. It had passed a similar declaration for Ireland in 1719. Not a
good omen.

The strains and differences between the colonies and England and among
the colonists would continue to grow sporadically in the ensuing years.
Josiah Junior, now heir to Oxenbridge Thatcher's high-profile practice,
still very much a junior attorney, had taken no public part but would in
the future, and it would be a daring defense of the use of force. It would
harm him professionally. Samuel would remain quiet on the controversies
and escape mob outrage.

For now, life settled back into its familiar and more comfortable pat-
terns. Ruggles would remain in the legislature, and other moderates like
Samuel Quincy could quietly pursue their callings with little disrup-
tion. Samuel Adams fretted that his goals had not been achieved. But in a

few years the inhabitants of Massachusetts would move from a quiet accommodation with the British imperial system to massive rebellion against it. Threats and intimidation would reappear. And many friends and relatives would feel the need to distance themselves from the cause, some figuratively, some literally.

SEVEN

Personal and Public Trials 1768 and 1769

A great Variety of useful Learning might be brought into an History of that Case [Rex v. Corbet]—and the great Curiosity of the World after the Case, would make it sell . . . The great Questions concerning the Right of Juries in the Colonies . . . and concerning the Right of impressing Seamen for his Majestys Service . . . and might possibly procure us for the future the Benefit of Juries in such Cases. And the World ought to know, at least the American part of it, more than it does, of the true foundation of Impresses, if they have any.
—Rex v. Corbet, John Adams, *Legal Papers, 2*, vol. 2

Panton and Corbet [Rex v. Corbet] ought not to have been forgotten. Preston and his soldiers [Trial of Soldiers for Boston Massacre] ought to have been forgotten sooner.

—John Adams to Jedidiah Morse, January 20, 1816

Charles Townshend died a year after passage of the act [Townshend Acts] "but, young as he was, he had already lived for a year too long. His foolish trifling with a great problem set all America seething once more."
—J. W. Fortescue, *History of the British Army*, vol. 3

I n the years 1768 and 1769 there were painful personal trials and critical public trials. Josiah Junior had begun writing essays a year earlier against the new Townshend Act's taxes on a range of British goods, urging the boycott of these. But the years were moving toward the painful division of the country and the Quincy family, and in these years they experienced both personal and public trials. The first was very much a family tragedy and not completely unexpected. By this point in time, Josiah Senior's oldest son, Edmund, had been battling pulmonary disease for many years. Indeed, he and his youngest brother, Josiah Junior, both were frail and suffering from the same disease. Only middle brother Samuel was hardy and escaped the family illness. Up until 1766 Edmund was able to continue his shipping business, going on strenuous voyages to Britain and Europe. He also kept up active friendships and correspondence with some of the most distinguished and well-respected men of the time. If, as Oscar Wilde wrote, you can always judge a man by the quality of his enemies, you can also judge him by the quality of his friends. Edmund, "Ned," was a promising, talented, and intelligent young man. He was a fervent champion of colonial freedoms, and among his friends were two especially distinguished advocates of liberty, the Boston minister Jonathan Mayhew and Englishman Thomas Hollis, both known for their zealous commitment to freedom. Mayhew, a Congregational minister, was a fierce opponent of the Stamp Act. A decade before the Act, in 1750 and 1754, he had preached a series of famous election sermons on the cause of liberty and duty to resist tyranny. He urged the colonies to work together toward that end. His sermons were widely published both in Boston and London, and his "Discourse Concerning Unlimited Submission," delivered on the anniversary of the execution of King Charles I, was judged afterward as the first shot of the American Revolution. Some thought there may have been a connection between his rousing sermon against the Stamp Act declaring that the essence of slavery consisted of subjection to others, "whether many, few, or but one, it matters not," and the mob's attack the very next day on Thomas Hutchinson's house. Mayhew died in 1766, at the age of forty-six, the year the Stamp Act was repealed. But in that time he had made a significant contribution to the struggle for the rights of Americans. His published sermons were kept in print for years.

Edmund's other distinguished friend, Thomas Hollis, was a student at Lincoln's Inn but, like many gentlemen, never practiced law. He was a friend of Mayhew, who probably introduced him to Edmund. In his travels to Europe Hollis met leading French philosophers of the day and Italian painters. He was a member of the Royal Society of Arts and a fellow of the Royal Society, a friend of John Wilkes and the elder William Pitt. His contribution was in advancing English liberty by republishing many books on the limits of government from the 17th century, as well as recent works of John Adams and others hostile to the Stamp Act. These he sent to libraries in England and Europe. Hollis was wealthy and also sent both money and books to American colleges. It is a mark of their respect for Edmund Quincy that Mayhew and Hollis kept up a correspondence with the bright younger man busily writing essays on liberty.

In 1766, the year the Stamp Act was repealed, Edmund's pulmonary condition grew worse. He had planned to be married that summer to Rebecca Lloyd. He had spent time the previous summer with her family on Long Island courting her, successfully. But since his health had worsened, the marriage was postponed. Edmund's doctor, Joseph Warren, who had trained with Rebecca's uncle, James Lloyd, encouraged him to take a trip to the Caribbean in hopes the warm, sunny climate would improve his condition.

1768 was a sad year for the Quincys. The family was counting on Edmund's voyage south and sojourn in the Caribbean to restore his health. But in the end there would be no wedding for Edmund and Rebecca. The sun and warmth of the West Indies failed to provide the anticipated cure, and poor Edmund never returned home. He died at sea on March 31, 1768. He was just thirty-five years old.[1] It was a terrible blow to his parents and his entire family that a promising and beloved member should be taken from them at such a young age. Samuel wrote a moving Latin lament in

his brother Edmund's memory that survives in published tracts.[2] It had
the following lines:

> *That heart which late, inflamed with patriot zeal,*
> *Braved the bold insults of his country's foe,*
> *No more its pious frenzy can reveal,*
> *Nor e'er in Freedom's cause again shall glow.*

It would be up to his father, his surviving brothers Samuel and Josiah Jr.,
and sister Hannah to take up the cause.

Edmund's fiancée, Rebecca Lloyd, moved on and a year after Edmund's
death married John Broome, a patriot, who would have a distinguished
military and public career, serving as lieutenant colonel of a New York
City regiment during the coming war, sitting in the New York Provincial
Congress, later a delegate to the New York State Constitutional Convention. After the war Broome would be elected lieutenant governor of New
York three times. The Quincys found it harder to move on.

Edmund's death was especially sad in that the voyage had promised
to restore his health. A death at sea, dying amid strangers, with no final
resting place was particularly painful for his family and friends. There
would, of course, have been a special service on the ship with the ship's
company paying their respects as the captain concluded, "We therefore
commit [his] body to the deep, . . . in sure and certain hope of the resur-
rection of the body, when the Sea shall give up her dead." Into the beautiful
turquoise blue waters of the Caribbean he slipped. But Edmund would
have no resting place among his ancestors. Josiah Senior's two other sons
would also die at sea.

Like Edmund, the trial that took place in 1769 is not as well-known
as it deserves to be, doubtless in both cases because more dramatic
persons and events would soon follow and obscure the memory. When
war breaks out, much that gradually led to it tends to get overlooked.

Under the pseudonym "Hyperion," Josiah Junior, now a protégé of
that radical Adams, Samuel, began writing a series of essays, published

in the *Boston Gazette*, against the Townshend Acts. They passed in June 1767 to take effect in November, imposing taxes on a variety of British goods—glass, paper, paint, tea. [3] The funds were earmarked for royal agents in the colonies and the British troops there. The rules for the hated writs of assistance were made stronger. There was ample reason for upset, and a vigorous boycott was orchestrated with often heavy-handed intimidation of merchants and customers to avoid purchasing the taxed goods. Josiah's "Hyperion," written in late September and early October, warned professional men not to be swayed by British offices and flattery but urged that "calmness and deliberation are to guide the judgment; courage and intrepidity command the action." Did he have his own brother Samuel in mind as one "swayed by British offices?" If so, Samuel was not dissuaded from accepting a position. In November 1767, as the Townshend Acts took effect, Samuel was appointed to the important legal post of solicitor general for Massachusetts to defend the royal government.

Josiah's essays went further than this cautionary warning, urging armed resistance to the tax acts. [4] His description of the grievances the colonists were experiencing was unrestrained, designed to awake and inflame his readers. "Oh, my countrymen!" Josiah wrote, "what will our children say, when they read the history of these times, should they find we tamely gave away, without one noble struggle, the most invaluable of earthly blessings? As they drag the galling chain, will they not execrate us? . . . If we would not be despised by the whole world;—let us, in the most open, solemn manner, and with determined fortitude, swear,—we will die,—if we cannot live freemen!" Even radical Sam Adams shied away from this impetuous call to arms, preferring, at least for the moment, the economic warfare of boycotts and the statesmanlike language of petitions. Josiah was more passionate than politically astute. He may have been physically frail, but he was a zealous patriot. This use of emotional rhetoric was apparent years earlier when Josiah was chosen to deliver the English oration at Harvard as he received his master of arts. He selected "Liberty" as his subject, but his oration was said to have been more on the subject of patriotism. It was long remembered for his rousing spirit. It stuck in the memory of its listeners a half-century later and was one reason he was later dubbed "the Patriot." Resorting to armed defense was a remedy he readily and almost casually advocated.

Josiah had planned to marry Abigail Phillips, but with Edmund's death the couple decided to wait a respectful interval while the family was in mourning and until Josiah was feeling fit once more. They were eventually married October 4, 1769. Abigail came from the prestigious Phillips family of Boston. Her father, William Phillips, was a successful and patriotic merchant, and the young couple shared interests in literature and a wide variety of subjects. It was a fine match.

Early in the New Year, Sam Adams and James Otis penned a circular letter to be sent to the other colonial legislatures insisting that the Townshend Acts were against the British Constitution because the colonists were not represented in Parliament. Parliament might be the supreme legislature for the British Empire, but since the colonists were "separated by an ocean of a thousand leagues" from the Mother Country, only their own assemblies, where they were represented, could lawfully tax them. The Massachusetts assembly approved the letter, and it was sent to other colonies, where it met with a positive response. The letter was sent the month before Edmund died. The secretary of state for the colonies, Lord Hillsborough, ordered the General Court—the Massachusetts legislature—to revoke the letter. Instead, they voted 92–17 not to do so. Massachusetts governor Francis Bernard then dissolved the legislature and mob violence ensued. As in the Stamp Act riots, customs officials were attacked. As order broke down, Hillsborough sought to restore it by dispatching four regiments of British soldiers to Boston, a decision bound to make matters worse.

Mob violence was a dangerous option and alienated many moderate, patriotic Americans. Everyone could agree that legal cases were a completely legitimate means of bringing the abuse of colonial rights to the attention of the population and the British government. Josiah, a lawyer himself, insisted the law would be on their side. And so it was in the case of *Rex v. Corbet* in 1769. The case raised two crucial issues for the colonists, the right to trial by jury even in an admiralty court, and the freedom of the colonists from British naval impressment. The defense attorneys were James Otis, famous for his role in the writs of assistance case, and John Adams, a close friend and neighbor of the Quincys.

Impressment of men into the Royal Navy was a perverse practice for a people proud of their individual liberties. But the Royal Navy was continually short of crew and legally authorized to impress able-bodied men. The Crown claimed a right to seize men of seafaring experience for the Royal Navy, and the practice was legal and increasingly common during the naval wars of the eighteenth century.[5] In the Napoleonic Wars at the end of the century, after American independence, the British captured and impressed thousands of Americans but, even before the American Revolution, they were impressing American sailors. To Americans it was a violation of all their rights as freeborn men. The Declaration of Independence would cite this as one of the complaints against George III. Usually, the press gangs prowled English dockside pubs seeking men with some naval experience and persuading them to enlist or simply seizing them. They were placed on a ship about to sail. The victims would wake up out at sea with little option but to serve on the ship's crew. Americans were tempting victims and at least spoke English.

The incident that sparked the trial, started when the British frigate HMS *Rose* was on a routine voyage off the coast of New England in 1769 on the lookout for smugglers. The *Rose* was sailing off the coast of Marblehead, north of Boston, when the crew spotted and stopped the brig *Pitt Packet*, manned by a crew of Irishmen sailing homeward from a voyage to Spain with a cargo of salt.[6]

Henry Panton, the chief officer of the *Rose*, and some of his sailors boarded the *Pitt*. Panton asked to see the vessel's papers while his men began searching the ship. Four members of the *Pitt*'s crew, Michael Corbet, Pierce Fenning, John Ryan, and William Conner, were discovered hiding in the forepeak, the small space under the weather deck. They were variously armed with what came to hand: a hatchet, a musket, a harpoon, and fishing tackle. Lieutenant Panton demanded they come out. When they refused, Panton threatened to tear the bulkhead down to get at them, summoning reinforcements from the *Rose* to do it. There is disagreement about what happened next. As John Adams later recalled, the four men in the forepeak refused to come out, and one of them, Michael Corbet, drew a line in the salt, threatening that if Panton stepped over it Corbet would consider it an intention to impress him. He warned Panton if he approached "by the eternal God of Heaven, you are a dead man." Lieutenant Panton was not put off by this threat, and after casually taking a pinch of snuff from his pocket stepped over the line and attempted to seize Corbet. Corbet then thrust his harpoon with great force at Panton, severing his carotid artery and jugular vein. The British officer dropped dead.

The question of whether this was murder, deserving of hanging, or legitimate self-defense would be central to the case. The trial testimony differed markedly from a self-defense scenario, and is more likely to be accurate, although the end result was the same. In this recounting Lieutenant Panton was sitting on a bale of salt while Corbet and his three colleagues tried to stop Panton's men from tearing apart the forepeak they were sheltering in. Suddenly a pistol was fired into the crowded space. In the confusion Corbet launched the harpoon hitting Panton, who bled to death on the deck. Corbet and his three shipmates were subdued and handed over to the authorities.

Clearly an offense at sea belonged in the jurisdiction of an admiralty court. A special court of admiralty was convened. Five commissioners were sent to the *Rose* to take the testimony of witnesses. The court consisted of high-ranking officials from Massachusetts and other New England colonies—the governor and two councillors from New Hampshire, a judge from the Rhode Island Court of Vice Admiralty, and two collectors from Boston, one from Salem and one from Portsmouth.

James Otis and John Adams were defending Corbet. Adams raised the question whether there ought to be a jury. The law over the years had gone back and forth on the subject.[7] The Court adjourned to consider the issue and commenced again on June 14.

The second, and perhaps more important, question was whether an American seaman could be impressed into the Royal Navy. And, depending on the answer, whether Corbet had killed in self-defense to avoid an illegal impressment. Two Boston newspapers covered the case and took competing positions. The dramatic story, the important issues at stake, and the famous attorneys involved meant there was a great deal of public interest in the trial. Adams wrote:

> No trial had ever interested the community so much before, excited so much curiosity and compassion, or so many apprehensions of the fateful consequences of the supremacy of parliamentary jurisdiction, or the intrigues of parliamentary courts. No trial had drawn together such crowds of auditors from day to day; they were as numerous as those in the next year, at the trials of Preston and the soldiers. [8]

Otis and Adams pressed for a jury trial but were overruled. There were three days of testimony. None of the accused testified. However, Adams's search of the laws on impressment resulted in the discovery of a statute that forbade impressment of American seamen.

The upshot was that on June 17, as Adams rose to begin his defense that the killing had been in self-defense and therefore justifiable homicide, Governor Hutchinson moved to adjourn. The court retired and four hours later returned with its verdict that the killing of Panton had been justifiable homicide, and the prisoners were set free. Adams believed it was fear of establishing the non-impressment of Americans that swayed the Court, who were keen to keep that news quiet. Hutchinson argued that since neither Panton nor any of his superior offers were, in fact, authorized to impress, the Court agreed the accused had a right to defend themselves and should be acquitted of murder. Adams and Otis had prevailed. It was a triumph. Adams always felt this case was more important than that of the following year, where he famously defended the soldiers involved in the so-called Boston Massacre. [9]

That renowned case, the Boston Massacre of 1770, seemed to realize the worst suspicions of the colonists fearful of a professional army based among civilians, and brought the two surviving Quincy brothers into court on opposing sides.

EIGHT

The Soldiers' Trial: Brother Against Brother

Thus were we, in aggravation of other embarrassments, embarrassed with troops, forced upon us contrary to our inclinations—contrary to Magna Charta, contrary to the very letter of the [English] Bill of Rights . . .

—Dr. Joseph Warren[1]

[T]he magistrates and the mob were so plainly in the wrong that two of the revolutionary leaders [John Adams and Josiah Quincy Jr.] came forward to defend Preston and his men, of whom all but two were acquitted, and those two but lightly punished. . . . thenceforward this trial was always paraded as a specimen of the impartiality of American justice.

—Fortescue, *History of the British Army*

I n his testimony before the Committee of the Whole of the House of Commons, Benjamin Franklin testified regarding the Stamp Act, being asked, "Can any thing less than a military force carry the stamp-act into execution?" Franklin responded, "I do not see how a military force can be applied to that purpose." He then went on to say, "Suppose a military force sent into America, they will find nobody in arms; what are they then to do? They cannot force a man to take stamps who chooses to do without them. They will not find a rebellion; they may indeed make one." Franklin's warning was prophetic.

The March 1770 confrontation between a Boston mob and royal soldiers, resulting in the shooting and killing of five Boston residents, was a major step on the road to revolution. This incident, which Americans quickly dubbed the "Boston Massacre," illustrated the peril of posting British troops in the midst of a city such as Boston, a lesson finally learned in 1775. Samuel and his brother Josiah appeared on opposite sides in the dramatic trials that followed the shooting. The growing and very public Quincy family split occurred in the following quite unexpected way.

Josiah Junior's essays starting in 1767 damned those who accepted, or were even tempted, by British posts. He was young and, with the black-and-white opinions of youth, deaf to any moderate or alternative views. As he saw it, on the controversies over British governance men were either willing to take arms in opposition to this oppressive regime or prepared to live as slaves and traitors. But this militant public scolding did not deter Samuel. Despite his brother's unforgiving diatribes, in November 1767 Samuel accepted the post of Massachusetts solicitor general. Samuel was a fine essayist himself but less inflammatory and more prudent than his brother, and does not seem to have published any retort, other than in private letters.

The brothers appearing on opposite sides in the historic trial of the soldiers was startling, particularly because Josiah had been scathing about the military he was now defending. But many lawyers took on clients as their profession required. Perhaps, therefore, too much should not be made of the Quincy brothers appearing on opposite sides. In his role as solicitor general, Samuel was ordered to prosecute the British soldiers accused of the murder of unarmed civilians in Boston on March 5. Samuel's co-counsel was Robert Treat Paine, a staunch patriot. But apart from the brothers opposing each other in court, this alignment of prosecution and defense was an odd political juxtaposition. Josiah and the Sons of Liberty were defending the soldiers who perpetrated what they dubbed the Boston Massacre, while the Crown was prosecuting its own troops. The Sons of Liberty vigorously denounced the "massacre" and continued to publicize it for propaganda purposes. Paul Revere, a Boston silversmith and Son of Liberty, produced an engraving that showed the soldiers lined up shooting on their captain's orders and killing, not the apprentices and dockside laborers of March 5, but neatly dressed gentlemen. The engraving was widely distributed. Nevertheless, the Sons of Liberty meant to demonstrate that the soldiers could get a fair trial in America by defending them. The British, on the other hand, feared that if they did not punish their troops' violence toward riotous residents, however justified, the enraged townspeople would assault the outnumbered Boston garrison. And so it began, the personal and public family division in the Quincy family spilling over into one of the most explosive incidents leading to war.

To understand the deep feelings colonists felt about this incident, it is important to understand the hostility with which professional soldiers were viewed in England and America. In the 16th and 17th centuries, European monarchs raised and commanded larger and larger professional armies. When they were not fighting the king's wars, they were used to subdue the country's legislative assemblies and quash individual rights. In England, Parliament was reluctant to approve funds for a standing army except in time of war. Their kings had to rely on a citizen militia commanded by the landed nobility. In 1687–88 James II, using secret funds from the powerful French monarch Louis XIV, was able to swell the size of his army without Parliament's approval. He then disarmed local squires who opposed him as he worked to convert the realm to Catholicism. Englishmen grew alarmed for the future of their faith and liberty, and a group of nobles invited James's Protestant son-in-law, William, the Prince of Orange, to save the country. William and his wife Mary, with some English and Dutch troops, invaded England. The populace rallied to William, James's army deserted him, and he fled. A special convention parliament was elected. Members aimed to protect the rights and religion of the realm by drafting a bill that elevated William and Mary to the throne, together with a list of rights for the new monarchs to accept. This English Bill of Rights included the article that there could be no standing army in time of peace without the consent of Parliament. To further their control of any professional military, Parliament also passed a Mutiny Act that required the army to return to Parliament annually to renew its right to try cases of desertion and mutiny and have its budget renewed. A century later William Blackstone, in his bestseller *Commentaries on the Laws of England*, published on the eve of the American Revolution, warned, "In a land of liberty it is extremely dangerous to make a distinct order of the profession of arms."[2] He advised Englishmen to look upon their professional soldiers, "as temporary excrescences bred out of the distemper of the State, and not as any part of the permanent and perpetual laws of the Kingdom."[3] The fear of government by an army was very real. The English Bill of Rights was meant to safeguard Englishmen by keeping the control of the military in civilian hands.

The troops that were sent to Massachusetts and bivouacked in Boston were a constant reminder of the danger of soldiers to individual liberty. It was, after all, a time of peace. The soldiers were deeply resented and frequently taunted and ill-treated by the residents, who were sometimes treated badly in return. The soldiers themselves had hard lives even without this constant public irritant. They endured brutal army discipline, received low pay, sometimes taking other jobs while serving to make ends meet, and—apart from their officers, whose commissions were usually purchased—tended to be drawn from the poorest of the population. Furthermore, in America they were ordered to tolerate the abuse hurled at them. With the dangers of rule by an army in the minds of the colonists and continual friction between the British troops and the town's residents, it was unwise to station them in the midst of the Boston population, during peacetime, with the difficult mission to preserve order and help collect taxes.

Clashes between the residents and the soldiers escalated that winter. On March 2 hand-to-hand fighting erupted when one of the workers at John Gray's Ropewalk asked a passing soldier whether he wanted work. When the soldier said he did, the employee told him, "Wee then, go and clean my shithouse."[4] The soldier came back later with some dozen troops and a fistfight began. More serious trouble was bound to occur.

The shooting that was dubbed the Boston Massacre took place on the evening of March 5, 1770. It immediately became so overladen with outrage and propaganda that the facts became buried between the popular view that the Crown's troops had brutally shot and killed peaceful, unarmed members of a Boston crowd, and the view that the soldiers, assaulted and threatened by a group of young dockside toughs throwing ice, snowballs, and sticks, shot in self-defense. With the soldiers immediately damned by an outraged public, their trial was delayed for seven months to allow passions to cool. In preparation for the court proceedings, some 125 individuals were called to give their depositions. Captain Thomas Preston, the officer present, was tried separately from the soldiers. His trial opened on October 24 and concluded October 30. The trial of the soldiers followed and lasted nine days. Some four civilians were tried afterward. We have the depositions of witnesses as well as excerpts of the defense and prosecution attorneys' statements to the jury in these trials. As in modern trials the memory of witnesses, and in this case bias as well, can vary. The jury took careful note of the evidence and the law of self-defense.

But first, an account of the event itself, as precisely as can be gleaned from the contradictory testimony of the many witnesses: follows. March 5 was a bitterly cold evening in Boston, with a new moon, the ground covered with a layer of ice and deep snow. The streets around King Street Customs House and the Brattle Street soldiers' barracks some 300 yards away were full of sailors and apprentices strolling about—the latter invariably described as boys, fourteen or fifteen years old, meanly dressed—and a small group of British soldiers. About eight o'clock that night the sailors and apprentices got into a shouting match with the soldiers, and a fight erupted near the Brattle Street Church. The crowd rained ice, snowballs, canes, and sticks upon the soldiers, who defended themselves. A boy was lifted into a window of the Meeting House (the church) to ring the alarm bell, and there were shouts of "fire!" Coming on the fight a passing officer, Captain John Goldfinch, ordered his men back into their barracks,

promising no more men would be out that night.[5] Citizens who rushed
out with their fire buckets, finding no fire, went home.

A small group of apprentices and sailors moved on to the Customs House,
guarded by a lone sentry marching back and forth.[6] Other strollers con-
verged, and quite quickly a crowd of some fifty people confronted the sentry.
The crowd knew that soldiers were not permitted to fire on civilians without
the approval of a magistrate. One witness, Dimond Morton, said the crowd
cried, "You dare not fire; and others said, fire and be damned; then the boys
gave two or three cheers."[7] Several witnesses claimed the crowd was armed
with sticks and cudgels and pelted the lone sentry with ice and snowballs
"as big as your fist; hard and large enough to hurt a man." The sentry called
for help and several minutes later Captain Thomas Preston, the officer of
the day, rushed to his aid with eight soldiers. Their guns were unloaded but
their bayonets were fixed. Pushing through the crowd, the soldiers formed
a half circle around the sentry. When Preston arrived, he called for the
crowd to disperse, but they continued pelting the soldiers, hitting one of
the soldiers' guns. Crispus Attucks, a forty-seven-year-old man of mixed
race, rushed forward and grabbed the bayonet of one of the soldiers, Hugh
Montgomery, knocking Montgomery to the ground.[8] Montgomery got up,
shouting, "Damn you, fire!" and fired at the crowd. Cries of "Fire!" rang out
in the dark and, with more men moving toward the troops, other soldiers
fired, killing four men outright, including Attucks, and wounding seven
more. Five men would die. Captain Preston ordered his men to stop firing.

Complicating the facts was the story of Charles Bourgate, a servant of
Edward Manwaring, Esq., who testified that hearing the bells ring, "which
I took to be for fire," he rushed to the Customs House, where his master had
gone.[9] He knocked on the door and went inside. He was led to an upstairs
room where a group of men were assembled. Someone handed him a loaded
gun. He claimed he was threatened with serious punishment if he did not
fire out of an open window, which he then did, twice. His master entered
the room and fired as well. Bourgate fled home, and he was "licked" the
next day by his master "for telling Mrs. Waldron about his firing out of
the custom-house, but for fear that I should be licked again I did deny all

that I said before Justice Quincy [Josiah's uncle], which I am very sorry for."
Several witnesses corroborated Bourgate's story. Gillam Bass, for example,
claimed, once firing began, to have seen "two or three of the [gun] flashes so
high above the rest, that the deponent verily believes they must have come
from the Custom-house windows."[10] Francis Read reported, "Casting my
eyes about after the firing was over, I saw the smoke of two discharges high
above the rest."[11] Benjamin Frizell, a mariner from the county of Lincoln,
testified to the firing of five guns, two by soldiers to his right hand, "the
other three, as appeared to the deponent, were discharged from the balcony
or the chamber window of the Custom-house, the flashes appearing on the
left hand and higher than the right hand flashes appeared to be."[12] Those
firing from the Customs House probably meant to frighten off the crowd
since they don't seem to have killed anyone. But the king's treasury funds
were stored there, and protecting the money may have been the motiva-
tion. Edward Manwaring, Bourgate's master, and his friend John Munroe,
both in the Customs House when the shooting occurred, were among four
civilians later accused of firing at the crowd.[13]

Thomas Hutchinson, the acting governor, rushed to the scene as soon as he
learned of it. He confronted a shaken Captain Preston. Wounded members
of the crowd lay bleeding in the street. Hutchinson reminded the captain
that he had no power to fire on any public body without being ordered to by
a civil magistrate. Of course, in an emergency like this, that would have been
exceedingly difficult and much too late to avoid injury to the soldiers or the
crowd. Hutchinson returned to the town house and assured other council
members who had gathered there that he would see justice done. He then
stepped out onto a balcony and pleaded with the crowd for patience: "Let
the law have its course. I will live and die by the law."

The soldiers might have been tried in a court-martial, but English tradition was adamant that such a court might favor soldiers and that soldiers,
like everyone else, must be tried in a common law court. The ordinary
routine of the law proceeded.

The next morning, in the wee hours of March 6, Justices Richard Dania
and John Tudor handed the sheriff a warrant for the arrest of Preston. The

two then interrogated Preston for an hour and concluded they had enough evidence to arrest him. He was sent to jail for what turned out to be seven long months to await trial. The eight soldiers involved were also jailed. Ordinarily there would not have been such a long wait, but Hutchinson was in no hurry for a quick trial. He delayed, he said, "so that people may have time to cool." In the meantime, while the Sons of Liberty kept the incident fresh in the public mind, the two regiments of soldiers were moved out of the city to Castle William, on an island in Boston Harbor.

Josiah Junior must have been astonished when the day after the shooting, he received a message from the jail that Captain Preston wished to see him. Just twenty days earlier Josiah had published "The Independent," an essay passionately defending the nonimportation agreement against the Townshend Acts. In it he takes his usual radical position:

> From a conviction in my own mind, that America is now the slave of Britain; from a sense that we are every day more and more in danger of an increase of our burdens, and a fastening of our shackles, I wish to see my countrymen break off,—*off forever*! All social intercourse with those, whose commerce contaminates, whose luxuries poison, whose avarice is insatiable, and whose unnatural oppressions are not to be borne. . . . Whether the arts of policy, or the arts of *war* will decide the contest, are problems, we will solve at a more convenient season. He whose heart is enamoured with the refinements of political artifice and finesse, will seek one mode of redress; he whose heart is free, honest and intrepid, will pursue another, a bolder, and more noble mode of redress.[14]

Yet Preston asked Josiah to defend him and his soldiers. It really was hard to get anyone to defend Captain Preston and his soldiers. Indeed, the captain and his men very likely believed the government that employed them would defend them. After all, they were posted to Boston to keep order and were doing their best. Imagine their dismay when they discovered that, for reasons of its own, the government intended to prosecute them. A sergeant had gone to Samuel Quincy's house, doubtless assuming that as solicitor general Samuel would be taking their case. With little alternative, since the government would not defend them, Preston was driven to ask their opponents for help. Josiah's extreme rhetoric and popular reputation would be helpful to demonstrate the limits of those views, that in the end law and order must prevail. John Adams, an equally zealous patriot but less given to extreme pronouncements than Josiah, was Preston's choice to be their senior advocate. Samuel Quincy and John Adams were friends, and one or both probably recommended the younger man.

Josiah was of two minds about accepting the offer:

> On the one hand were the obligations of humanity, official duty, and the strong desire that justice should not fall a sacrifice in her own temple, to the passions of the moment. On the other hand, the confidence of political friends, popularity, and that general affection which his public course had attained for him, in so remarkable a degree, among his fellow-citizens, were to be hazarded. [15]

Before agreeing to take on the case, Josiah consulted with John Adams, his close friend. John Adams and Josiah Quincy also consulted with friends and political colleagues and, on their urging, agreed to take on the soldiers' defense. Adams claimed to have taken the case because no one else would do so, which may have been true. [16] He may have persuaded Josiah to join the defense. A third attorney, Robert Auchmuty, joined them. In 1767, the year Samuel was appointed solicitor general for Massachusetts, Auchmuty was appointed judge of the vice-admiralty court of Massachusetts and New Hampshire. Unlike Adams and Quincy he was a loyalist and in 1776 went into exile in England.

The entire colony must have been astonished to learn that the government was preparing to prosecute its own soldiers, while radical patriots were to defend them. Among those startled and upset by Josiah's decision was his father, whose political views are plain in the shocked letter he wrote his son: "I am under great affliction, at hearing the bitterest reproaches uttered against you, for having become an advocate for those criminals who are charged with the murder of their fellow-citizens. Good God! Is it possible? I will not believe it."[17] He had been informed that a sergeant had inquired for Josiah at Samuel's house, but "had no apprehension that it was possible an application would be made to you to undertake their defence . . . I must own to you, it has filled the bosom of your aged and infirm parent with anxiety and distress, lest it should not only prove true, but destructive of your reputation and interest; and I repeat I will not believe it, unless it be confirmed by your own mouth, or under your own hand." He signed, "Your anxious and distressed parent, Josiah Quincy.[18]

Four days later Josiah replied, insisting he had little leisure and less inclination "either to know, or to take notice, of those ignorant slanderers, who had dared to utter their 'bitter reproaches' in your hearing against me, for having become an advocate for criminals charged with murder."[19] The slanderers, he wrote, should have "spared a little reflection on the nature of an attorney's oath, and duty. . . and some small portion of patience in viewing my past and future conduct." These so-called criminals, he reminded his father, are "*not yet legally proved guilty*" and "are entitled by the laws of God and man, to all legal counsel and aid." He admitted that, at first, he declined being engaged but "after the best advice, and most mature deliberation," he agreed, although he informed Preston "my real opinion, on the contests . . . of the times, and that my heart and hand were indissolubly attached to the cause of my country." Josiah had also been urged to undertake the defense by unimpeachable patriots, "an Adams, a Hancock, a Molineux, a Cushing, a Henshaw . . . a Warren . . . and a Phillips," all Sons of Liberty or their supporters. Josiah hoped that his father "and this whole people will one day REJOICE, that I became an advocate for the aforesaid 'criminals,' *charged* with the murder of our fellow-citizens."[20] Indeed, J. W. Fortescue, author of the classic history of the British army, writes bitterly, "This trial was always paraded as a specimen of the impartiality of American justice."[21]

Josiah closed his letter to his father with the observation, "There are honest men in all sects,—there are wicked bigots in all parties,—I abhor them." This unusually moderate statement is at odds with Josiah's previous condemnation of those who supported the British. Josiah Senior would have had no worries about his older son Samuel prosecuting the accused soldiers. Samuel, at least, was in tune with the popular view of the terrible conduct of the "criminals."

Both prosecution and defense had a mix of radical and loyalist attorneys. For the defense there were John Adams and Josiah Quincy, along with admiralty judge Robert Auchmuty. For the prosecution Samuel Quincy, solicitor general, and Robert Treat Paine, a staunch patriot who would later sign the Declaration of Independence. The lawyers all knew each other. Samuel Quincy and John Adams were classmates and friends. However mixed the politics of the lawyers, they did their best, in the highly charged circumstances, to represent their clients fairly. As it turned out so did the jurors.

It was one thing to have taken a legal side for strategic reasons and another to suddenly be arguing against your deeply held views. Samuel had to prosecute soldiers who he had reason to believe had defended themselves against a motley group of ruffians. Josiah had to defend soldiers whose use and task he feared and despised. Both Quincy brothers did their duty as attorneys and argued against their own personal opinions on behalf of their clients.

There are no surviving notes from the trial of Captain Preston, just Preston's own previous deposition and Robert Treat Paine's closing statement for the prosecution. The captain was accused of ordering the soldiers to fire, a charge he adamantly denied. The case against Preston was confused by the shouts of "fire" from many quarters. Fortunately, we do have notes, edited by John Adams, on the trial of the soldiers. With these materials we can at least cobble together an account of these key and lengthy trials.

The opening statements on both the prosecution and the defense stressed the need for the jurors to remain impartial as they evaluated the evidence.[22] The trials had been delayed for seven months in hopes that emotions would cool, but even after seven months there was still great outrage at the shooting, continually stoked by the Sons of Liberty, while members Adams and Josiah Jr. now defended the soldiers. In modern times there might have been a change of venue, but in 1770 the trial remained in Boston. The jurors were sequestered and survived on a diet of biscuits, cheese, and cider, along with "sperites licker."[23] In truth this may have not differed much from their regular winter diet.

The captain was to be tried separately from the soldiers. When they learned this the eight soldiers on trial wrote to the court pleading to be tried with the captain: "We poor distressed prisoners beg that ye would be so good as to let us have our trial at the same time with our Captain, for we did our Captain's orders, and if we do not obey his command should have been confined and shot for not doing it."[24] The court was not prepared to change the arrangements. The soldiers seem to have discounted the plea of self-defense for themselves. They were right, though, that their interests and those of their captain posed a conflict of interest for them and their defense team. But it was too late now, and Adams and Quincy were committed to defending them all. The trial of the captain and later the soldiers took place in Boston's Queen Street Courthouse.

Captain Preston's trial was first. As counsel for the Crown, Samuel Quincy opened the case, reminding the jurors Preston was charged with having ordered his men to fire on the unarmed crowd without prior permission from a magistrate. Preston adamantly denied having done so. The problem for the prosecutors was the confusion that night and the noise and chaos just before and at the time of the shooting. There were shouts of "fire" from townsmen, including some who were pelting the soldiers. It was unclear whether Preston had given an order to fire or the soldiers, hearing the word "fire" shouted, fired, or had begun firing to protect themselves from the angry mob. In any event Preston insisted he had not given the order to fire.

The opening statements from the soldiers' trial are probably similar to those for Captain Preston. The following excerpts are from the statements at the trial of the soldiers.

As counsel for the Crown, Samuel Quincy opened the trial for the soldiers.[25] He repeated the charge that the soldiers were "induced from some cause or other to fire on the inhabitants of this town, in King Street. They are charged with five distinct indictments with the willful premeditated murder of five different persons . . . to each of these indictments, they have severally pleaded, not guilty.[26]

"I am aware," he told the jurors:

> How difficult, in cases of this sort, it ever is, and more especially so in these times and in this trial to preserve the mind perfectly indifferent; but I remember, we are bound, not only by the natural obligations towards God and man, but also by an oath to examine into the evidence of fact without partiality or prejudice . . . It has become my duty, it shall therefore be my endeavor, to acquit myself in the course of this trial with decency and candor; reflecting, that however interesting the question may be, the object of our inquiry is simply that of truth, and that this inquiry is to be conducted by the wisdom of the laws and constitution.[27]

Next Josiah addressed the jury for the defense, also pleading for impartiality. He pointed out that the persons slain were described in the indictment as "being in the peace of God, and our lord the king, at the time of the mortal wounds given," an inaccurate description if the crowd was hurling missiles of various sorts at the soldiers.[28] The soldiers had all pleaded not guilty. Josiah treated the jury to a sympathetic description of a soldier's life, at odds with his previous condemnation of their profession. The soldiers were men and deserved to live, he stated.

> An opinion had been entertained by many among us, that the life of a soldier was of very little value; and much less value than others of the community. The law, gentlemen, knows no such distinction; the life of a soldier is viewed, by the equal eye of the law, as estimable, as the life of any other citizen.[29]

Josiah continued:

> I cannot any other way account for what I mention, but by sup-
> posing that the indigence and poverty of a soldier,—the toils of
> his life,—the precarious tenure by which he is generally thought
> to hold his life, in the summary decisions of a court-martial,
> have conspired to propagate a sentiment of this kind; but a little
> attention to the human heart will dissipate this notion.

"The reputation of the country depends much on your conduct, gentlemen; and may I not add, justice calls aloud for candour in hearing,
and impartiality in deciding, this cause, which has, perhaps, too much
engrossed our affections; and, I speak for one, too much excited our
passions."[30] Josiah then reviewed recent history that gave the colonists
ample reason for animosity. Five or six years ago, he explained, "measures
taken in Great Britain," presumably the Stamp Act, caused Americans to
fear "that our dearest rights were invaded." Many regarded "the soldiers
as fastening, and riveting for ages, the shackles of their bondage." But,
he warned, "it is not our business here to inquire touching these delicate
points . . . however interesting or important in themselves, we must keep
far away from us, when in a court of law. It poisons justice, when politics
tincture its current."[31] They were jurymen not statesmen. The soldier had
not stopped being a citizen when he became a soldier. "How stinging was
it to be stigmatized, as the instrument of tyranny and oppression?"[32] On
the other hand the citizens had been told their rights were being quashed
and had every reason for antagonism toward the soldiers.

In the captain's case, Preston was led through the information in his
deposition. In that deposition Preston swore that when he heard the bells
ringing he believed that was a summons to the inhabitants to attack the
troops.[33] As he was officer of the day, he repaired at once to the main
guard, on his way hearing people uttering cruel and horrid threats against
the troops. A crowd was heading to the customs house, "where the king's
money is lodged." The lone sentry there was surrounded, and the mob was

threatening him with clubs and other weapons "to execute their vengeance on him." Preston was told the crowd meant to carry the sentry off and probably murder him. He feared they might also be aiming to plunder the king's chest. In the emergency he urgently dispatched a non-commissioned officer and twelve [*sic*] men to protect the sentry and the king's money. Then he hurried after them "to prevent, if possible, all disorder, fearing lest the officer and soldiers, by the insults and provocations of the rioters, should be thrown off their guard and commit some rash act." The rash actions of the mob would have stirred his men to protect themselves. Preston's insistence he never gave an order to fire was supported by three defense witnesses, while four prosecution witnesses insisted that he did. Preston said that some "well-behaved persons" asked him if the men's guns were charged, and he replied yes. Then he was asked if he intended to order the men to fire and answered no, "observing to them that I was standing in front of the soldiers, and must fall a sacrifice if they fired. . . . and my giving the word fire under those circumstances would prove me to be no officer."[34] At that point, Preston continued, one of the soldiers received a severe blow with a stick, a fact corroborated by witnesses, stepped to one side, and fired. Preston, turning, asked him why he fired without orders, when suddenly Preston himself was struck with a club on his arm. "Had it been placed on my head," he commented, "most probably would have destroyed me." This assault seemed to trigger a general attack on the soldiers by men in the crowd, many armed with heavy clubs and snowballs. At the same time someone called from the back of the crowd "damn your bloods—why don't you fire." This shout also jibed with witness testimony. Preston felt all their lives were in imminent danger. Three or four soldiers fired, then three more "in the same confusion and hurry."

After all the witnesses were examined, Robert Treat Paine summed up the case for the Crown against Captain Preston:

> It's importance Gentln. is not confined to ye small Circle of a
> few Individuals, but concerns ye very foundation of Civil Gov-
> ernment. In their Defense every Source of Eloquence & Art

has been exhausted; which I don't mention as a fault in them. But to guard you against mistaking ye Flowers of Rhetoric for Reason & Argument. This Prosecution is founded on one of ye most essential Laws of Nature: Murder is such a daring violation of ye first Law of Society, . . . your enquiry Gentn. in this important Affair will be directed to these two points—did the Prisoner give Orders to fire, in consequence of which ensued ye Death of any or all ye Persons named in ye Indictments? If so, has he offered any thing to reduce this Crime to a lower Species of homicide than Murder?[35]

Treat went over the evidence and the manner in which soldiers were patrolling the streets, brandishing weapons and threatening innocent inhabitants "with Bloodshed & Slaughter."

But Preston's testimony, along with that of defense witnesses, left the jurors in doubt whether Preston had ever given an order to fire. After a few hours of deliberation, the jury unanimously agreed to acquit Preston of all charges. It was a great victory for John Adams and Josiah Quincy. But the verdict was a surprise to the public, including the Sons of Liberty, who wanted to prove the soldiers could get a fair trial, but didn't expect Preston to be found not guilty.[36]

Captain Preston was a native of Ireland, and after the trial retired from the military and returned to his home country. Years later, in the 1780s, when John Adams was a United States minister to Great Britain, he saw Preston in London.

Eight weeks after Preston's trial, the trial of the eight soldiers, the case of *Rex v. Weems et al.*, took place. It was a more difficult argument for the defense than the trial of Captain Preston had been. All eight soldiers pleaded not guilty. Yet five members of the crowd had been killed. They claimed they had all fired in self-defense. This time we have detailed records of the trial.

Again, Samuel Quincy opened for the prosecution, Josiah for the defense. Josiah gave a long opening statement, then he and Adams spent the next four days examining some forty witnesses. Josiah began his defense by carefully separating the behavior of the crowd that had provoked the shooting from the general population of Boston. No longer were those who were shot victims, but a threatening rabble. "The inhabitants of Boston," he explained, "by no rules of law, justice, or common sense, can be supposed answerable for the unjustifiable conduct of a few individuals, hastily assembled in the Streets. . . . Who can, who will, unnecessarily interest themselves to justify the rude behaviour of a mixt and ungovernable multitude?"[37] He added that the law "puts the citizen and soldier under equal restraint."[38]

Josiah then closed, apologizing for the time taken, but had done so "from a sense of duty to the prisoners; they, who in some sense may be said to have put their lives in my hands; they, whose situation was so peculiar, that we have necessarily taken up more time, than ordinary cases require . . . remembering that they, who are under oath to declare the whole truth, think and act very differently from bystanders, who, being under no ties of this kind, take a latitude, which is by no means admissible in a court of law. I cannot close this cause better than by desiring you to consider well the genius and spirit of the law, which will be laid down, and to govern yourselves by this great standard of truth." [39] For good measure he quoted Shakespeare's reference to the "quality of mercy."

Samuel Quincy summed up the evidence for the prosecution. All the soldiers charged had been in the group on March 5 when members of the public had been shot. The difficulty with the witness statements was the uncertainty as to which of the soldiers had fired: "The five persons named in those indictments were killed by some or other of that party. But who they were that killed those several persons, may not be precisely ascertained, except in the case of *Killroy*, against whom I think you have certain evidence."[40] He then mentioned a key legal rule bearing on this case: "That it is immaterial, where there are a number of persons concerned, who gave the mortal blow, all that are present, are in the eye of the law, principals." He added, "No man shall be the avenger of his own cause . . . If a man might at any time execute his own revenge, there would be an end of law."

If attacked he should retreat if possible. He concluded, "I shall therefore rest the case as it is, and doubt not but on the evidence as it now stands, the facts, as far as we have gone, against the prisoners at the bar, are fully proved, and until something turns up to remove from your minds, the force of that evidence, you must pronounce them *GUILTY.*"

John Adams then summed up the evidence for the soldiers in an eloquent speech that explained that this was a case of self-defense:

> I will enlarge no more on the evidence, but submit it to you. Facts are stubborn things; and whatever may be our wishes, our inclinations, or the dictates of our passions, they cannot alter the state of fact and evidence: nor is the law less stable than the fact; if an assault was made to endanger their lives, the law is clear, they had a right to kill in their own defence; if it was not so severe as to endanger their lives, yet if they were assaulted at all, struck and abused by blows of any sort, by snow-balls, oyster-shells, cinders, clubs, or sticks of any kind; this was a provocation, for which the law reduces the offence of killing, down to manslaughter, in consideration of those passions in our nature, which cannot be eradicated. To your candour and justice I submit the prisoners and their cause.

In addition to the uncertainty over which soldiers had fired, Adams and Quincy made a compelling case for the soldiers acting in self defense. The result was an astounding triumph for John Adams and Josiah Quincy. Six of the soldiers were acquitted and the remaining two had their charges reduced to manslaughter, and their punishment was to be branded on the thumb. However most colonists felt about this result, both the Sons of Liberty and the Crown government could boast that impartial justice had been done.

Samuel Quincy was obviously less pleased than Josiah at the result, although he had no choice in prosecuting the Crown's soldiers and, at the time, popular opinion was behind him. The third trial dealing with the Boston Massacre, the trial against the four men who had shot from the Customs House window, took place on December 13. Samuel Quincy had the unfortunate duty of prosecuting them. In writing to his co-counsel, Robert Paine, he referred to being "imbarked in another Windmill-Adventure, & came off as you will readily suppose like poor Quixote in a like Instance."[41] Since the only witness he brought forward gave false testimony and was later convicted of perjury, the four men were acquitted.

The March 5 riot and killings and resulting trials were over. There was shock that apart from two soldiers whose charges were reduced to manslaughter and each had a branded thumb, no one had been punished for the deaths of five colonists and injuries to several others. The soldiers based in Boston had been moved from the city to an island in the harbor. The two Quincy brothers had opposed each other in court. No one's reputation was tarnished, as Josiah Senior had feared. Both had behaved in a professional and dignified manner. For the time being life went back to its familiar routines. In his memoir of his father's life, Josiah Junior's son concluded: "The passions of the moment, restrained in her courts, waited patiently for her decision, and submitted to a judgment, in which neither the feelings nor the sentiments of the time acquiesced. The multitude was silent, though not satisfied, under the authority of the laws."

The results of the soldiers' trials certainly made the soldiers happy. But the aftermath had a perverse impact not pleasing to either Quincy brother or their supporters.

NINE

Battling the Doldrums

I shall be no more perplexed, in this manner. I shall have no journeys to make to Cambridge—no general court to attend—but shall divide my time between Boston and Braintree, between law and husbandry. Farewell, politics.

—John Adams, diary entry for April 20, 1771

Report sent to London after trials of soldiers, "disposition in all the colonies to let the controversy with the kingdom subside . . . Hancock and most of the party are quiet; and all of them, except [Samuel] Adams abate of their virulence."

—Thomas Hutchinson, governor of Massachusetts

By the beginning of 1771 everyone was emotionally exhausted. The activists for and against the British government and the Massachusetts public were thoroughly tired of politics. The "massacre" in early March of 1770 and the trials months later didn't end until late December, taking nearly all of that year. Outrage and anger can only last so long, despite the energetic efforts of the Sons of Liberty to keep the memory of the incident fresh and raw. Nearly a whole year and what a disappointing climax. To begin with, the result of the trials did not please the law-yers who argued them. It was Jonathan Sewell, the attorney general of Massachusetts, not Samuel Quincy who was supposed to prosecute the soldiers, but Sewell declined, leaving Samuel to take on the chore. The prosecution of the king's men clashed with Sewell's personal view that the soldiers were innocent, and he left the tensions of Boston for his home in Middlesex County for what was to become a yearlong exile.[1] Samuel's prosecution of the troops was, and was meant to be, popular with the public. But to his and their disappointment, he lost all three cases. The captain, the soldiers, and the four civilians all were freed, to the dismay of the colonists. Samuel had done his duty as solicitor general and was well-respected in government circles. He and his wife, Hannah, lived in a fine house in the best section of Boston with their three young children: little Hannah, now eight; Samuel, six; and Thomas, four. Samuel may have been frustrated with the results of the trials, but the British government got what it wanted, domestic peace. It had demonstrated its willingness to discipline its troops and had removed them from the city to reduce chances of any repeat of the March shooting.

John Adams and Josiah Jr. had taken the unpopular side to prove a point, and to the dismay of the public won the cases; their clients were free. Most colonists felt that justice had not been done. Men had been shot dead, and the shooters were found innocent. It all seemed for nothing. John Adams was sunk in gloom and resolved to retire from politics. He refused to seek reelection for his seat in the Massachusetts House of Representatives, but might not have won in any case since there was still anger at him for defending the soldiers. It would have been humiliating to lose the election. Instead, he prepared to dedicate himself to law and farming, to support his family. Feeling emotionally and physically low he moved back to Braintree and went to Taunton Springs for treatment, writing Isaac Smith in London, "Your Friends are all well, excepting myself. I hope very soon to be better . . . and have determined to shake off a little of that Load of public and private Care which has for some Time oppressed me. If I had not, I should soon have shaken off this mortal Body."[2]

As calm returned, Samuel Adams, that great stirrer of pots, fretted that many people were left "with little to complain about." The Townshend Act taxes had been removed in 1770, except the tax on tea. He was concerned "about the political lethargy in Massachusetts,"[3] and wrote Arthur Lee, a Virginia diplomat in London, bemoaning affairs of America: "Such is the indolence of men in general, or their inattention to the real importance of things, that a steady and animated perseverance in the rugged path of virtue at the hazard of trifles is hardly to be expected."[4]

The British had figured out a way to make use of their military without placing their troops in the midst of a city. The soldiers based in Boston had been transferred to an island in the harbor, but Admiral Samuel Hood, commander of the British fleet in North America, made Massachusetts Bay the fleet headquarters, and by August of 1771 twelve British warships carrying some 260 guns were anchored in Boston Harbor within firing range of the city.[5]

Josiah Senior was comfortably ensconced in his lovely new home in Braintree, its large windows overlooking the harbor. He watched over his growing brood, grateful the court trials with his two sons pitted against each other were finally finished. He was sixty years old in 1770 and apparently in good health, certainly compared to his son Josiah, yet he routinely referred to himself as "old and infirm." Yet many men of his era lived well beyond sixty. Benjamin Franklin would live into his eighties. It is unclear what Josiah's infirmity was, perhaps mobility issues. Old and infirm he may have been, but he would live another fourteen years. He was as sharp and keenly involved in family and public business as ever. There were certainly enough family matters to occupy him. Every one of his adult children posed a different problem.

Son Samuel was prospering and living well with a happy marriage and three fine children. Not every attorney had the income and prospects Samuel did. The only concern for Josiah was Samuel's devotion to the British government. But for the moment at least, that didn't pose an intolerable problem. One could be loyal to both the government and colonial liberties. Families needn't argue about it.

Daughter Hannah's husband, Bela Lincoln, a physician and, like most colonists, a farmer, was having a hard time managing his finances. He took time off, however, for politics. His views were simple and shared by Josiah. He was a zealous patriot, furious at the Stamp Act, and was one of a group of men carrying a petition to Parliament against the Sugar Act on behalf of the Massachusetts General Court. All this took time from his medical practice and his farm. His wife's family was wealthy, but Bela was not.

On a personal level the Quincy family was seriously concerned as Bela continued to treat poor Hannah cruelly. It is not clear what made the "good" doctor such a vicious husband to his once lovely, intelligent, and kind wife. By the spring of that year, Bela began suffering from a serious digestive illness. His illness, of course, made his financial problems worse. He could not attend to patients or to his farm. Although Hannah dutifully cared for him as his health failed, an ungrateful man became an ungrateful patient. They say doctors make the worst patients, a truism certainly accurate in his case. Bela remained as nasty and unsympathetic as ever. He and Hannah had no children, probably a good thing in the circumstances. When Hannah managed to slip away from his bedside to visit her father that spring, Josiah was dismayed to see his once lively and beautiful daughter sad, careworn, and haggard. She had just left Bela at a hospital on George's Island in Boston Harbor and had to hurry back to return to him.[6] Despite Hannah's care and the hospital treatment he was receiving, Bela's condition grew steadily worse. It was difficult for a Christian to know what to hope for in his case, other than praying that if he survived, he would become more gracious, and kind to his family and poor Hannah.

Young Josiah Jr. was an exception to the political apathy pervading the colony. His frail, slender body harbored an inexhaustible spirit and a fierce dedication to liberty. Somehow, despite being plagued by the family pulmonary disease and seldom in good health, and always being busy with family responsibilities and his law practice, he still found time to pen essay after essay, on the salaries of judges and many other topics, under a batch of patriotic pseudonyms.[7] Perhaps he was spurred on by Samuel Adams, but more likely his many essays that appeared in the *Gazette* on the

threats to their liberties were meant to assure his readers and himself that
his defense of the British soldiers did not diminish his dedication to the
preservation of colonial freedoms.

By February 1771, less than two months after the last of the "Massacre"
trials, he had already shaken off his role as defender of British soldiers, and
writing as "Mentor" complained of hearing "so little discourse relative to a
decent, manly, and instructive commemoration of the melancholy tragedy
of the 5th March, 1770."[8] To remedy such forgetfulness he recommended
a regular public observance of that event, illustrating the "fatal effects
of the policy of standing armies, and the natural tendency of quartering
regular troops in populous cities in time of peace."[9] The idea was taken
up, and an annual assembly on March 5, with stirring speeches, took
place in Boston for many years. It came to replace the traditional British
November 5 bonfires of Guy Fawkes Day, celebrating the rescue of Parliament and king from a group of Catholic terrorists. In 1772 Dr. Joseph
Warren, Josiah's doctor and an active patriot, gave a rousing speech on
the anniversary of March 5 to an overflowing crowd.

That winter, in February of 1772, Josiah and Abigail welcomed the
birth of their first child, a little boy they named Josiah after his father and
grandfather. Little Josiah would one day write a memoir of the life of the
father he never really knew. By the end of 1772 Josiah was forced to lay
aside his work as his pulmonary illness returned in force. A letter to his
father at that time explains the ravages of the disease. He put an optimistic
gloss on his condition so as not to upset Josiah Senior:

> My fever the last two days and nights seems almost wholly
> to have left me; my slumbers are sound and undisturbed, and
> the light of the morning finds me refreshed. I find my bodily
> health less impaired than I could expect. Indeed I have per-
> ceived of late no propensity to that fainting and languor, which
> the last year troubled me so much. Dr Warren thinks that my
> symptoms are favourable, and my prospect of health (humanly
> speaking) certain.[10]

Samuel Adams, determined to keep the pot of dissent stirred, had devised a plan to encourage correspondence among the thirteen colonies so they could share views on Parliament's latest taxes and other policies and coordinate their response. Josiah Jr., ill as he was, was prepared to promote the effort. A Committee of Correspondence was established in Boston in the summer of 1772, and Josiah was elected a member. On February 8, 1773, a year after Josiah's letter to his father and struggling with a renewed bout of pulmonary disease, he set sail for Charleston, South Carolina. The idea was to travel back by land in order to meet and discuss political issues with the leading men in each colony on his journey home. Abigail and baby Josiah were invited to Braintree to stay with his father while he was away. February was not the kindest month to travel, but the hurricane season eliminated the months of August through October, and something needed to be done. He badly needed the warm weather of South Carolina, and the Massachusetts Committee of Correspondence was eager for insights into the views of those in the southern and middle Atlantic colonies.

For public consumption Josiah's journey was said to be solely for his health, just as his brother Edmund had sailed south in hopes a warmer climate would improve his. But Josiah's trip had the hidden agenda of sounding out and reporting on the attitudes of patriots in other colonies. The Committee of Correspondence armed him with a packet of letters of introduction to important colonial leaders in the colonies he would be visiting. Massachusetts had been in the forefront of opposition to British policies. It was important that she not stand alone. [11]

Abigail supported her husband's journey that winter despite its hazards. Josiah's conversations and the observations he meticulously recorded in his journal would be invaluable, but as for his health, such a mission by sea that time of year and long trek back on land was more harmful than helpful. At his father's urging Josiah made out a will before leaving, with his doctor, Joseph Warren, as a witness. [12] The stormy voyage that followed showed the wisdom of that precaution.

On February 8 Josiah set sail in the *Bristol Packet* for South Carolina, the ship passing in sight of his father's house in Braintree. [13] His father and

brother Edmund had been seasoned travelers, having journeyed across
the Atlantic several times. But Josiah had never had a sea voyage or been
out of the sight of land. He writes unsparingly in his journal of the first
part of the voyage:

> A more disagreeable time can hardly be conceived, than the
> season of my first days and nights. Exhausted to the last degree,
> I was too weak to rise, and in too exquisite pain to lie in bed.
> Unable to take any manner of food, I remained wholly confined
> to my state-room, till pain forced mee to make one effort to
> get fresh air. Assisted by two people, I reached the foot of the
> companion stairs. But was not able to proceed further. The fresh
> air, instead of refreshing, at first overcame me, and after several
> fainting turns, I was carried back to bed. My sickness came on
> with redoubled violence the night passed heavily away, and my
> cabin was so sultry and hot, that to rise or perish seemed the
> only alternative. I knocked for the watch upon deck, and with
> the assistance of two of them, was seated on a hen-coop, by the
> side of the binnacle. [14]

On deck he found a dark, sultry, windy night, with distant flashes
of lightning and peals of thunder, "instead of stable earth, the fleeting
waters—the little hall of right and wrong is changed for the wide, expanding
immeasurable ocean. . . . waves contend with waves, and billows war with
billows; seas rise in wrath, and mountains combat heaven." He found the
tumult a "vast field for contemplation." Rain and cold quickly followed but,
unwilling to return to his cabin, he sent for his cloak and spent the night
with the sailor singing at the helm to cheer him until dawn.

Terrible weather returned at the end of the voyage. Within thirty leagues
of port a torrential hurricane struck with fierce rain, hail, sleet, and snow,
lasting several days. Josiah had to tie himself to his bed to keep from
being thrown out of it. "Seas broke over us often; now and then one would
strike with enormous force . . . I believe every soul on board expected to

perish." The ship was near the latitude where the remains of Josiah's brother Edmund had been deposited in the ocean. The *Bristol Packet*, with its passengers and crew, survived the tumultuous voyage. Josiah returned to land a relieved and wiser man, who now appreciated the terrors of ocean travel and the joy of survival. It was quite the adventure, full of new experiences, ones landsmen like himself never knew. The Boston Committee of Correspondence had pinned its hopes on this spirited but frail young man.

Three weeks after setting out, the little ship lay off the port of Charleston. Josiah wrote Abigail on March 1 of his safe arrival, not sparing her from an account of the terrifying dangers he had endured. "A voyage more disagreeable, dangerous, and terrible, perhaps was never passed, than that which landed me upon this distant shore."[15] He was full of praise for the soundness of his ship and the skills of its captain and crew, which had brought them safely to their journey's end.

Josiah brought to the mission the expectations and prejudices of a born and bred New Englander seeing for the first time the very different culture and government of each colony he visited. Charleston, his first destination, came off well. He was astonished at the beauty and grandeur of Charleston, its buildings, commerce, shipping, "and indeed in almost every thing, it far surpasses all I ever saw, or ever expected to see in America."[16] Everything there seemed focused on trade and magnificence, great state, and "much gaiety, and dissipation." He attended a concert and sent Abigail a detailed comparison of the ladies of South Carolina with the ladies of Massachusetts. In the following days he toured the town, met a number of leading citizens, eventually including one half of their assembly, and was privy to their political views. One gentleman was loud in his conviction that Massachusetts meant to subjugate all the other colonies.[17] Josiah was intrigued by the different formalities of the South Carolina legislature and interested in their laws and manners. He found that "the constitution of South Carolina is in very many respects defective, and in an equal number extremely bad."[18] He noted that while "the whole body of this people" seemed averse to the claims and assumptions of the British legislature over the colonies, one seldom heard any "animated expressions against

the measures of administration." Further he found a "general doubt of the
firmness and integrity of the northern colonies" including that of Massachusetts. [19] He questioned how representative the assembly was when it did
not represent the laborers, mechanics, tradesmen, farmers, or yeomen. "The
representatives," he noted, "are almost wholly rich planters," whose interests,
of course, were well represented. Any representative could represent any
part of the colony as long as he had property there, which he found "a fatal
kind of policy." As a result, a majority of the House lived in Charleston
"during the sickly months." He reckoned the number of slaves to white
people some seven to one, maybe greater, which he found one of many
"mischiefs of slavery." British officials were instructed that the property of
those who did not reside in the colony should not be attached for recovery
of debts, different from legal practices in England. Josiah was happy to meet
some like-minded men who were enthusiastic about the plan of correspondence. After three weeks in Charleston, he journeyed north, meeting with
cordial and gracious hospitality from wealthy and distinguished families.
He found little of interest in North Carolina where, for some reason, he
claimed there were no courts "of any kind in this province, and no laws
in force by which any could be held."[20] He did, in fact, find five laws in force
for the province. Presumably the common law provided for everything
else. There were fewer slaves in North than South Carolina; its population
different, its crops less valuable. Herds and flocks were more numerous,
people were working their own land, and products were produced for the
shipping trade of Virginia. Both South and North Carolina in his opinion
needed repeal of their laws on religion. He headed north to Virginia.

It was early April as he traveled into Virginia, where he commented on
the excellent farms with large cleared tracts of land, well fenced and tilled.
It was lovely, full of flowering trees. "Peach trees seem to be of spontaneous
growth in these provinces and I saw them all along in the finest bloom."[21]
"The melody of the fields and woods through Virginia," he added, "is greatly
beyond that of the Carolinas."[22] He was not impressed by the capital, Wil-
liamsburg, with "nothing of the population of the north, or of the splendour
and magnificence of the south." He liked the college there though, and

the statehouse, and purchased "a very handsome" edition of Virginia laws. He attended the General Court but found the constitution of the courts of justice and equity "amazingly defective, inconvenient, and dangerous, not to say absurd and mischievous."[23] He learned that the Virginia council was appointed from the richest landed men but added "their views, connexions, interests, or inclinations, have generally been such, as to keep them from baser betrayments of their trust, and the more atrocious prostitution of their enormous power and authority."[24] As Josiah traveled, he seemed to gain an ever higher estimation of the laws and customs of his own province. Only in the fruitfulness of their farmland did he find a great deal to admire compared to the indifferent Massachusetts soil and harsh weather.

Next came Maryland, which he found more hilly, with fields devoted to tobacco, which, with that of Virginia, was much prized. In both colonies tobacco crops were being replaced with fine fields of wheat and other grain, and "afford great pleasure to the lover of mankind and the useful arts; and the exquisite verdure which at this season covers their fields, present a prospect highly gratifying to the love of nature." He met with Daniel Dulany, the attorney general, attended the supreme court, and felt the residents were friendly to strangers and "tolerably industrious;—but I saw nothing to lead me to suppose that they in any measure surpassed the New Englanders in either of these respects."[25]

On April 23 he entered Pennsylvania, where he found much to praise, including the well-laid and maintained public roads, evidence of good policy and laws, or a "well regulated province." The countryside was devoted to cattle grazing, and the prospect approaching Philadelphia presented a "most delightful scene" with the scent of blooming orchards that "gave a rich perfume, while sweetest melody of birds was truly charming to the ear." He enthused that the country was "a perfect garden, I had almost said an Eden." He met the supreme court judges, lawyers, John Dickinson (author of the famous essay "The Farmer"), and other interesting residents. Josiah characterized the Philadelphians as commercial, keen, and frugal, "replete with benevolence, hospitality, sociability, and politeness, joined with that prudence and caution, natural to understanding people, who are alternately visited by a variety of strangers, differing in rank, fortune, and character."[26] Its streets were laid out at right angles, the "best laid out city in the world." He did worry about the proprietary interest from which he found the province in great danger, although the Quaker interest operated against that in land cases. Indeed, he thought all general questions and points carried by the Quakers worth considering. The Quakers were public-spirited in matters of public buildings and institutions. Among the farmers he judged a spirit of industry and useful improvement.

On to New Jersey, where he described Princeton and its college as flourishing and handsome, the soils of the entire state "equal if not superior to any yet settled in America."[27] He traveled through Connecticut by water to spare his horses, already fatigued by their journey. Being so close to home he waived details of judgments on New York and Rhode Island.

Looking back on his journey he wrote:

> Were I to lament any thing, it would be the prevalent and extended ignorance of one colony, of the concerns of another;— were I to breathe a wish, it would be, that the numerous and surprisingly increasing inhabitants of this extensive and fertile continent, may be thoroughly attentive to, and suitably actuated by the blessings of Providence, the dangers which surround them, and the duties they owe to God, themselves, and posterity.[28]

Several weeks after his arrival home, he wrote in response to a letter from George Clymer, a Philadelphian concerned, like Josiah, for the fate of colonial liberties, "Let us forgive each other's follies, and unite while we may. To think justly, is [certainly] not sufficient—but we must think *alike*, before we shall form a union;—that truly formed, we are invincible."[29] There would be a serious crisis by the end of 1773 to test that unity, one sufficient to gladden the heart of that old troublemaker, Samuel Adams.

TEN

No Tempest in a Teapot

W hen Josiah returned in May refreshed from his journey south, it was to a world sliding rapidly toward the conflict he had been urging. Josiah may have egged it on, but two prominent Massachusetts residents were largely responsible for what happened next: that perennial agitator, Samuel Adams, no surprise there, and the colony's governor, Thomas Hutchinson, who had been fingered by the prime minister, Lord North, as a significant contributor to the tensions leading to the outbreak of war. Hutchinson, who had already been a victim of a mob, would now become one of the first casualties of the war. Sam Adams, on the other hand, was to be a proud father of the impending conflict. Josiah Junior, once home again, was in the thick of the debate, egging on resistance to the government's increasing power. As the political waves were about to break over the Quincys and their friends, they had more immediate family matters of life and death to deal with.

The spring of 1773 was an exceptionally sickly season. It was smack in the middle of what has since become known as the Little Ice Age, with its brutally cold winters. The annual wave of contagious diseases—measles, yellow fever, and smallpox—taxed the knowledge of the best-trained medical men, with their satchel of remedies. While Josiah was still on his travels, his little half-sisters were sick with the measles. Their mother, Anna, was also ill, although it is uncertain whether she also had measles. Thankfully they all recovered. But Josiah's doctor, friend, and fellow Son of Liberty Joseph Warren was not so fortunate. Despite his medical skills he could not save his dear wife, Elizabeth, who died that April leaving him with four children, the youngest just one year old. Two weeks later the wife of Paul Revere, also a Son of Liberty and courier for the Committee of Correspondence, died, leaving him with eight children. He remarried and became the father of another eight little Reveres. Along with these unexpected deaths there was an expected death. In July Hannah's husband Bela Lincoln died on George's Island, where he was being treated for the intestinal disease that had ravaged him for two years. He was buried in Hingham, his family home. Hannah, now a widow and childless, returned with relief to her father's house in Braintree. There, with the gentle support and love of her family, she gradually recuperated from the exhausting task of caring for a cruel and petulant husband and began to regain her old lively and confident manner. Happily, Josiah Jr.'s wife and infant son were well.

The political situation began to pick up dangerous momentum. In contrast to public apathy in the aftermath of the soldiers' trials, 1773 saw a return to heated opposition to British policies. Boston's Committee of Correspondence urged the colony's towns to form their own committees of correspondence and town meetings to vote on the issues.[1] By that April nearly half of the 260 Massachusetts towns and districts had complied. Their focus was on a boycott of taxed items. The Townshend taxes had been withdrawn except for the tax on tea.

The response of the Braintree town meeting passed in March included the following statements:

> All Taxations by what name soever called, imposed upon us without our consent by any earthly power are unconstitutional, oppressive & tend to enslave us.

That as our Fathers left their native Country & Friends in order, that they and their Posterity might enjoy that civil & religious Liberty here which they could not enjoy there We their descendants are determined by the grace of God that our consciences shall not accuse us with having acted unworthy such pious and venerable Heroes and that we will by all Lawfull ways and means preserve at all events all our civil and religious rights and priviledges.

That all Civil officers are or ought to be Servants to the people & dependent upon them for their official support, and every instance to the contrary from the Governor downward tends to crush & destroy Civil liberty.

The resolution concluded with a mix of lawful fealty and a warning:

That we bear true loyalty to our Lawfull King George the 3d and unfeigned affection to our Brethren in Great Brittain & Ireland and to all our Sister Colonies, and so long as our mother country protects us in our Charter rights & privilidges so long will we by divine assistance exert our utmost to promote the welfare of the whole British Empire which we earnestly pray may flourish uninterruptedly in the path of righteousness, till time shall be no more. [2]

When it came to the tax on tea, however, the gloves were off in other towns. The town of Lexington, west of Boston, approved the following statement that spring, insisting on a boycott on tea:

that if any heade of a family of this Towne, or any person shall from this time Forward until this duty be taken off purchase any Tea, or use, or consume any Tea in their families, such person shall be looked upon as an enemy to this Towne, & to

this country, and shall by this Town be treated with neglect &
contempt.[3]

The little town of Lincoln, wedged between Lexington to its east and
Concord to its west, chose a committee to "take into consideration the
present circumstances of the town with respect to their constitutional
rights and privileges in common with all other towns in the Province."
Lincoln residents were somewhat more cautious than those of Braintree and
Lexington, and it wasn't until late 1773 that they pronounced "the present
gloomy cituation of our publick affairs" and duty on tea "alarming."[4] They
copied Lexington's language, "not to purchase or use any tea nor suffer it
to be purchased or used in our families so long as there is any Duty laid
on such tea by an act of the British Parliament—and we will hold and
esteem such as do use tea enemies to their country—and we will treat
them with the greatest neglect." Should the boycott of tea fail to persuade
Parliament to repeal the Tea Act they added:

> We trust we have courage and resolution sufficient to encounter
> all the horrors of war in the defense of those rights and privileges
> civil and religious which we esteem more valuable than our lives
> and we do thereby assure not only the town of Boston but the
> world that whenever we shall have a clear call from heaven we are
> ready to join with our brethren to face the most formidable forces
> rather than tamely to surrender up our rights and privileges into
> the hands of any of our own species not distinguished from
> ourselves except it be in disposition to enslave us.[5]

Between Lexington's resolution in spring and the "clear call from heaven"
that the Lincoln town members began to hear in late 1773, there had
been a crucial event that sharpened their anxiety. Their governor, Thomas
Hutchinson, was an unwitting instrument in that summons.

Thomas Hutchinson was a brave, sensible man. Unlike many royal governors he was an American born and bred, the fourth of twelve children.

His family had been active in Massachusetts affairs for generations. He imbibed the American jealousy of their individual rights and colonial self-government. After graduating from Harvard, he became a successful merchant and entered politics, first elected as a Boston selectman in 1737 and taking on increasingly important posts. He had been lieutenant governor and now, in his sixties, the governor. In 1734 he had married Margaret Sanford, daughter of a family with a long history of connection with his, and a third cousin. He and Margaret had twelve children, but tragedy struck repeatedly, and only five of them survived to adulthood. Margaret died in 1754 during childbirth. After her death Thomas threw himself into his work. Although he would later be considered the most important figure on the loyalist side in prerevolutionary Massachusetts, Hutchinson was a fair-minded governor, ready to oppose what he felt were unfair taxes and advising the royal government on other parliamentary laws. Indeed, for a man whose elegant family home had been wantonly and mercilessly vandalized by a mob furious at the imposition of the Stamp Act of 1765 (with he and his family fleeing for their lives), he was amazingly fair.[6] He was at his sensible and courageous best in a crisis. On the night of the Boston Massacre, Hutchinson had promptly appeared before an outraged crowd, promising that justice would be done, and saw that it was. He ordered that the British regiments be removed from Boston to Castle William in the harbor. Hutchinson's plain honesty often made him unpopular. Late in 1772 he pointed out to the Massachusetts assembly that they could not have all the rights of Englishmen; the province either must be subject to Parliament's authority to make laws for it in all cases whatsoever, or be independent.[7] Assembly members were outraged, but would embrace that very view. Their reply, written by John and Samuel Adams and Joseph Hawley, insisted the province's charter already had made Massachusetts autonomous.

Upsetting as Hutchinson's comments were, there were two far more serious political problems for him in 1773. The first came with the publication of private correspondence among him, his son-in-law Andrew Oliver, and Thomas Whately, an assistant to British prime minister George

Grenville. These letters were written in 1767 through 1769, the years when the Townshend Acts were riling Americans and British troops were landing in Boston. They were confidential letters, reports he was required to submit of American events and his opinions on the situation. They were also written only two to three years after Hutchinson's mansion had been destroyed and his and his family's lives threatened by a frenzied mob.

In 1772 someone anonymously sent the packet of Hutchinson's and Oliver's private letters from those years to Benjamin Franklin, agent for Massachusetts and Pennsylvania, then resident in London.[8] Like Hutchinson, Benjamin Franklin had been born and raised in Boston but then moved to Philadelphia. There he established himself as a printer and author. He was an amazing man, talented and brilliant and increasingly involved in public affairs. From the mid-1740s to the mid-1770s, Franklin served as a colonial agent for Pennsylvania and later for the House of Representatives of Massachusetts Bay, in London. Franklin eventually came to be regarded as the spokesman for American interests there. He had opposed the Stamp Act and testified in the House of Commons as Parliament discussed repealing the act. When he read the packet of Hutchinson and Oliver letters from 1767–1769, Franklin immediately realized how explosive the reaction would be if they were made public. In enabling that exposure there is the suggestion Franklin wanted to divert attention from Parliament to the writers.[9] If that was his aim, it was certainly accomplished, at least in regard to the writers. In December 1772 Franklin sent the letters to Thomas Cushing, the speaker of the Massachusetts assembly, insisting—presumably for deniability—that they not be published or widely circulated because he was not "at liberty to make the letters public."[10] Sending them to Cushing ensured they would be made public. Cushing wrote to Franklin asking him to ease the restriction on the circulation of the letters. Samuel Adams was then serving as clerk of the assembly, and the packet of correspondence soon got into his hands. On June 2 the letters were revealed to the Massachusetts assembly. Sam Adams saw that they were then published in the *Boston Gazette* and reprinted throughout the colonies to give them the widest possible circulation. Their readers saw Hutchinson as clearly trying to destroy American liberties. In the uproar that followed he was burned in effigy for what seemed confirmation of a plot to deprive Americans of their rights.

The news of the publication of these letters and volatile reaction to them reached the British public. There was such heated debate in England over how these letters found their way to the Massachusetts assembly that apparently two gentlemen actually got into a duel on the issue. "For the prevention of further mischief," Franklin confessed that he was the person who obtained and transmitted the letters to Boston.[11] He pointed out that they were not private letters between friends but "written by public officers to persons in public station, on public affairs and intended to procure public measures; they were therefore handed to other public persons who might be influenced by them to produce those measures." Their tendency, he added, was "to incense the Mother Country against her Colonies, and, by the steps recommended, to widen the breach, which they effected." The caution expressed in them about privacy was meant "to keep their contents from the Colony Agents, who the writers apprehended might return them . . . to America. That apprehension was, it seems, well founded; for the first Agent who laid his hands on them, thought it his duty to transmit them to his Constituents." It remains unknown to this day who sent the letters to Franklin or why, after they reached the leaders of the Massachusetts assembly, they waited several months before revealing their contents. But, as they say, the rest is history.

Just what did Hutchinson write? His letters tended to belittle the colonists. He urged Britain to exert more control. In 1768, for example, he referred to "principles of government absurd enough, spread thro' all the colonies, but I cannot think that in any colony, people of any consideration have ever been so mad as to think of a revolt":

> It is not strange that measures should be immediately taken
> to reduce the colonies to their former state of government and
> order. . . . Many of the common people have been in a frenzy,
> and talk'd of dying in defence of their liberties, and have spoke

and printed what is highly criminal, and too many of rank above the vulgar, and some *in public posts* have countenanced and encouraged them until they increased so much in their numbers and in their opinion of their importance as to submit to government no further than they thought proper. . . . There has been continual danger of mobs and insurrections, but they would have spent all their force, within ourselves, the officers of the Crown and some of the few friends who dared to stand by them possibly might have been knock'd in the head, and some such fatal event would probably have brought the people to their senses."[12]

In a 1769 letter Hutchinson's comments were still more upsetting:

This is most certainly a crisis. I really wish that there may not have been the least degree of severity, beyond what is absolutely necessary to maintain. I think I may say to you the *dependence* which a colony ought to have upon the parent state; but if no measures shall have been taken to secure this dependence, or nothing more than some declaratory acts or resolves, *it is all over with us.* The friends of government will be utterly disheartened and the friends of anarchy will be afraid of nothing be it ever so extravagant. . . . I never think of the measures necessary for the peace and good order of the colonies without pain. *There must be an abridgment of what are called English liberties.* I relieve myself by considering that in a remove from the state of nature to the most perfect state of government there must be a great restraint of natural liberty. I doubt whether it is possible to project a system of government in which a colony 3,000 miles distant from the parent state shall enjoy all the liberty of the parent state. . . . I wish the good of the colony when I wish to see some further restraint of liberty rather than the connexion with the parent state should be broken; for I am sure such a breach must prove the ruin of the colony.[13]

For years Josiah, Sam Adams, and other writers insisted a plan was afoot to deprive the colonists of their liberties. That now seemed confirmed by the leak of Hutchinson's letters. Samuel Adams had included just the letters he wished for publication. In one that was not included, Hutchinson followed up on his observations above making no proposals on what the royal government ought to do, instead commenting thoughtfully, "I can think of nothing but what will produce as great an evil as that which it may remove or will be of a very uncertain event."[14] Hutchinson closed with the plea: "I must beg the favor of you to keep secret every thing I write, until we are in a more settled state, for the party here either by their *agent* or by some of their emissaries in London, have sent them every report or rumor of the contents of letters wrote from hence. I hope we shall see better times both here and in England."

Although Hutchinson did not make any specific suggestions for increasing control of the colonies, Oliver certainly did. Oliver's idea was that the governor's council, currently elected by the assembly with the governor's consent, be changed to one whose members were appointed by the Crown. He suggested the colonial government be made independent of the assembly and urged the reduction of English liberties "by degrees." More troops should be sent to enforce government control and new repressive measures taken against the radical leaders. Although these suggestions were not carried out, one did not have to be a careful reader to find an intent to destroy colonial liberties in these comments.

The uproar over the publication of these letters was as great in Britain as in America. The Privy Council debated a petition from the Massachusetts assembly to remove Hutchinson and Oliver at a meeting attended by a throng of distinguished observers and speakers for and against the petition. After a eulogy of the great services of Hutchinson, the discussion turned to Franklin, who had admitted he had obtained the letters and sent them to America. Franklin, then sixty-seven, a well-respected writer and philosopher, representative of the most important colonies, stood motionless in front of the audience of distinguished Englishmen and listened to himself being viciously attacked for nearly an hour as a thief and an accomplice of thieves.[15] They dismissed the Massachusetts petition to remove Hutchinson and Oliver and dismissed Franklin from his post as deputy postmaster general of the colonies.

The second uproar occurred with the arrival of ships bringing tea to Boston in accordance with the Tea Act, which imposed a tax on tea. After the repeal of other Townshend Act taxes in 1770, only the tax on tea remained. It was really benevolence on the government's part. The tea tax was intended to solve the financial problems of the East India Company, which then had some 17,000,000 pounds of tea stored in England, the result of the effective American boycott of the Townshend Act taxes. As usual in the weeks when Parliament was mulling over a new act, rumors were rampant in the colonies about this proposed statute. The East India Company would be given a monopoly on the sale of tea to the colonies, but this would not raise its price for consumers. Indeed, they would be able to buy its tea more cheaply than competitors and smugglers, even with the tax on it. The tax on the tea would be taken when it was landed.

The Sons of Liberty were perplexed about how to combat this new challenge. Ordinary people would be happy to pay less for this legal tea than for smuggled tea. On November 28, 1773, the *Dartmouth*, the first of four merchant ships carrying tea from England to Massachusetts, arrived in Boston Harbor. Two more ships, the *Beaver* and the *Eleanor*, arrived within days, while a fourth ship was wrecked in a storm off Cape Cod. Other East India Company tea was on its way to other American ports, but the ships en route to Boston arrived at Boston Harbor first. The three ships were all owned by Americans. Two were owned by members of a family who were patients of Dr. Warren. The three ships carried a cargo of 340 tea chests containing more than 45 tons of tea with a value of some £9,000, a vast sum ($1,592, 670 in today's money).

Hurried meetings took place with the governor, the ship owners, and tea consignees against a background of public protests. Since the tax on the tea was to be paid when the cargo was landed, the Sons of Liberty urged Hutchinson to refuse to permit the ships to unload the tea, and to send it back to Britain. Although other cargo was landed without fuss, Joseph

Warren and Paul Revere organized a watch to prevent the tea from being unloaded. Time was of the essence, as twenty days were allotted from the time the first ship entered the harbor for the duty to be paid.

Hutchinson was a man who went by the book. He was intent on following his orders and refused to send the ships back without unloading their tea. In New York, Philadelphia, and Charleston tea agents had resigned and merchants refused to purchase the tea. Had Hutchinson been more conciliatory, the crisis, or at least this tea crisis, never would have happened. But he felt duty-bound to carry out orders.

The twentieth day arrived on December 16. An emergency meeting organized by the Sons of Liberty, with about sixty men, took place at one of the churches. After a final meeting with Hutchinson proved fruitless, their decision was to board the ships and destroy the tea. Donning blankets and headdresses, painting their faces and hands, and otherwise disguising themselves as Narragansett Indians, armed with hatchets, they quietly marched down to Griffin's Wharf that night under a bright moon and boarded the three ships. They asked the ships' captains for the keys to the hold, received them, and began bringing up the tea chests. Once on deck they broke the chests open with their hatchets and began dumping the 92,000 pounds of tea into the harbor. It took about three hours of heavy work and was accomplished with no damage to the ships, their crew, or other property, except for one broken padlock that was the personal property of one of the captains and promptly replaced the next day by the patriots. All went surprisingly peacefully, despite a harbor filled with British warships. This was, of course, the event dubbed the Boston Tea Party. A crowd of citizens watched the proceedings from the wharf.

One of the disguised participants, George Hewes, paints a vivid picture of the event: "We were surrounded by British armed ships, but no attempt was made to resist us." [16] Some residents were sorry to see good tea wasted. Hewes remembered: "There were several attempts made by some of the citizens of Boston and its vicinity to carry off small quantities of it for their family use."

To effect that object, they would watch their opportunity to snatch up a handful from the deck where it became plentifully scattered, and put it into their pockets. One Captain O'Connor, whom I well knew, came on board for that purpose, and when he supposed he was not noticed, filled his pockets, and also the lining of his coat. But I had detected him and gave information to the captain of what he was doing We were ordered to take him into custody, and just as he was stepping from the vessel, I seized him by the skirt of his coat . . . he made his escape. He had, however, to run a gauntlet through the crowd upon the wharf, each one, as he passed, giving him a kick or a stroke. Another attempt was made to save a little tea from the ruins of the cargo by a tall, aged man who wore a large cocked hat and white wig . . . . He had slightly slipped a little into his pockets, but being detected, they seized him, and taking his hat and wig from his head, threw them, together with the tea, of which they had emptied his pockets into the water. In consideration of his advanced age, he was permitted to escape, with now and then a slight kick.

The next morning, after we had cleared the ships of the tea, it was discovered that very considerable quantities of it was floating upon the surface of the water; and to prevent the possibility of any of its being saved for use, a number of small boats were manned by sailors and citizens, who rowed them into those parts of the harbor wherever the tea was visible, and by beating it with oars and paddles, so thoroughly drenched it, as to render its entire destruction inevitable.

The disguises and dumping of the tea, the failed attempts to rescue some for family use, all seemed a bit of theater. But the repercussions were anything but laughable. What followed would lead to war.

Was Josiah Junior one of the organizers of the destruction of the tea? Although he is unlikely to have been one of the disguised participants,

Governor Hutchinson accused him of being one of its planners and branded him guilty of "High Treason."[17] Josiah was furious. "Who is the Traitor, who is the Betrayer of Government?" he asked, "He who *openly* assembles with his brethren to consider public affairs; who speaks his sentiments freely, and determines his conduct in the face of all men?—Or he who conspires against the very being of the State . . . and who writes Secret and confidential letters to the enemies of his country, blasts its reputation with calumny, and points the way to its overthrow and ruin?"[18] In a widely read essay, he went further and threatened the use of violence against Hutchinson and other friends of the government, albeit under the pseudonym "Marchmont Nedham": "When THIS PEOPLE are driven to desperation, they who thus abuse them, will no longer dwell in safety."[19] It is a reminder that Josiah had no hesitancy about the threat and use of force against political opponents.

One further upset, late in 1773, seemed to confirm in the patriots' suspicion that the Crown meant to follow the suggestion that American rights be cut step by step. This issue involved the colonial judges and the entire jury system. Trial by jury was especially important to Americans. Through it they had a legal route to protect their rights and defend their compatriots. It was also an aggravation as the writs of assistance made clear. One governor of Massachusetts had complained, "A customs house officer has no chance with a jury," and another had grumbled, "A trial by jury there is only trying one illicit trader by his fellows, at least his well-wishers."[20] It was important that the judges be independent, but as the old saying goes, "who pays the piper calls the tune." This was especially true when the judges held their offices at pleasure, which enabled them to be removed if they displeased those that had appointed them. This judicial policy was carried out through instructions to colonial governors and Crown refusal to allow colonial acts that provided for judicial tenure during good behavior.[21] Massachusetts judges were appointed by the legislature, the council, and the governor and paid a salary by them. Late in 1773, however, the Crown took advantage of a clause in the Revenue Act of 1767 to use the Townshend taxes "for

making a more certain and adequate provision for defraying the charge
of the administration of justice."[22] The king now granted a salary to the
judges of the superior court and forbade them to receive their salaries
from the House of Representatives, council, and governor. While the
patriots were afraid of the power this gave the Crown over the judiciary,
the Crown feared the power the Massachusetts legislature currently had
over the judges.[23] John Adams argued that if the judges were dependent on the Crown "for Bread [as] well as office," with the governor
dependent on the Crown and the Council in danger of becoming so,
"the Liberties of the Country would be totally lost, and every man at
the Mercy of a few Slaves of the Governor."[24] Both Crown and colonists
insisted the judges had to be independent but realized whoever paid
their salaries would control the judiciary. The king's government argued
the salary of the supreme court judges in Massachusetts was inadequate,
"even their Doorkeeper had a large stipend," while the judges had to
travel on circuit seven months each year, covering from 1,000 to 1,500
miles.[25] The king was simply "taking the cases of the judges into consideration, and from his known justice and benevolence, ordered their
salaries to be paid out of his revenues in America, such salaries as would
keep them above want, and below envy."[26] Most of the judges agreed to
accept the salary, but four living near Boston, "the focus of tarring and
feathering," refused to accept it. Chief Justice Oliver, after seventeen
years in the service, agreed not to accept the grant and to resign from the
bench if the assembly would reimburse him one half of his loss in their
service, some £1,000. He lived some thirty miles from Boston. Samuel
Adams, clerk of the assembly, insisted Oliver give an explicit answer.
When Oliver replied that he would accept the king's grant, articles of
impeachment for high crimes and misdemeanors were brought against
him that Governor Hutchinson refused to enforce.[27] In the standoff
the Worcester, Boston, and Charlestown grand juries refused to serve
under him until he answered the charges. In 1775 Chief Justice Oliver
sailed into exile, never to return. He died in Birmingham, England, in

October 1791. He soon had company in England from other members of the bench. Of the five judges of the Massachusetts Superior Court, four remained loyal to the Crown when the Revolution began.

Deep divisions and hasty and sad departures would quicken in the New Year.

ELEVEN

Divisions Hit Home

When I consider the Spirit which at present prevails throughout this conti-nent I really detest that restless ambition of those artfull and designing men which has thus broken this people into factions—and I every day see more and more cause to deprecate the growing Evil. This party Spirit ruins good Neighbourhood, eradicates all the Seeds of good nature and humanity—it sours the temper and has a fatal tendancy upon the Morals and under-standing and is contrary to that precept of Christianity thou shallt Love they Neighbour as thy self.

—Abigail Adams to Mercy Otis Warren,
February 27, 1774

I t wasn't until January that news of December's destruction of tea reached London. At home there was an uneasy pause as Americans waited to see what the British response would be. Tea had been shipped to other American ports. But other governors yielded to protests and agreed to send the tea back across the Atlantic. The New York Sons of Liberty sent one tea ship back, but in April a second ship arrived and had its cargo of tea dumped into the harbor. Only in Boston, however, did the colonial governor insist the tea be unloaded and taxed. The result was that in Massachusetts desperate opponents of the tax boarded three ships and destroyed the tea. Despite the pleas of local merchants and other worried citizens, legislative leaders refused to compensate the owners for the thousands of pounds of tea lost. The vandalism, after all, was the act of a few zealots. In the past the population was not held responsible for mob violence, and the men who destroyed the tea were disguised. The legislature was unwilling to reimburse the shippers. Massachusetts had made itself a target and was to feel the full brunt of British anger.

Sam Adams, that architect of revolution, was jubilant. He wanted extreme measures. As he saw it, the destruction of the East India tea was just the bold act of defiance that could galvanize the public and lead to war. "You cannot imagine the height of joy that sparkles in the eyes and animates the countenances as well as the hearts of all we meet on this occasion," he wrote Arthur Lee in London. [1] Benjamin Franklin, Massachusetts's agent there, thought otherwise. He saw what the British would see, wanton vandalism, lawlessness, "an act of violent injustice." He pleaded with the patriot leaders in Boston to repay the damages. Sam Adams was unmoved. "Franklin might be a great philosopher," Adams conceded, but he was a "bungling politician." The destruction of the tea and refusal of Boston to pay for the damage had the result Sam Adams hoped for. It provoked the fury of king and Parliament and brought on the whirlwind that would divide well-intentioned but moderate Americans from more radical family and friends. The Quincy family was caught up in the discussions and divisions, from the elderly Colonel Josiah to firebrand Josiah Junior and moderate government official Samuel.

The new year found the Boston Committee of Correspondence urging the cities and towns of the province to respond to recent events. Boston did not want to be alone. On a frigid January day the Braintree town meeting members dutifully assembled, "to take into consideration the circumstances of our Publick affairs, (in which not only every Town but every individual is interested) and to consider in particular the affair of the East India Company, sending their Teas into America subject to a duty here for raising revenue out of us against our consent." [2] Members voted to elect a committee of five men, one from each of the town's precincts, to draft their formal response. Colonel Josiah Quincy, aged and infirm though he claimed to be, was named its chairman. The committee adjourned briefly and prepared a quick report, but those waiting felt "the season being very cold & uncomfortable," that their draft should be considered at a later, presumably warmer, time. Perhaps it was a sense of caution rather than cold that prevailed, for various drafts were considered subsequently but the vote postponed.

It wasn't until the annual Braintree town meeting on March 11, its members still uncertain but clearly worried about what the British would do, that the town passed the resolution Col. Josiah's committee had prepared.[3] It began on a somber note: "We have reason to be alarmed when all that is dear to us is at stake and there can be nothing more influencing than the danger of losing our civil & Religious Privileges, Benefits in themselves truly valuable and obtained at such expense of treasure & toil attended with such Hazards & hardships as not parrall'd in History."[4] They then charged that Parliament's claim, in the 1766 Declaratory Act, to legislate for the colonies in all cases whatsoever was "evidently repugnant to the views of our Predecessors . . . and should it take place must leave us & our Posterity nothing to hope but every thing to fear, that a prejudiced or corrupt Ministry should see good at any time to impose on us." This was an odd complaint to raise now since that act had been passed eight years earlier, but its full implications were suddenly realized. All laws, the meeting insisted, were to be made with the consent of the people. "By the will of God," they were determined "to stand fast in the liberty wherewith we are made free, and to hazard life itself rather than submit to foreign taxation." Not everyone agreed with this provocative approach. The resolution lamented "the want of a truly Patriotic spirit and that private views & interest are so apparently the governing motive of so great a part in this day of Distress & Danger." Disagreement with their view was dismissed as merely a selfish, private interest keeping some people from a true patriotic spirit. Josiah must have had Samuel, his eldest son, in mind in denying the patriotism of those who held more cautious views.

Portrait of King George III, studio of
Alan Ramsay, 1763. *From Wikimedia.*

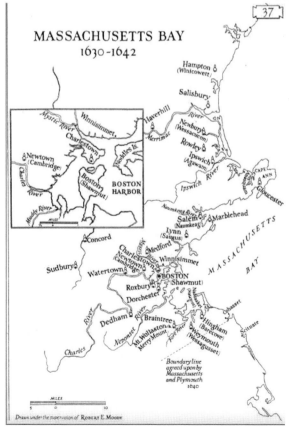

Map of Massachusetts Bay,
1630–1642. *Drawn for Robert
E. Moody.*

Col. Josiah Quincy by
John Singleton Copley, 1767.
*Courtesy of the Dietrich
American Foundation.*

Josiah Quincy Jr., "the patriot,"
painted by Gilbert Stuart, 1825,
fifty years after his death.
From Wikimedia.

Samuel Quincy, painted by John Singleton Copley, c. 1767. *From Wikimedia.*

Hannah Hill Quincy, Samuel's wife. Painted by John Singleton Copley, 1761. *From Wikimedia.*

Hannah Quincy Lincoln Storer, Skipworth, 1804. *Courtesy of Harvard University portrait collection, Gift of Francis Storer Eaton, great-grandson of sitter, to Harvard College, 1955. Ob. No. H559.*

ABOVE: Josiah Quincy House, 1770. *From Wikimedia.* BELOW LEFT: Abigail Adams by Benjamin Blyth, circa 1766. *From Wikimedia.* BELOW RIGHT: John Adams, 1766. *From Wikimedia.*

TOP: Samuel Adams by John Singleton Copley, 1772. *From Wikimedia.* CENTER LEFT: James Otis by Joseph Blackburn, 1755. *From Wikimedia.* CENTER RIGHT: Jonathan Sewell, 19th century, anonymous. *From Wikimedia.* BOTTOM: Major General Benjamin Lincoln, Charles Wilson Peale, 1781–82. *From Wikimedia.*

Governor Thomas Hutchinson
by Edward Truman, 1750.
From Wikimedia.

Ebenezer Storer by John
Singleton Copley, 1767.
From Wikimedia.

TOP: Boston Stamp Act, engraving, August 1765. *From Wikimedia.* CENTER: Boston Massacre, 1770, Paul Revere. *From Wikimedia.* BOTTOM: Boston Tea Party, 1773. *From Wikimedia.*

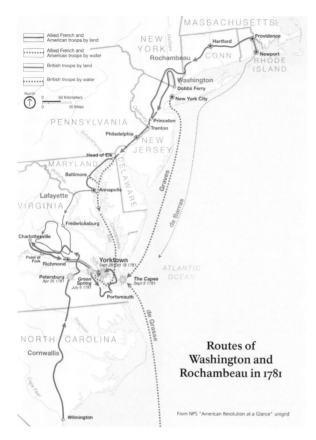

ABOVE: Routes of Washington and Rochambeau in 1781. *From Wikimedia.* BELOW: Surrender of Lord Cornwallis by John Trumbull, 1820. *From Wikimedia.*

While the people of Braintree and other Massachusetts towns pondered their responses to the Tea Act and deplored their divisions, Parliament was busy debating its response to what its members saw as the increasing lawlessness of the colonists. What had repeal of the Stamp Act bought England? Many members had thought it a mistake to appease the Americans and repeal the Stamp Act, and the repeal only passed narrowly. But a solid majority of members approved the Declaratory Act's assertion of power over the colonies. A majority now believed it was past time to deal firmly with their ungrateful and lawless colonists in all cases whatsoever.

Two weeks after Braintree finally passed its resolution, the first blow fell. Parliament passed the Boston Port Act, the first of the so-called Coercive Acts that were to shut the port of Boston, rip up the Massachusetts charter, and reduce the inhabitants to a state of dependency. The Port Act demanded Boston residents pay for the thousands of pounds of tea dumped in the harbor. Until that time, all commercial shipping was barred from Boston Harbor except for a few authorized shipments of food and fuel to keep residents from starving and freezing. The Port Bill was to take effect on June 1. Local workers were quickly put out of work—some 3,500 sailors, fishermen, and shipyard workers and hundreds of others at all levels in the shipping business that fueled Boston's economy. The city of Boston was connected to the mainland by a narrow causeway and easily cut off by land. Any ships violating the prohibition would be confiscated and become the property of the Crown. Of course, closing Boston's harbor would be a boon to other American port cities, so it was crucial that other ports (New Haven, New York, Philadelphia, Baltimore, and Charleston) made common cause with Boston. Would the other colonies stand with Massachusetts? When news of the Port Bill reached Virginia, Thomas Jefferson wrote, "We were under conviction of the necessity of arousing our people from the lethargy into which they had fallen, as to passing events."[5] Boston citizens faced starvation, its businesses faced collapse, the residents' individual rights were being trampled. Other leading Virginians, Patrick Henry, Richard Henry Lee, launched an appeal to Heaven asking every colony to declare June 1, the day the Port Bill was to take effect, a day of prayer and fasting.

At this dire time when resolution was called for, no one was more resolute than Josiah Junior. His pulmonary symptoms had increased, made
worse by the cold, damp weather bringing sleepless nights, fevers, weak-
ness. His wife tended him with the medicines Dr. Warren recommended
but was unable to restore his health. Despite his illness and legal work,
time was of the essence. So, Josiah picked up his pen and wrote a fiery
response to the Port Act, "Observations on the Boston Port Bill, with
Thoughts on Civil Society and Standing Armies."[6] It was published on
May 14, just four days after details of the act reached Massachusetts.
Unlike his past essays, which appeared with various pseudonyms, Josiah
signed his own name. As he explained: "He who shall go about to treat of
important and *perilous* concerns, and conceals himself behind the curtain
of a feigned signature, gives an advantage to his adversaries; who will
not fail to stigmatize his thoughts, as the notions of an unknown writer,
afraid or ashamed to avow his sentiments. . . . Therefore I give to the
world both my sentiments and name."

The essay, in Josiah's typical fashion, was a spirited defense of Americans and, like earlier essays, a call to arms. Although he pointed out it
was "thrown together in haste" by "one of infirm health," both true, it was
replete with historical and legal arguments. He defended Boston, noting
that popular commotions had occurred in most English maritime towns
and the destruction of the tea in Boston was a "mere temporary" event.
Some residents were tumultuous, but there was no evidence that the town of
Boston "aided, abetted, or participated in these tumults." On the contrary,
town records proved the inhabitants "discountenanced and disavowed all
riot and disorder." No court tried, let alone convicted, the population. By
canceling all shipping contracts, the Port Act was an ex post facto law,
anathema to common law. He went on to warn against the dangers of
standing armies and in favor of a citizen militia. Finally came a call to
action: "I speak it with anguish—Britons are our oppressors; I speak it
with shame—I speak it with indignation—WE ARE SLAVES." But he
predicts America will have "Patriots and Heroes, who will form a BAND
OF BROTHERS;—men who will have memories and feelings—courage

and swords:—*courage,* that shall inflame their ardent bosoms, till their hands cleave to their swords—and their SWORDS to their enemies hearts." Josiah then concludes by modestly admitting to being "several years on this side of the meridian of the age of man and will no doubt be found to have many indiscretions and faults for those of *riper* years and cooler judgment to correct and censure," but he publishes "from a sense of duty to GOD and his Country." He sent a copy of the essay to his brother Samuel.

How was Samuel, the Crown's solicitor general, coping with the increasing attacks on the British government he was sworn to defend? He was concerned, but unlike his impetuous younger brother, he did not publish his thoughts or urge residents to reach for their swords. His personal response to Josiah's essay was hopeful and surprisingly measured.[7] Samuel describes a letter that accompanied the essay as "doubly acceptable" as it assured him "of your desire to live in amity with an only brother. Such a testimony of your respect I cannot fail of remembering with pleasure. The convulsions of the times are in nothing more to be lamented, than in the interruption of domestic harmony. We have hitherto, I trust, happily seconded the friendship of blood, by the friendship of the heart and affections; and though our intercourse is not so free, or frequent, as it could be wished, yet the caution we have preserved when together, in conversing on the subject of politics, will continue to prevent a clashing of the fiercer passions."[8] It is a caution many current American families know well.

Samuel contrasted his and Josiah's different temperaments, in one a love of ease—presumably himself—in another a "zeal and fervour of imagination, strength of genius, and love of glory, shall snatch at the wreaths of fame, through the turmoils of publication." Their ideas of government and religion may vary, and their external conduct may vary, but Samuel hopes that "cannot be fairly imputed to either of us, as a defect of conscience, or uprightness of intention . . . . should we at any time disagree upon matters that require an explanation, it will be my study to obviate the effect of such an infelicity." Samuel closes with a generous and emotional prayer:

God preserve you in health and longevity, the friend and patron,
and at length the father of your country, and the éclat of your
own times record you with honour to the memory of the latest
ages, and especially, the prayer nearest my heart, may you continue, and have reason to continue, the friend and companion
of your most cordially affectionate brother.

Sadly, that hopeful prayer for brotherly affection would not be realized.
On July 26 Josiah was elected to the Boston Committee of Safety.

In the meantime, Samuel had a clash in opinion nearer to home.
His wife, Hannah, like the rest of her wealthy merchant family,
was an ardent patriot, and while she basked in the handsome living
Samuel earned—the mansion in the best part of Boston, fine clothes,
luxuries—she took exception to her husband's loyalty to the government.
In early autumn, after further British actions to punish Massachusetts
had been enacted, Abigail Adams wrote John about the political split
in the Quincy family. Abigail and her children had been invited to spend
the day at Colonel Josiah's fine home, overlooking Boston Harbor, along
with other family members. After she arrived, Samuel's wife, Hannah, and
Josiah Junior and his wife appeared: "a little clashing of parties you may be
sure," Abigail noted. But the clash did not occur. Samuel's wife seemed to
agree with the rest of the party: "She thought it high time for her Husband
to turn about, he had not done half so clever since he left her advice."[9] On
the other hand she and Samuel both admired the bishop of St. Asaph's
speech in the House of Lords arguing against the draconian Massachusetts
government bill, and for more lenient treatment of the colonists.[10]

While the colonists fretted and passed resolutions, Parliament was
devising more controls. If bad things come in threes, this would be an
avalanche of punishing laws. Since Boston residents were not prepared to
reimburse the East India Company for its considerable loss, Parliament
was ready to exercise its powers over the colony on a variety of fronts.
Four regiments arrived in Boston on May 13. A week later, on May 20,
Parliament passed the extraordinary Massachusetts Government Act. The

Massachusetts Charter of 1691, under which the colony government had been operating for more than eighty years, was revoked. The governor and his council were now to be appointed by the king. The governor's power was increased, that of the elected legislature reduced. The Massachusetts legislature could no longer withhold approval to legal and judicial offices. Even town meetings needed the approval of the governor to meet at all. Indeed, the governor could, if he wished, reduce these assemblies to an annual meeting to elect officers. This act in particular seemed to break the bonds of loyalty to Britain by arbitrarily severing the charter that spelled out the structure of the Massachusetts government and promised residents the same rights as Englishmen, as if born and abiding in England. Perhaps another form of government was needed to ensure those rights since the Mother Country seemed willing to cancel them at its discretion.

The same day the Government Act was passed, Parliament passed the Administration of Justice Act. The soldiers were in place, the government strengthened, but the officers of the law needed to be protected. The act claimed Massachusetts was "disordered." The aim was "the impartial administration of justice in cases of persons questioned for any acts done by them in the execution of the law, or for the suppression of riots and tumults."[11] Since local juries were likely to convict Crown officers, trials of British officials charged with capital crimes could be moved to England or another colony.

In June the Parliament renewed and expanded the Quartering Act. The Quartering Act of 1765 had required colonists to provide barracks for British soldiers. In the 1766 version the barracks were to include, if necessary, the housing of soldiers in inns and empty buildings. The new Quartering Act applied to all the colonies and permitted the governor, rather than colonial legislatures, to find housing, presumably empty houses, barns, and other buildings, to quarter British soldiers.

Parliament also was finally ready to deal with the governance of French Canada, won in 1763 in the French and Indian War. In June 1774 it passed The Quebec Act. This act contained a number of features that upset and disappointed the people of the thirteen colonies who, after all, had helped win that conflict and celebrated the victory. First the act expanded the territory of Canada to include land that would become the states of Illinois, Indiana, Michigan, Ohio, Wisconsin, and parts of Minnesota, limiting or quashing land claims by existing colonies and colonists. While treating the thirteen colonies harshly, Parliament was sensitive to the culture and religion of the 99 percent of Canadian residents who were of French descent, by permitting use of French civil law for private cases, with common law for public law, court procedure, and criminal prosecution. They removed reference to the Protestant faith from the Quebec oath of allegiance. Instead, the act granted the Catholic Church the power to collect tithes. Worse from a constitutional point of view, Quebec was to be governed by an appointed governor and council, but unlike the American colonies there was not to be an elected legislative assembly. Americans feared this was the pattern Britain planned to impose on them. This act would be listed as one of the colonial grievances in the Declaration of Independence, "abolishing the free System of English Laws in a neighbouring Province, establishing therein an Arbitrary government . . . enlarging its Boundaries . . . an example and fit instrument for introducing the same absolute rule into these Colonies."

All these arrangements, combined with the Coercive Acts, which stripped Massachusetts of its charter, left Americans dismayed and deeply troubled.

To return to the Port Act, Massachusetts happily did not stand alone in surviving the shutting of its chief harbor. Nearby towns and other colonies sent food, herds of sheep, and other supplies to the people of Boston to compensate for the closing of Boston Harbor. From Farmington came rye, corn, and olive oil. Barrels of fish arrived from Marblehead. More than £1,000 worth of flour came from New York and Norfolk. Portsmouth in Virginia sent a ship carrying corn, pork, bread, and flour. Henrico County, Virginia, sent wheat, corn, and flour.[12] The colonists also began planning for a Continental Congress to be held in Philadelphia.

Early in 1774, as the Braintree meeting mulled its response to events, General Thomas Gage was appointed military governor of Massachusetts. He was fifty-six at the time, a veteran of years of service in North America and commander in chief of the British forces in the American colonies. He was the second son of Viscount Gage, scion of an ancient family based in Sussex. Second sons like Thomas frequently joined the military. After a fine education he enlisted in the British army and served to defeat the Scots' Jacobite uprising. His regiment sailed to North America in 1755, during the French and Indian War, to expel French forces from the Ohio territory. He had served alongside a young George Washington, and the two corresponded for some years. Charles Lee, one of the British officers who later joined the American army, wrote Gage: "I respected your understanding, lik'd your manners and perfectly ador'd the qualities of your heart."[13] Gage was later military governor of Montreal. He was not a great military strategist but a solid, fair-minded administrator. In addition, he was married to an American, Margaret Kemble, the lovely daughter of a wealthy New Jersey family. With his calm and genial temperament, Gage was popular in both Britain and America. If anyone could quiet the tensions in Massachusetts and bring the colonists to a sensible appreciation of good order and obedience it was, or seemed to be, Thomas Gage. Despite his popularity in America Gage had told an exasperated George III that the Americans "will be lyons, whilst we are lambs; but, if we take the resolute part, they will undoubtedly prove very meek."[14]

Thomas and Margaret Gage arrived in Boston in mid-May, about the time the new regiments were to arrive and in advance of the Government Act. They stopped first at Castle Island in Boston Harbor, where the regiments were based, before moving on to Boston. There Gage was politely received by many citizens, even by the radical Hancock. He was the more welcome as he was to replace the deeply unpopular Governor Thomas Hutchinson. Hutchinson was also unpopular in Britain, being blamed for refusing to send the tea ships back, which produced the Tea Party and the political commotions that followed. Hutchinson was being recalled for what was tactfully labeled "consultation."

Before Hutchinson left, however, he received many complimentary addresses from leading citizens in Boston and other towns. The signers of these missives became known as "Addressers" and were later persecuted.

On May 30, just days after Samuel's kind response to Josiah's essay on the Port Act, in which he prayed the two brothers could remain in affectionate relationship, Samuel signed the "Address of the Barristers and Attorneys of Massachusetts to Gov. Hutchinson."[15] The brothers' opinions on Hutchinson could not be more at odds. The "Address of the Barristers and Attorneys" was lavish in its praise for Hutchinson. Despite the vicious attacks on him by the radicals, the signers declared their "firm persuasion" of his "inviolable attachment to the real interest of this your native country, and of your constant readiness, by every service in your power, to promote its true welfare and prosperity." Heaping praise on praise they commended his "great abilities, adorned with a uniform purity of principle and integrity of conduct" and expressed the "grateful acknowledgments of every true lover of his country, and friend to virtue," with the hope his presence at the royal court will help bring about "the relief of this province and particularly the town of Boston, under their present distresses, we find it a consolation which no other human source could afford."

On June 1, a beautiful spring morning, Hutchinson left his fine home on Milton Hill and gazed over his sizeable farm with its peaceful prospect across to the Blue Hills, unaware he was seeing it for the last time. Smiling to his neighbors, he walked down to the Lower Mills, greeting those of all political persuasions.[16] He crossed the river at the foot of the hill and met his carriage, which conveyed him to his ship. (The carriage was to be confiscated the following year and appropriated for Washington's use.[17]) Hutchinson loved his country and his home and earnestly hoped good sense and amity could be achieved. In exile in Britain, he took seriously the role of consultant and did his best to apprise the government of the situation in America. He later found himself, like other exiles after him, defending his countrymen.

Gage's commission was bound to be difficult, no matter how engaging and well-intentioned a man he was. His task was to enforce the harsh Coercive Acts. The Americans would have been less welcoming if they knew Gage had advised George III on the importance of firmness in the face of lawlessness.

Over the summer, committees of correspondence throughout the colonies began sounding out opinions, galvanizing opposition to Parliament's
acts against Massachusetts, and warning of the precedent they must
now oppose. British troops had been reinforced, and colonial military
preparedness was essential for their own protection. Groups of men were
advised to form militia companies and to drill regularly and, if need be,
defend their families and their towns. Weapons and ammunition were to
be stockpiled. The militia was under strict orders, however, to act only in
defense. Indeed, even Sam Adams and Joseph Warren, who were so pleased
with the destruction of tea, saw the need to warn against the use of riots
or attacks on property "as being subversive of all order and government."[18]

In August, Massachusetts and other colonies began selecting delegates
to travel to Philadelphia for a Continental Congress in September. The
cousins Sam and John Adams and Thomas Cushing, representatives for
Massachusetts, journeyed together by coach for the 300-mile trip to Philadelphia, then the largest city in the colonies. They were greeted by friendly
crowds along the way. Samuel Adams's aim for the Congress was to unite
all the colonies in opposition to the British, with his eye particularly set on
Virginia. The delegates were a mix of radicals like Samuel, who opposed
British control of America, and moderates like their fellow-delegate Thomas
Cushing and Pennsylvanians like James Wilson, who were hoping for compromise and reconciliation. Few Americans wanted independence, or war.

Everything was now happening very fast. As delegates traveled to Philadelphia, Massachusetts committees of correspondence met in opposition to
the Massachusetts Government Act and urged that all the province's counties close their courts. By early October seven of the nine contiguous mainland counties in Massachusetts did so. Each county published its resolve,
explaining its reason. The most famous and well-drafted was the Suffolk
Resolves, the county that included Boston, written by Joseph Warren and
Samuel Adams and submitted at a meeting on September 6. Three days
later, after various edits, the Suffolk resolves were approved. Paul Revere
was assigned to deliver the resolves to the Continental Congress as quickly
as possible. The resolves were forceful and precise. They denounced the

Coercive Acts and urged a complete boycott of British goods—no imports or exports, and a refusal to use British products. They pledged to ignore the Massachusetts Government Act and Port Bill and demanded officials appointed under the Massachusetts Government Act resign. This approach had worked with the Stamp Act, with intimidation, boycotts, and protests. Citizens were to refuse to pay taxes until the Massachusetts Government Act was repealed and should instead support a Massachusetts government free from royal authority until all the Coercive Acts were repealed. Preparation for military action was recommended. Every colony was to raise militia regiments of local men ready to protect home and country. The danger of armed violence was clear.

That point was driven home on September 1, when Gage's troops seized the weapons stored by the Sons of Liberty and residents of Charlestown, the town across the bay from Boston. The first news to reach Congress about the confiscation of the arsenal was truly alarming, claiming that six people had been killed by British troops and that Boston had been leveled.[19] Later, relieved delegates learned that while thousands of armed militiamen had rushed to the scene, they were under strict orders from the Committee of Correspondence to act only in defense. There was no firefight or fire. Known as the Powder Alarm, it was a lesson to both sides how dangerous the situation had become.

For Gage the lesson of the Powder Alarm was that "if force is to be used at length, it must be a considerable one, and foreign troops must be hired, for to begin with small numbers will encourage resistance, and not terrify; and will in the end cost more blood and treasure."[20] Gage seized the powder and for extra security placed troops and 28 cannons along the narrow, 120-yard causeway into Boston.

Despite the mixed political views of the Continental Congress's delegates, news of the close call over the powder seizure hardened opinions, and the Suffolk Resolves were unanimously endorsed. The delegates were careful, however, to reiterate their loyalty to the British Crown but not Parliament's right to tax the colonies. The Congress adjourned on October 26, 1774.

With its adoption of the Suffolk Resolves, both sides had dug in very publicly. Parliament would not repeal the Coercive Acts until Massachusetts agreed to reimburse the owners of the tea and yield to the law. Massachusetts and its sister colonies would not repay the damages and obey the Parliament or government until the Coercive Acts were repealed. It was not only a stalemate, but a dangerous one.

The question was how the British saw the American situation. There were fears that Oliver, the lieutenant governor, and another prominent Tory were off to England to inform the government of their own side of events. It was important someone from the patriot side provide their side of the story and sound out leading members of Parliament and other prominent individuals. There was still hope that some means of reconciliation might yet be found to restore peace and that the English people, suffering from endless taxes themselves, might even make common cause with the colonists.

Joseph Warren, Josiah's friend and doctor, felt someone must be dispatched to Britain as an emissary for a peaceful compromise. He had considered going himself but felt his provincial and local responsibilities precluded that.[21] He asked Josiah to undertake that secret mission. This was an odd choice. No one knew better than Warren the precarious state of Josiah's health. On the other hand, Josiah had undertaken a useful journey to the southern and middle Atlantic colonies in 1773 to sound out opinion on British policy. Since the publication of his essay on the Port Act, leading men had been sending him letters of encouragement. Josiah's politics were sound. He was not diplomatic, but volatile and hot-headed, however, ever ready to urge a resort to arms. Despite these problems Warren asked Josiah to undertake the mission. For Josiah it was a flattering but risky invitation. His health was poor, and he remembered with a shudder the terrible sea journey he had weathered on his trip south along the coast. An ocean voyage in the fall, the hurricane season, was likely to be worse. But the task was vital to the future of his country. He accepted. As delegates were converging on Philadelphia for the Continental Congress, Josiah Junior began preparing for an ocean voyage.

The mission was kept a closely guarded secret "lest the enemies of the patriotic cause should take measures to counteract the effect of his presence and representations in England."[22] His journey was concealed from all but his nearest relations, and the political friends who had proposed the measure, or so they thought.

Josiah bid his wife and baby son a loving farewell and, armed with a batch of letters of introduction, boarded a ship in Salem, north of Boston, on September 28 bound for England. His ship crossed the turbulent Atlantic safely and docked on November 8 at Falmouth, in Cornwall, on England's rugged southwest coast. On November 17 Josiah arrived in London.

Despite the effort to keep Josiah's errand a secret, General Gage knew of his journey days before he set sail. Indeed, on September 25, three days before Josiah left Salem, King George wrote Lord Dartmouth, "I understand that a Person whose Name is kept secret goes on the same Vessell, and that there is something mysterious concerning the Object of his Voyage."[23] A letter from Josiah Senior to his son a month after he had set sail, but while he was still at sea, anxiously sought reassurance. "News, that would be almost as joyful [as his health restored] and reviving to your aged father, as to hear that, through your mediation peace and harmony were restored between the parent state and her injured and oppressed children upon this continent." He informed Josiah he was especially concerned that "all the tories and some of the whigs, resent your clandestine departure. Many of the former say, that as soon as your arrival is known, you will be apprehended and secured."[24] There was general confusion about the purpose of his voyage. "Your friends say, your principal motive is the recovery of your health, which if Providence should please to restore, they rest assured of your best endeavours to procure a redress of the grievances, and a speedy removal of the intolerable burdens, with which your native country is and has been long oppressed." The letter concluded with the prayer, "God Almighty grant, if your life and health are spared, that you may succeed in every respect."[25] Much rested on Josiah's efforts.

TWELVE

Partings: Two Ocean Voyages and a Death

The die is cast. Yesterday brought us such a Speech from the Throne as will stain with everlasting infamy the reign of G[e]orge the 3 determined to carry into Execution `the acts passd by the late parliament . . . even without giving us an opportunity to be heard in our defence. . . . and the attempt to bring beggary and Slavery is avoued or can be no longer concealed. When this happens the Friends of Liberty, should any such remain will have one option still left, and will rather chuse no doubt to die [the] last British freemen, than bear to live the first British Slaves.

—Abigail Adams to Mercy Otis Warren,
Braintree, Mass., February 1775[1]

You are quite mistaken in supposing anything conciliatory toward America is intended. The ministers, with their leader are violently blowing the coals into a flame, that will lay waste the whole British Empire. From the destruction of so vast a body, new empires and new systems of government must arise. In short a civil war is inevitable.

—William Lee, friend of Josiah Quincy
in England, March 4, 1775

W as Josiah's mission a fool's errand? King George III, "the tyrant" according to the Declaration of Independence, was not really a tyrant of course, but that did not change the fact that he had had enough. He was a dutiful monarch who stayed within his constitutional bounds, a good husband, father of thirteen, and a conscientious administrator. Kings, not Parliament, had granted the colonies their charters. The American colonists had long assumed, or prudently pretended to believe, as generations of British subjects before them, that it was not the king but wicked ministers giving him bad advice. Now that Parliament was more powerful, it was not just evil councilors who were the villains; it was Parliament, too.

But the king's own opinions had changed. That final straw that provoked him to get personally involved in imperial policy was the Boston Tea Party. Clearly the previous policy had been too lenient. The colonists were like naughty children. King George, along with many members of Parliament, believed repealing the Stamp Act in 1766 because of the colonists' resistance was a mistake. It was appeasement, and appeasement was always unwise and merely led to future problems. For that reason, after the repeal the king and Parliament enthusiastically endorsed The Declaratory Act, making clear Parliament was not conceding an iota of its power to pass laws for the colonies "in all cases whatsoever." Somehow the colonists, in their joy at the repeal of the Stamp Act, did not seem to have noticed the peril in that assertion, or maybe they thought it could be circumvented. There might be another fight another day, but for now they had won.

The destruction of the tea was that next fight. King and Parliament demanded reparations and decided a change in tactics was urgent. The gloves were off. George heartily endorsed the Coercive Acts, and as soon as Massachusetts's former governor Thomas Hutchinson reached England, the king spent two hours quizzing him about his advice and the state of affairs in Massachusetts.[2] Hutchinson agreed that the Port Act, closing the port of Boston, was a sensible step. Firmness was imperative, especially since the radical colonists seemed to be moving toward rebellion and, even worse, republicanism. The British government needed to take a hard line to restore order and obedience.

With king and Parliament agreeing on this stern approach, was Josiah's mission to change minds too late? It seemed wishful thinking that leading British politicians and people of influence, even the average overtaxed Englishman, would make common cause with the Americans. But many did want to pull back from war. Not long after Josiah arrived in England, Massachusetts's new governor, General Gage, recommended a more conciliatory approach and the suspension of the Coercive Acts.[3] The king thought this an absurd idea. But several leading ministers and lords agreed with Gage. Like the urgent American efforts to preserve the peace, Lord North, the prime minister, wanted to draw back from war. He suggested sending commissions to America to make inquiries and evaluate the situation. At the very least sending commissioners would demonstrate a good faith effort to allow the colonists to present their side of the case. Distinguished opposition MPs such as Edmund Burke, William Pitt the Elder, and the Second Marquess of Rockingham also opposed use of force. British merchants, worried about their American business, also lobbied for negotiations. In April 1775 John Wilkes, the lord mayor of London, the London livery company, trade associations, and the Common Hall of the City of London all joined the call for the Crown to find a peaceful solution. A year later, even after fighting had begun, the Continental Congress sent the "Olive Branch" petition, still hoping for some exit from war. Through it all King George remained unmoved. "We must with Vigour pursue the means of bringing the Deluded Americans to a Sense of their Duty," he demanded, which only force could do.[4] Sadly, all these efforts to avert bloodshed and the anguish of division would be too late.

———

Josiah was an unfortunate choice for this delicate mission. Beneath the physical liability of his frail health was an impulsive and volatile temperament. John Adams, who Josiah had assisted in defending the British soldiers, wrote Abigail that he had been dismayed by Josiah's "too youthful ardour" and found the younger man "allways impetuous and vehement."[5] Nevertheless Adams, along with numerous prominent patriots, wished him "a prosperous voyage, and much of the exalted pleasure of serving your country."[6] At this point even a more experienced diplomat might not have succeeded, but Josiah's journal of his mission mirrors Adams's gloomy assessment as Josiah swung from optimism to anger, from extreme to moderate politics and back again, and finally to despair.[7]

Josiah's limited experience of sea voyages had not been a happy one. Unlike his father and older brother, Edmund, he had never crossed the Atlantic, but his voyage south along the American coast was buffeted by days of stormy weather and his own illness. It took special fortitude on his part to sail the ocean to Britain. He could praise God that his ship arrived safely in England, on November 11, and that he was in good health. Josiah's first impression of the Mother Country was to marvel at the "riches and powers of this great nation," which "I should not have believed." On his journey to London, he passed mile after mile of little villages and market towns surrounded by well-tended fields, each with its ancient stone church. They were a wonder for a young man from Massachusetts Bay. Unlike Massachusetts buildings, the houses and farms were mostly made of wattle with oak beams, or stone, material to be expected in a country with little timber. Some older houses were capped with thick layers of thatch to keep out the cold, which gave them the aspect of returning to the ground from which they had come. Handsome manor houses dotted the countryside, each with an adjoining village. It took a full week of travel to reach London. London was then the largest city in Europe with a teeming population of nearly one million people. Compared to Boston's 15,000 people and Philadelphia, the largest American city, with 40,000, Josiah could be forgiven for feeling astonished and overwhelmed by the size of this great capital.

His first meeting when he arrived was with Benjamin Franklin, the Massachusetts agent in Britain. Josiah had doubted Franklin's fidelity to colonial concerns. While Josiah had applauded the destruction of the tea, Franklin had been shocked by it as a "violent Injustice on our part." But on meeting Franklin, Josiah found him "warm in our cause," "an American in heart and soul."[8]

Josiah saw his task as countering hostile information by explaining the American point of view and wasted no time attending a host of meetings with members of the governing ministry, opposition members of Parliament, and London radicals. He suggested that Americans would be ready to contribute to the British Empire if they were "sole judges of the time and quantity of their grants."[9] He sent a flurry of letters about his activities and impressions to his wife, "My best Friend," to be shared with leading friends of the cause. Despite his best efforts his conversations failed "to correct the falsehoods" he believed had been relayed by Hutchinson, or to alter government policy. The discussions with opposition leaders involved him more and more in their politics. While on November 24 he wrote that both opposition and government leaders made "great professions of friendship," he was frustrated by the lack of progress, and switched from counsels of diplomacy to radicalism, cautioning Congress against negotiation.[10] Negotiations, to his mind, would cause friends to become despondent, and economic measures such as had been used in the past would not succeed since the British government ignored even their own merchants. In early December he met with Corbin Morris, who was intimate with the ministry. Morris invited him to suggest an approach the colonists would agree to that would lead to a settlement, but Josiah distrusted the man and the approach, fearful he was being manipulated. Instead, he pinned his hopes on the parliamentary opposition. In a frenetic letter home on December 7, he urged Americans to prepare "for the worst," claiming that their forbearance and delay had brought evils upon them, then immediately seemed to correct himself, writing: "You see my heart gets the better of my head; my feelings rise paramount to my discretion. This will always be with those who are warm in the cause of their country,—their zeal banishes caution. You see however, I still retain some discretion, but even that I had lose than be 'unpregnant of my cause or lack gall to make oppression bitter.'"[11] Only if the Americans show they are in earnest and resolved to endure all "with a spirit worthy of the prize for which they contend" he argued, will they have active and powerful friends in Parliament. Members of the Continental Congress must have been shaking their heads at the receipt of this missive and probably regretted sending so inexperienced and impulsive a man to represent the interests of their country.

A week later even this frenetic approach seemed insufficient to Josiah. Writing on December 14 he argued for violence: "Let me tell you one very serious truth in which we all agreed, *your countrymen must seal their cause with their blood.*"[12] He seemed to be calling for war: Americans "must now stand the issue; they must preserve a consistency of character; THEY MUST NOT DELAY; they must—or be trodden into the vilest vassalage, the scorn, the spurn of their enemies, a byword of infamy among all men."[13] However, he claimed this approach would bring peace, because once his countrymen had demonstrated resolve, "whether successful or not, your foes will diminish, your friends amazingly increase, and you will be happy in the peaceful enjoyment of your inheritance." In the same letter, Josiah reported the rumor that Lord North had sneered, "that I have my price." He had insults of his own to share. He saw the British commercial world as "infested with 'conspirators' against American happiness." He bristled that many Englishmen dismissed Americans as "all cowards and poltroons" but in turn sneered that Englishmen "in variety and abundance of fraud and deceits far surpass any part of N. America."[14] Writing Joseph Reed in Philadelphia he admitted that he believed they must "seal their faith and constancy to their liberties with blood." January found him more hopeful of a change, as he sat in the gallery to listen to eloquent members of the opposition plead for repeal of the coercive acts. But by late January it was clear that the support and oratory of America's friends in Parliament would not change policy. The friends of America were, after all, members of the opposition, not the governing party. A torrent of parliamentary defeats for conciliation followed. Petitions of merchant groups from Britain's chief trading cities, the largest petitioning campaigns of the time, signed by thousands for and against war, were consigned to what Edmund Burke labeled a "committee on oblivion." Despite his growing discouragement, Josiah pushed himself to keep a busy schedule of meetings, increasingly with British radicals. But Parliament had lost patience. On February 1 the Lords consigned Chatham's eloquent motion for conciliation to the same oblivion, in a vote of 61 to 32. The following day the House of Commons, by a vote of 296 to 106, declared Massachusetts in rebellion.[15]

As this depressing flood of events continued, Josiah responded to repeated concerns from family and friends about his health. In mid-January he assured his wife, "My health was never better."[16] But a week later, he confided to his journal, "This night, for the first time since my arrival, I was taken very ill with a fever and spasms."[17] In the best of times British winter weather is bone-chilling, damp, and unhealthy, and 1775 was in the midst of what we now know as the Little Ice Age. Doctor Fothergill came the next day to see Josiah, refusing to take any payment, and came frequently thereafter. Josiah went to stay with a family in Islington "while in my present feeble state of health," where he was kindly cared for and visited by friends and well-wishers. But by February 26 he had, against his own "private opinion and inclination," agreed to sail home. Josiah met with Franklin for a private conversation before he left. Watching the frail, passionate young man attempting to carry out his mission, Franklin mused, "It is a thousand pities his strength of body is not equal to his strength of mind. His zeal for the public, like that of David for God's house, will, I fear, eat him up."[18]Franklin favored boycotts and economic measures over force, while Josiah fluctuated from moderate to radical solutions with changing conversations and events.

It was all too depressing and too late. Josiah's hopes for success sank along with his health, and on March 4 he boarded a ship for home.[19] He had wanted to stay in England to take the waters at Bristol as his doctor advised, but the entreaties of fifteen or twenty of his friends urged him to immediately leave for Boston.[20] The very day Josiah left, his friend William Lee agreed with Josiah's own gloomy assessment: "You are quite mistaken in supposing anything conciliatory towards America is intended. The ministers, with their leader are violently blowing the coals into a flame, that will lay waste the whole British Empire. From the destruction of so vast a body, new empires and new systems of government must arise. In short, a civil war is inevitable."[21] Before Josiah reached Massachusetts, war had already begun.

Back home, as 1774 turned into 1775, tensions over political differences boiled over with intimidation and mob violence driving families and friends apart. Deep family tragedies loomed. Josiah Senior, his children, and their spouses and friends were not alone in the impending danger of painful partings. John Adams and Jonathan Sewell had been close friends since they first met, instantly feeling a special rapport. Both studied law in Judge Russell's office and later enjoyed exchanging ideas and traveling together from court to court.[22] When apart Adams and Sewell corresponded frequently. It was Sewell's post as Massachusetts attorney general that Samuel Quincy later held. Sewell was married to Samuel and Josiah's cousin Esther Quincy. Esther's younger sister Dorothy, married that staunch patriot, John Hancock.

In 1774 as Adams and Sewell were strolling along the Great Hill in Portland, Sewell tried to convince his friend not to attend the first Continental Congress. Adams replied, "The die is now cast, I have now passed the rubicon; sink or swim, live or die, survive or perish with my country, is my unalterable determination." That year after Sewell's Cambridge home was attacked by a wild mob, he and his family fled to Boston, where others loyal to the government had found safety. In 1775 Jonathan Sewell and his family sailed into exile in England. The two dear friends did not meet again until twelve years later, when Adams arrived in England to serve as a minister for the new nation. The two old friends met in Sewell's rooming house in London. He was there on his way to New Brunswick, Canada, to serve as an admiralty judge. Sewell wrote that "when Mr. Adams came in, he took my hand in both of his, and with a hearty squeeze, accosted me in these words—*how do you do my dear old friend!*—our conversation was just as might be expected at the meeting of two old sincere friends after a long separation."[23] They talked warmly for three hours and parted. Neither man had altered his views of the other's political choices, but it no longer mattered. Privately, however, Sewell judged Adams unsuited for his role as a courtier, while Adams thought Sewell a sad exile whose only purpose was rearing his children. Sewell and his family moved to Canada, where he took up his post. They never returned home. Some years later when Sewell died Adams attributed it to a broken heart.[24]

James Otis, famous in England as the champion of American rights, was married to Ruth Cunningham, the daughter of a wealthy merchant and a "High Tory." Despite her politics Otis loved her dearly. When war broke out, she became a loyalist. The couple had three children, a son James, who had died tragically at the age of eighteen, and two daughters, Elizabeth and Mary. Like the Quincy sisters, they married men on opposite sides in the war. Elizabeth married a British army captain and spent her life in England, while her sister Mary wed Benjamin Lincoln, Hannah Quincy Lincoln's nephew, whose father would become one of Washington's leading generals.

Then there is the American founder Gouverneur Morris, a congressional delegate from New York, who signed the Articles of Confederation and the United States Constitution. Morris stayed connected with his two loyalist sisters. His mother and most of his brothers-in-law and half-brothers were also loyalists. Yet he prosecuted loyalists and apparently advocated their public executions to frighten neutrals into joining the patriot cause.[25] If war makes strange bedfellows, it makes even stranger enemies.

Late in 1774 General Thomas Gage changed his mind. In 1775 members of Parliament were laughing that Americans "were neither soldiers, nor could be made so; being naturally of a pusillanimous disposition, and utterly incapable of any sort of order or discipline."[26] Colonel James Grant, who had fought in the French and Indian War, sneered that five thousand British troops could march from one end of America to another without any serious opposition. But Gage, who had lived in America for twenty years, was married to an American, and was witness to the popular militancy of the people of Massachusetts, knew better than the arrogant members of Parliament. He advised the government to suspend the Coercive Acts for which he was branded cowardly by army comrades and labeled the "Old Woman."[27]

As his troops were being reinforced that spring, Gage was under pressure to act against the ringleaders of the Massachusetts opposition and to seize the growing arsenal of weapons being stockpiled at Concord, some twenty miles west of Boston. He was a careful man. Before taking any action, he sent spies to Concord and as far west as Worcester, some forty-eight miles from Boston, to discover the attitudes of residents toward the government. One of Gage's spies, John Howe, set off to discreetly sound out the government's friends and opponents, dressed like a local with leather breeches, mixed stockings, and a scarf tied at his neck. His advice to Gage on his return was that a troop of mounted men, in a lightning nighttime raid, might be able to destroy the weapons at Concord and return safely, but he warned "to go with 1,000 foot to destroy the stores the country would be alarmed" and the greater part of the troops "would get killed or taken."[28] Gage ignored Howe's advice and sent some 900 infantry to Concord, confident so large a force of professional soldiers would cow any resistance. One of the officers leading the expedition believed "one active campaign, a smart action, and burning two or three of their towns will set everything to rights."[29] As a precaution the foray was kept secret.

In the dead of night on April 18, Gage's regulars set out with orders to seize Sam Adams and John Hancock, then staying in Lexington, and to destroy the weapons cache at Concord. The troops moved stealthily, wading through swamps and taking byways to avoid alerting the militia in the farms and towns along the way. But they might not have bothered. Paul Revere and other Sons of Liberty had been closely monitoring the activity of the Boston soldiers, and when they learned the troops were to be on the march that night, went riding out to alert the special minutemen militia and residents along the road to Concord.[30] Sam Adams and Hancock were warned to flee.

The minutemen were under strict orders to fire only if fired upon. The Continental Congress had stressed that the people of Massachusetts avoid any offensive moves, but stay "peaceably and firmly . . . on the defensive," lest some rash action lead to "the horrors of a civil war" while there were still hopes of peace.[31]

A small band of seventy local men gathered at dawn on the Lexington green to confront Gage's 900 troops. The regulars could have gone around the small group, but their lead officer ordered them to take battle positions.

He ordered the Americans to disperse. As they began to do so, someone fired—it is unclear who—and shooting began. Eight of the Lexington men were killed and ten wounded. The British troops gave their traditional cheer and marched off to Concord.

News of the shooting at Lexington spread, and by the time the British got to Concord hundreds of armed men awaited them with dozens more racing there. The Americans cautiously stood at a distance and watched the troops. The British began gathering and burning some wagons and military equipment. Seeing the smoke and thinking they were setting the town on fire, the militia attacked. Then stopped. After a stalemate of two hours, while the British waited in vain for reinforcements, they began the twenty-mile march back to Boston. The entire way they faced withering fire from the meadows, from windows of homes, from behind stone walls, and from stands of trees. They responded by shooting at an unseen enemy, sometimes into houses. The British troops, like European soldiers at the time, were trained to fight in the open, not in this "Indian style" of warfare. The death toll was high. By sunset, when the running battle was finally over, the British had suffered 73 men killed, 174 wounded, another 26 missing. Their dead and wounded littered the road from Concord. Some 50 Americans were killed or died later from their wounds, another 39 were wounded, and 5 were missing. Those American casualties came from twenty-three Massachusetts towns.

The campaign was a disaster for the British forces but also for all those hoping for peace and reconciliation. The day after the fight the Massachusetts Provincial Congress sent out a desperate plea:

> Our all is at stake. Death and devastation are the certain consequences of delay. Every moment is infinitely precious. An hour lost may deluge your country in blood and entail perpetual slavery upon the few of our posterity that may survive the carnage.[32]

The Congress summoned men to converge on Cambridge, just across the Charles River from Boston, to prevent the British troops bivouacked there from returning to take revenge. Thousands of armed men and boys answered the call. Gage and his troops found themselves besieged.

Josiah's journey back across the Atlantic was turbulent, the fresh sea air more dangerous than healthy. While the ship was still in the English Channel, he wrote "the sea runs high and I can scarcely write legibly" and his cough was "far from better."[33] The poor man lacked comfortable quarters and was at sea for more than five weeks. His fate was in the hands of Heaven. A kindly sailor had been looking after him. To this man he confided that his one desire was "that he might live long enough to have an interview with Samuel Adams, or Joseph Warren;—that granted, he should die content."[34] Sadly, this prayer was not to be answered. Three days' sail from land, Josiah lay dying. He summoned his "friend on board" and dictated a final message for his family and friends. [35]

> Ever since I have been out, almost every thing has been different from what I expected. Instead of pleasant weather, the most inclement and damp, which removed me entirely from the deck, and when I was flattered with the hope of getting into port six days ago, I am yet here, as distant from it as when the encouragement was given me . . . I am persuaded that this voyage and passage are the instruments to put an end to my being. His holy will be done!"

The sailor-scribe added a postscript:

> "Mr Quincy is so low, that he probably will not be able to read a word of the foregoing, but it is to be hoped it will be intelligible with a little pains."

On April 26, within sight of his beloved country, Josiah died. Just hours later the ship entered Gloucester harbor. He never knew that a week earlier, while he was at sea, war had begun.

In the confused aftermath of that first Revolutionary War battle his family, eagerly awaiting his arrival, were heartbroken when they later learned of his death. They were unable to pay their last respects to him. His "best friend," his wife Abigail, had been in Boston with their two young children, both deathly ill. Their little daughter had died on April 13. Worried and alone, Abigail took her sick little son to her parents' home on Beacon Street, where her sisters Mary and Hannah had a carriage waiting to take them to Norwich, Connecticut, where their brother William had found a house for them all.

When the people of Gloucester were unable to reach Josiah's family promptly, he was buried in a Gloucester cemetery, where the kindly residents gave him a proper funeral, remembering his contributions and sorrowing for his loss. Sometime later Abigail journeyed to Gloucester to retrieve Josiah's trunks with his journals, clothes, and other possessions. He had brought two rings he had specially made in London, one for Abigail, one for his father. Hers was set with diamonds, and Josiah Senior's had the image of Liberty with the motto "Oh, save my country!" Abigail hoped to speak with the sailor who had cared for Josiah, but he was already off on another voyage.[36]

Josiah's last letter asked that his remains be buried in a special tomb to be built in his hometown of Braintree. When the theater of war had moved from Massachusetts to other colonies, his grieving father complied with his son's wishes and removed his remains to the family burial ground in Braintree. Abigail never remarried and, years later, complying with Josiah's last wish, was buried beside him when she died. The inscription on a monument to them was composed by John Quincy Adams. Of Josiah he wrote:

BRILLIANT TALENTS, UNCOMMON ELOQUENCE,

AND INDEFATIGABLE APPLICATION,

RAISED HIM TO THE HIGHEST EMINENCE IN HIS PROFESSION,

HIS EARLY, ENLIGHTENED, INFLEXIBLE ATTACHMENT

TO THE CAUSE OF HIS COUNTRY,

IS ATTESTED BY MONUMENTS MORE DURABLE THAN THIS . . .[37]

THIRTEEN

Parting Ways

The unhappy event which took place yesterday, was as unexpected as it was distressful; my concern for your safety, as well as my anxiety for the agitation of my dear partner, wounded me to the heart. Oh, cruel separation. I had many things to say; I could have talked with you for ever; but the will of Heaven forbade it. . . . God preserve you in health and every earthly enjoyment, until you again receive the salutation of your friend and brother, Samuel Quincy.

—Samuel Quincy to his brother-in-law,
Henry Hill, Esq., Boston, May 13, 1775

E veryone seemed to be fleeing. It was one thing to talk boldly about defending liberty and another to experience a shooting war. Boston Harbor was crowded with British ships and the city full of soldiers, while local men in every village were armed and drilling. Hundreds of people living in Boston or on the seacoast took their children and a few prized possessions and fled inland. There were invariably numerous false alarms. Abigail Adams wrote her friend Mercy Otis Warren that Josiah Senior's family in Braintree "have several Times been obliged to flee from their house and scatter themselves about."[1] "Our Hearts are bleeding for the poor People of Boston," John wrote Abigail from Hartford. "What will, or can be done for them I cant conceive. God preserve them."[2] In late May the sight of three British ships near Weymouth, five miles from Braintree, caused panic. Believing 300 British troops had actually landed and were marching inland, Abigail wrote, "People women children from the Iron Works flocking down this Way—every woman and child above or from below my Fathers" in Weymouth. "My Fathers family flying, the Drs. in great distress as you may well imagine for my Aunt had her bed thrown into a cart, into which she got herself, and orderd the boy to drive her of to Bridgewater which he did."[3] Refugees from Boston stopped at the Adams farm, "tired and fatigued, seek an assilum for a Day or Night, a week—you can hardly imagine how we live."[4] Some 2,000 men dashed to defend Weymouth, but the goal of the British expedition causing the alarm was just to land at Grape Island in the harbor to get hay.

After the Battle of Lexington and Concord, the city of Boston was crowded, dangerous, and unpleasant. The causeway from Boston to the mainland was cut off by a huge, ragtag army of some 15,000 men and boys stationed across the river in Cambridge. Patriots such as Josiah's wife, Abigail Phillips, and her family fled from Boston; loyalists like Jonathan Sewell and his family arrived there seeking British protection from the mob. Some loyal to the government began to flee abroad, to Canada or England, and became "absentees." With more families arriving in Boston than leaving, and a rapidly growing force of troops, the city's population swelled to bursting. Fine homes were commandeered by army officers, and as food became scarce prices soared. Sewell and his family were fortunate to find a spacious house. John Andrews, a Son of Liberty living in Boston, complained that for those lucky enough to buy food it was a diet of "pork and beans one day" and "beans and pork another."[5] Worse, in the unhealthy and crowded conditions in the city, smallpox threatened and many residents were dying daily of dysentery.[6] Funerals were so frequent, Sewell jested darkly, that "for a month past you meet as many dead folks as live ones in Boston streets."[7]

Samuel, his wife Hannah, and their three young children, Hannah, Samuel, and Thomas, had been living comfortably in Boston for many years. As solicitor general for Massachusetts and also a justice of the peace, this last post quietly funded by the tea tax revenue, they had a handsome income.[8] In 1771 they sold their house on South Street to Thomas Hutchinson, the much-hated governor of Massachusetts, and built a handsome new home on Hanover Street, larger than Josiah Senior's new Braintree residence. They were prosperous and enjoying their prosperity, entertaining prominent people of all political persuasions. Samuel was, as he had written his brother, not a rabble-rouser. He was a skilled attorney, dutiful and prudent, and although an excellent essayist, refrained from publishing contentious essays. He was clear about the differences in his temperament and his younger brother Josiah's. Upon reading Josiah's essay on the Port Bill, he contrasted his own love of ease to Josiah's "zeal and fervour of imagination" and "love of glory."[9] Samuel had opposed the Stamp Act and celebrated its recall, and in 1769 joined a festive dinner with 350 Sons of Liberty to commemorate the successful protests that brought down that tax. He was not a member of the Sons of Liberty but sat happily at a table in an open field with his father, John Adams, Henry Hill, his wife's grandfather, and other leading opponents of the government.[10] While prominent loyalists had been attacked for their views and their offices and their homes vandalized and stripped, Samuel was left alone. Indeed, to many he was a hero for prosecuting the British soldiers involved in the Boston Massacre. The famous African American poet of the day, Phyllis Wheatley, included in her series on American heroes and events a poem in honor of Samuel, "To Samuel Quincy, a Panegyric."

After the destruction of the tea in December 1774, it became harder to be neutral. Samuel, as solicitor general of Massachusetts, and Jonathan Sewell, as attorney general, received orders from London to arrest the men the government saw as ringleaders of the Tea Party—John Hancock, Sam Adams, Joseph Warren, and Thomas Cushing—and charge them with "High Treason" and "High Misdemeanors."[11] Despite these orders Samuel reassured his anxious family that neither he nor Sewell would arrest the four men.[12] But Samuel dismissed it as preposterous when the radicals wanted to impeach Chief Justice Peter Oliver. Chief Justice Oliver's brother Andrew, who had served as lieutenant governor under Hutchinson, died two days before the popular annual commemoration of the Boston Massacre. There was fear that if his funeral took place so soon after the commemoration it would provoke an angry mob. Many government supporters, including Andrew's own brother the chief justice, planned to stay away from the funeral. Andrew was especially unpopular with the public due to his having been named the stamp master to implement the Stamp Act. Mobs had attacked and ransacked Andrew's home and office in the summer of 1765. Samuel was against the Stamp Act but furious at those reluctant to attend the funeral. Andrew had been a close personal friend, and Samuel was determined to attend the funeral to honor him. [13] When roused, Samuel could be faithful. Samuel and his sister Hannah differed on issues but were both adamantly against mob violence and intimidation. In his own modest way Samuel was an idealist, or at least an optimist, writing brother Josiah, "A consciousness . . . of having done his duty will support every man against the attacks of obloquy and reproach." [14]

While Samuel had written confidently about the importance of a man being conscious of having done his duty, it is unclear what he thought his duty was. Within a month after the Battle of Lexington and Concord, he decided to leave for Britain. This decision and its timing are difficult to understand. He had never been personally attacked by any mob. His house had never been ransacked. Yet shortly after that battle and barely two weeks after the tragic death of his brother Josiah, he had made up his mind. He traveled to Braintree to tell his family. The Quincy family was still in deep mourning for Josiah. They knew Samuel's views but hoped he would join them in support of the American side, or at worst stay neutral. Of his father's three sons, Samuel was now the only survivor.

Samuel's fellow loyalist Jonathan Sewell, who had to flee a mob attack on his home, did not leave Boston until three months after Samuel and, even then, felt it was actually improper to abandon his office until relieved of his duty. Samuel does not seem to have had the same reservations. Perhaps having ignored the order to arrest leading patriots and charge them with treason was a foretaste of more difficult choices to come. He would not be able to continue bridging the two sides and might lose his post and become a victim of the mob. If that was his concern, he did not mention it. Nor did he refer to any sense of duty to the government he served. Perhaps since Great Britain was likely to win any further confrontation, it seemed better to be in a position to take advantage of that result than sacrifice everything to a losing cause. The growing tensions in Massachusetts were truly frightening, and life in Boston was increasingly unpleasant for him and his young family. As for his grieving family at Braintree, their feelings and sense of abandonment were regrettable but did not deter him.

Samuel's father and sister Hannah were keenly aware he favored the British government but were distraught when he announced his plan to leave immediately for England. Both wrote him desperately trying to persuade him to change his mind.[15] In her letter Hannah used every means to appeal to him, hoping her note "may serve to convince you that I have not forgotten that you are my *only* brother."[16] She reminded him sea voyages were dangerous, their two other brothers died at sea, and she might never see him again. Their country was in great distress, and their families and close friends faced a chaotic and dangerous situation, as well as mourning the recent loss of their dear brother Josiah. Then she got angry: "Let it not be told in America, and let it not be published in Great Britain, that a brother of such brothers fled from his country—the wife of his youth—the children of his affection—and from his aged sire, already bowed down with the loss of two sons, and by that of many more dear, though not so near connections," and argued that his motive "to secure himself from the reproaches of his injured countrymen, and to cover such a retreat, obliged to enlist as a sycophant under an obnoxious Hutchinson, who is a tool under a cruel North, and by them to be veered about, and at last to be blown aside with a cool 'to-morrow, sir.'" She called on him to "arouse from your lethargy—let reason take the helm—disregard all greatness but greatness of soul;—then the little trappings that royalty can confer will lose their lustre, that false lustre which I fear inclines you to the *prerogative* side." Hannah may have been told that Samuel expected Hutchinson, then in London, to find him an advantageous position.

Samuel's decision to leave was most upsetting for his wife. On May 13, the day after confronting her, he wrote her brother, Henry Hill, of his decision. "I am going, my dear friend," he explained, "to quit the habitation where I have been so long encircled with the dearest connections," to "hazard the unstable element, for a while to change the scene—whether it will be prosperous or adverse, is not for me to determine. I pray God to sustain my integrity, and preserve me from temptation." His explanation for his departure, "for a while to change the scene," offered no justification for such a drastic break, only a glib statement of his plans. He hoped the venture would be prosperous. He said nothing about attention to his duty to the government or fear of harassment, just the opportunity to prosper. Several times Thomas Hutchinson, now in England, was mentioned as helping him find a lucrative post.

Samuel went on to describe "the unhappy event" the previous day when he discussed his departure with his wife, her response as "unexpected as it was distressful." He seemed strangely surprised at her reaction. Apparently, he had assumed Hannah and his children would accompany him to England, or that she would at least sympathize with his plan. Although he knew her political views were staunchly patriotic, he seemed quite unprepared for "the agitation of my dear partner," which "wounded me to the heart. Oh, cruel separation." Hannah absolutely refused to accompany him. Unlike most of those who fled the country with their families, Samuel was ready to go alone. In Hannah's need and distress her brother Henry and his wife, Amelia, had kindly agreed to take her and her three children into their own home in Cambridge.[17] The fine mansion Samuel Quincy had built for his family in Boston with its lovely furnishings would be abandoned.

Samuel hastened to reassure Henry of his innocent political intentions: "My political character with you may be suspicious; but be assured, if I cannot *serve* my country, which I shall endeavor to the utmost of my power, I will never *betray* it." There is a hint that he hoped to achieve some sort of reconciliation: "There never was a time when sincerity and affectionate Unity of Heart could be more necessary than at present. . . . in the midst of the Confusion that darkens our native Land, we may. . . by a rectitude of conduct, entertain a rational hope, that the Almighty Governor of the Universe, will in his own time, Remember Mercy." He thanked Henry for generously taking in his wife and children and ended with the hope that he and Henry might enjoy "that harmonious intercourse, I have been favored with since my union with your family. I will not despair of this great blessing in some future and not very distant period. . . . God preserve you in health and every earthly enjoyment, until you again receive the salutation of Your friend and brother, Samuel Quincy."

On May 24, Samuel boarded a ship bound for England, convinced he would be back by fall.[18]

In June, after reinforcements, which included three British major generals, had arrived in Boston, the Battle of Bunker Hill was fought. British troops crossed the Charles River to the Cambridge shore. When they were shot at from some of the houses in nearby Charlestown, they set the town on fire. Confident the barely trained Americans would flee when fired on, the British troops moved in close ranks straight up Breed's Hill and assaulted the Americans dug in behind a redoubt. The Americans beat them back with devastating results, time after time, until their ammunition ran out.[19] The British gained the hill but not before suffering more than 1,000 casualties, nearly half the troops in action. Nineteen British officers were killed and another seventy wounded. Among the 400 to 600 American casualties was Dr. Joseph Warren, a leader of the Sons of Liberty and a dear friend and physician to the Quincy family. When the death toll was taken, a stunned General Gage wrote a friend, "The loss we have sustained is greater than we can bear," the victory "too dearly bought."

In July Samuel had been in England for a month. He wrote Henry that he had not yet seen Lord North, the prime minister, nor Lord Dartmouth, "not because I could not," he explained rather imperiously, "but because I have not been sent for, and choose my own time if I do it at all." He added that he had just returned from a visit to "one of the first law officers, by whom I was very politely received."[20] As for politics, he wrote, "I say nothing; suffice it that my opinion of men and things remains the same, and is confirmed every hour." Clearly if his purpose in traveling to Britain was to help achieve some reconciliation, he was in no hurry to attempt it. Instead, his visit to a prominent law officer seems closer to the aim of the trip, to get business for himself. He had just learned of the Battle of Bunker Hill and added that everything "is peace here; I wish it may soon return to my dear, dear country."

The following month Samuel responded to a direct request by Henry, for "the love" of his country, to try to bring about a reconciliation. He impatiently rejected the feasibility of attempting or accomplishing any such thing: "My good friend I am unhappy to find that the opinion I formed in America, and which in a great measure governed my conduct, was but too justly founded. Every proposal of those who are friendly to the colonies, to alter the measures of Government and redress the grievances of which they complain, is spurned at, unless attended with previous concessions on their part. This there is less reason every day to expect, and thus the prospect of an accommodation is thrown at a distance."[21] For good measure he added, "The political subordination of the colonies is in this island a sacred tenet." An economic boycott of British goods, so helpful in the past, he considered not effective as British merchants were finding purchasers for their goods in Spain and "the Russian war." The Battle of Bunker Hill, with its devastating loss of life, may have demonstrated how serious an opponent Americans were, but Samuel noted it was met with determination "to send more supplies and men and Gage to return." By September, however, Samuel seemed in low spirits, writing his wife of his fears that his children would not remember him "as I do them, that is, with great Tenderness and Affection, and an earnest Solicitude to see them."[22] Of course at that point he could return if he wished and as she would continue to remind him. But more importantly his children knew that their father had left them and the stalwart Americans around them to find safety and employment in the country their families were fighting.

Friends and family attributed Samuel's motives in leaving America to his love of ease and desire for personal advancement. His sister Hannah's letter pleading with him to stay faulted him for the "little trappings that royalty can confer," which she feared inclined him "to the prerogative side." Abigail and John Adams, in their many letters to each other, didn't mention Samuel's departure when it occurred, but the following March, after the British evacuation of Boston, Samuel's fine house on Hanover Street was found to have been left in ruins. John saw it as a lesson: "let Us take Warning and give it to our Children. Whenever Vanity, and Gaiety, a Love of Pomp and Dress, Furniture, Equipage, Buildings, great Company, expensive Diversions, and elegant Entertainments get the better of the Principles and Judgments of Men or Women there is no knowing where they will stop, nor into what Evils, natural, moral, or political, they will lead us."[23] He added, "I pity his pretty Children, I pity his Father, and his sisters." Abigail didn't mince words. In her opinion Samuel's mansion fell victim to his "own merciless party," whose soldiers, upon preparing to depart from Boston, spared Hancock's home from "a Reverential awe for Virtue and patriotism, whilst they Detest the paricide and traitor."[24] Samuel had made a hard-headed gamble to take advantage of the coming war, confident the British were sure to win. The gamble was not without immediate costs, exile from family and friends and reputation. Time would tell whether it was the right move. Within months of his departure, loyalists and even those who wished to remain neutral were put under increasing constraints, ostracized, disarmed, even imprisoned. Had Samuel remained, the mob and the official Committee of Safety would have focused on him and his family. The suffering he had avoided with his departure would have arrived at his door.

Samuel spent Christmas in London with Jonathan Sewell and his family. The Sewells had arrived in England in August, three months after Samuel. Before they left, Samuel's uncle Edmund Quincy, Jonathan's father-in-law, had written to his daughter Dolly in Fairfield, Connecticut, to let her know of the imminent departure of her sister Esther and family for England. "I wish them a safe journey, and peace and comfort to Esther," Edmund wrote, "for of late, she could not enjoy any great share." He was afraid "I should lose a Daughter to the quarrel: But we must learn to submit to whatever may be the will of Heaven concerning us or ours."[25]

A month after the Battle of Lexington and Concord, a Continental Congress began to meet in Philadelphia. Boston managed to send delegates. News of the recent battle began to spread. Upon hearing the Boston delegates were nearing Philadelphia, a great number of people rode out several miles to greet them. The citizens gave them a rousing greeting when they entered the city, "very grand and intended to show their approbation of the conduct of the good people of that govt. in the distressing situation of affairs there."[26] Silas Deane, a delegate to Congress from Connecticut, wrote that he trembled when he thought of the "vast importance" of the meeting, ending a letter to his wife with the prayer, "May the God of Wisdom preside!"[27]

The citizen-army ringing Boston Harbor was chaotic, with men coming and going. At first they were under the command of Major General Artemas Ward, described uncharitably by the American general Charles Lee as "a fat old gentleman who had been a popular church-warden."[28] Ward was a veteran of the French and Indian War and always met with a council of senior officers before issuing orders. There was a housing problem, a discipline problem, and just a general lack of military experience among most of the impromptu army. John Adams labored to get the delegates to the Continental Congress to adopt these forces as its own. He pointed out to the Congress, "this extraordinary martial assemblage was the most singular condition ever presented by such a body. It could not be said that the officers commanded by any lawful title or authority, or that the rank and file obeyed otherwise than by virtue of their own willingness to do so."[29] They needed an experienced commander. George Washington, a dignified Virginia aristocrat, had been a young officer in the French and Indian War, and attended the meetings of Congress in his uniform, presumably as a reminder of his military expertise. Although John Hancock had hoped to be appointed, he lacked experience and there was wisdom in naming the Virginian, involving that colony closely in the New England struggle.

Events were happening so quickly Congress was forced to play catch-up. Despite Congress's hopes that colonists would act only on the defensive, in early May, the day before Congress met, a small contingent of men from

Connecticut and Massachusetts, led by Benedict Arnold and a group of Green Mountain Men from Vermont under Ethan Allen, seized the lightly guarded British forts at Ticonderoga and Crown Point. These forts guarded what the Indians called "the Great Warpath" from Canada, south down the Hudson River to the heart of New York. In the course of the next winter, Ticonderoga's prized cannon would be towed to Boston. The forts also provided an entry to Canada. Colonial revolutionaries hoped the Canadians would join the cause but used the threat of force if they refused.

On June 15 the Congress acted and appointed Washington to command the citizen army. While Washington and a group of Southern officers were riding north, the Battle of Bunker Hill took place. Washington arrived on June 25 to take command. Always the diplomat he applauded the Massachusetts Provincial Congress for the "virtue & publick Spirit of the whole Province of Massachusetts Bay" and their "firmness, & Patriotism without Example in modern History" but wrote privately to his nephew, "The officers generally speaking are the most indifferent kind of people I ever saw" and summed up the whole as "an exceeding dirty and nasty people."[30] He had his work cut out for him.

The New Englanders found reassurance in the tall, dignified forty-three-year-old Virginia planter with military experience and impressive martial bearing. He was described by a Connecticut delegate to Congress as "no harum-scarum, ranting, swearing fellow, but sober, steady, and calm."[31] Washington's goal was to transform this hastily gathered mob, more citizens than soldiers, into a disciplined and trained military force. They were, after all, to be fighting against the hardened veterans and Hessians of the powerful British Empire.

There were still hopes that some sensible arrangement could be made to avert full-scale war. On July 5 the Congress, pressed by more moderate members to find a peaceful solution, passed the "Olive Branch Petition" affirming American loyalty to Great Britain, followed a day later by a "Declaration of the Causes and Necessity Taking Up Arms." A copy of the Olive Branch Petition was rushed to Britain and delivered to the secretary for the colonies, Lord Dartmouth, on August 21, but the king refused to receive it. He had been anxious to declare the American colonies in a state of rebellion all summer, and now, two days after Dartmouth received the Congress's petition, he issued the Proclamation of Rebellion and Sedition, declaring the American colonies to be in a state of rebellion and ordering "all Our officers. . . and all Our obedient and loyal subjects, to use their utmost endeavours to withstand and suppress such rebellion." King George had good cause for his obstinacy. Massachusetts was still unwilling to pay for the destruction of the tea, and his troops had been fired upon and killed in the running battle at Lexington and Concord, a thousand killed in the Battle of Bunker Hill, Fort Ticonderoga seized, and later that year a full-scale attack on Canada. It was a bit late for a so-called Continental Congress to claim to represent an obedient and loyal people. With his brusque dismissal of the petition, Americans realized a bridge had been crossed.

Most on both sides in America and Britain believed any war would be short. People always think a war will be short. They have been wrong time and time again, and this conflict was to be no exception.

FOURTEEN

The Horsemen of the Apocalypse Arrive

You ask, 'When is the Continental Congress by general consent to be formed into a supreme legislature; alliances, defensive and offensive, formed; our ports opened; and a formidable naval force established at the public charge?' I can only answer at present that nothing seems wanted but that "General consent." The novelty of the thing deters some, the doubts of success others, the vain hope of reconciliation, many. But our enemies take continually every proper measure to remove these obstacles . . . every day furnishes us with new causes of increasing enmity, and new reasons for wishing an eternal separation, so that there is a rapid increase of the formerly small party, who were for an independent government.

—Benjamin Franklin to Josiah Quincy,
Saratoga, New York, April 15, 1776

We might have been a free & a great people together.

—Thomas Jefferson, rough draft of
Declaration of Independence

That summer and fall of 1775 it seemed as if the Four Horsemen of the Apocalypse had descended on New England's villages and towns. War had arrived with all its uncertainties and frights, its absences and privations. Pestilence and death were part of everyday life but struck with unusual force that autumn. Just famine was missing. For now. But the Crown had banned New England fishermen from trolling the Grand Banks of Newfoundland, and many thousands of men and their families were suddenly destitute.[1]

Fall and winter were traditionally sickly seasons, but this year was unusually rainy and cold. Crops failed. Hundreds of bushels of apples set aside for cider spoiled as very cold weather struck in November, including even some snow. Abigail Adams reckoned the "great and incessant rains we have had this fall, (the like cannot be recollected) may have occasioned some of the present disorders."[2] Throat distemper, known today as either diphtheria or strep, along with dysentery, were deadly, and struck Braintree and other little communities hard. As these abated, jaundice and rheumatism followed. Jaundice and other illness in the American army camp spread to the nearby towns. Smallpox was rampant in Boston, and Washington believed some refugees who were allowed to leave the city were purposely infected with the disease to spread it among the American troops.[3] John Adams, then in Philadelphia, learned that his Braintree home was "an hospital in every part" and that children of neighbors were dying—"Mrs. Randle has one child that is not expected to live out the night. Mrs. Belcher has another, Joseph Bracket another, Deacon Adams has lost one."[4] The Quincy family was more fortunate. Josiah Senior, daughter Hannah, and Josiah's little daughters survived the various sicknesses. Early in the New Year, while the country was struck with pleurisy fever, which was "very mortal," Braintree "was not very sickly." Still three grown persons had died near the Adams home in Braintree in a week and "many others lay bad—it [presumably pleurisy fever] carries them of in 8 days."[5]

The barrage of evils sparked appeals to heaven. Local governments and the Continental Congress designated special days of prayer and fasting. All people were sinners, but surely the colonists must have sinned mightily to be peppered with such trials. Abigail Adams, in the midst of diseases striking family and friends, mused, "We have done Evil or our Enemies would be at peace with us. The sin of Slavery as well as many others is not washed away."[6]

Slavery was legal in Massachusetts, at the time, and throughout the colonies, although there were few slaves in New England. Its modest family farms could be managed by the farmer and his wife with their large family of children. A big farm or a tavern might have one or two enslaved people to help. They could be married in church, their children were baptized, and they usually lived in the house and ate with their owners. They were often educated and trained in skilled trades. However mild this form of slavery seemed, they and their children could be sold. There had been petitions submitted to the Massachusetts legislature to end the terrible institution, but these typically floundered on the issue of financial reimbursement. It would take the text of the new 1780 constitution, written by John Adams when Massachusetts became a state, that declared all men were born free and equal. That text would be cited in a court case late in the war ending the shameful institution in the state.[7]

The war intruded on the work of the Braintree town meeting. The agenda was now punctuated with resolutions on payments to militia troops for time spent training, questions on whether military volunteers should be exempt from the poll tax, the cancellation of a meeting because inhabitants were busy guarding the shore, all interspersed with ordinary business like the annual vote on whether the hogs "may run at large within the said Town the ensuing year."[8]

A major attempt at stopping the precipitous slide into civil war came from the American side on July 8, 1775, a year before the Declaration of Independence, but only after battles and considerable bloodshed. The effort was a concession intended to persuade the moderate members of the Congress that their more militant colleagues were willing to give peace a chance. It was clearly necessary to make the gesture because the general public wanted "to prepare for a vigorous defensive War, but at the Same time to keep open the door of Reconciliation—to hold the Sword in one Hand and the Olive Branch in the other."[9] John Dickinson, a delegate from Delaware, was the author of the Olive Branch Petition. The Second

Continental Congress characterized this as a "humble petition" to the king's "Most Excellent Majesty" from his faithful subjects. They reminded the king of their expectations after the triumphant French and Indian War and their alarm when, instead, they were faced with a new system of statutes and regulations that filled their minds "with the most painful fear and jealousies." The petition exonerated the king from responsibility for this policy and repeatedly blamed "Your Majesty's Ministers," whose measures and hostilities "compelled us to arm in our own defense and have engaged us in a controversy so peculiarly abhorrent to the affections of your still faithful Colonists." In fact, of course, the king wholeheartedly approved of the measures his ministers had taken. The pretense he had been deluded by his ministers was more diplomatic than likely to be persuasive. The petition went on to assure King George of their attachment "to your Majesty's person, family, and government, with all devotion that principle and affection can inspire; connected with Great Britain by the strongest ties that can unite societies and deploring every event that tends in any degree to weaken them." To that end they beseeched the king to use his influence to return Mother Country and subjects "into a happy and permanent reconciliation" with the repeal of the statutes that immediately "distress any of your Majesty's Colonies." King George was urged to gauge the sense of the American people. They concluded by wishing the king a long and prosperous reign and that his descendants may govern his dominions with honor to themselves and happiness to their subjects. It was signed by John Hancock, president of the Congress, and delegates from twelve colonies.[10]

The petition was sent to London on July 8. Dickinson hoped the battles of Lexington and Concord combined with this "humble petition" would persuade the king to open negotiations.

While the petition, a last effort before full-scale war, was reluctantly approved by many activists in Congress as a concession to their more moderate colleagues, they were at pains to undermine any hope of success its dutiful expressions and wish for peace might have had. Congress had authorized an invasion of Canada only a week before the Olive Branch Petition was approved and followed the petition by a Declaration of the Causes and Necessity of Taking Up Arms. They had also voted two million dollars for supplies for an army and named several men as field officers, including George Washington, who assumed the post of commander in chief. There was a strong stench of hypocrisy about the whole episode.

On June 17 the Battle of Bunker Hill took place. The British troops won the day but suffered over a thousand casualties. They set the nearby town of Charlestown on fire. Congress learned of the battle on June 30.

The activists needn't have worried about ending the "dispute" without achieving their goals, since the king had no intention of even reading the petition. A copy of the Olive Branch Petition was presented to the colonial secretary on August 21. The original arrived on September 1. A letter written by John Adams to a friend, stating war was inevitable and complaining that the colonists should have raised a navy already and taken government officials prisoner, was intercepted, and arrived in England at the same time as the petition. Before that, on July 20, the king learned of the Battle of Bunker Hill with its more than 1,000 British casualties. He was in no mood to even read the petition. On August 23 King George issued the Proclamation of Rebellion, declaring the American colonies in a state of rebellion and ordering his officers and loyal subjects to suppress it. In a speech to Parliament in October, the king labeled the colonists' gestures toward reconciliation as "meant only to amuse, by vague expressions of attachment to the parent state, and the strongest protestations of loyalty to me, whilst they are preparing for a general revolt."[11] The chance of peace had slipped away. If there had been any serious possibility of reconciliation, it had been overtaken by events. Pride and overconfidence on both sides ruled.

The military situation was at a standoff until the spring of 1776. The British controlled Boston and its harbor but were besieged by the American army on the coastline ringing the harbor.

While Josiah Senior mourned the death of his youngest son and coped with the desertion of another, he plunged wholeheartedly into helping the patriot cause. He was a member of the Massachusetts Committee of Safety and when not busy with committee business spent much of his days sitting at the window of his Braintree home with its fine view of Boston Harbor, monitoring the movements of the British fleet and reporting to General Washington indications that the ships were on the move. The ships were dangerous. On October 10 Josiah scratched on one of its panes GOVERNOR GAGE SAILED FOR ENGLAND WITH A FAIR WIND. [12] Gage had been relieved of his command. Within three days of learning of the British troops' devastating losses at the Battle of Bunker Hill, the ministry replaced him with General William Howe and ordered Gage back to Britain, and no wonder. The total number of British casualties, some 1,054 of an estimated 1,200 troops engaged, was terrible, but the rate of officers killed was shocking. Over one-eighth of all British officers who would be killed during the American Revolution died at Bunker Hill. [13] General William Howe, who replaced Gage, viewed the "loss of so many brave officers with horror." Gage was also wrong in assuming resistance to the British government was confined to Boston and could easily be quashed. [14]

Josiah was correct. The British fleet posed a danger to New England's seaside towns. In October, when the town of Bristol, Rhode Island, refused to provide provisions for a British ship, the town was bombarded and burned. The townsmen then turned over the forty sheep requested. [15] That same month British ships bombarded and burned the town of Falmouth (now Portland), Maine. As long as the fleet remained off the New England coast, it was a menace.

Josiah sent Washington various suggestions about how to protect the coast. On November 4 Washington took time from transforming a chaotic group of men into an army to reply, very tactfully, to one of Josiah's suggestions for a scheme "you conceive to be conducive to the public service." He patiently explained that in the adoption of a defensive plan, "many things are to be considered to decide upon the utility of it." [16] There was "the expense of so many batteries as you propose, with the necessary defences to secure the channel" at the same time "we are in a manner destitute of canon, and compelled to keep the little powder we have, for the use of the musketry." Washington had already viewed the locations Josiah wanted protected. Replying to an invitation to visit, he responded, "Permit me to thank you most cordially for your polite invitation and to assure you that I am, sir, Your most obedient Humble servant, George Washington."

Washington hit the nail on the head. Cannons were key to victory against the British troops occupying Boston. It was the impetuous seizure of Fort Ticonderoga by Benedict Arnold and Ethan Allen and his Green Mountain Boys, three weeks after the Battle of Lexington and Concord, that solved that problem. Ticonderoga had been a choice target because it was lightly guarded and well-equipped with cannon. As the year ended and bitterly cold weather and icy conditions set in, the fort's fifty-nine cannon, weighing almost sixty tons, were placed on forty-two sledges drawn by oxen for the long trip to the Boston area. Henry Knox, who would become the army's self-taught artillery expert, and his men moved the ponderous load 300 miles in fifty-six days, arriving to great joy outside Boston on January 25, 1776. Washington fortified Dorchester Heights and mounted the cannon there. A redoubt was built in the army camp, and under cover of cannon fire 2,000 men moved it into place. On the morning of March 5, the British awoke to find American artillery threatening their ships. Two days later, as the army in Cambridge observed a day of prayer, fasting, and humiliation, the British began to evacuate Boston. Howe and Washington had struck a bargain that the Americans would allow the evacuation to proceed peacefully, and the British agreed not to burn Boston.[17] As they left, however, the British did blow up Castle William, the island fort guarding Boston Harbor, which hadn't been included in the agreement. Eleven hundred loyalists left with the British army.[18]

It was unclear where the British troops and fleet were heading when they left New England. Although no one knew it at the time, the fighting was to move to New York and New Jersey, to Pennsylvania and Delaware, farther and farther from home.

Just months after Samuel Quincy left for England, the pressure on Crown supporters—loyalists or Tories—became more insistent and punitive. Any toleration for differences of opinion or even for being noncommittal in 1774 had evaporated. In the spring of 1775, the Continental Congress ordered penalties against anyone who refused to publicly "associate to defend the

American rights by arms."[19] They were to be disarmed and even, if neces-sary, arrested. Perhaps Samuel was wise to leave when he did. Perhaps his absence spared his wife and children humiliation and danger. Horrible atrocities occurred against those who held government office or simply said something positive about the government. In some cases, violence was tolerated or orchestrated by Committees of Safety.[20] These powerful new committees energetically policed their territory to ferret out loyalists, searching their mail and homes, urging neighbors to denounce neighbors, resorting to public shaming. All the actions that would have been opposed with outrage had the royal government carried them out were now resorted to by its opponents. Press freedom was attacked. When the *New Hampshire Gazette* refused to reveal the name of an author who complained about the intimidation and repression, the paper was shut down.[21] Other newspa-pers took the hint and censored their content. Books and pamphlets that offended were burned and hunts launched for their authors. But in the spring of 1776, Congress itself was insisting that a public pledge of support for the patriot cause be subscribed and punishment meted out for those who refused.

New Yorkers were and remained very divided in their loyalties, and there were more than the usual fears of loyalist spies and sabotage. In October 1775 the president of the Continental Congress sent the New York Convention a resolution to act "respecting those who are in your Opinion dangerous by being at large."[22]

In January of 1776 Thomas Paine's powerful pamphlet, *Common Sense*, appeared. It was published and quickly republished, causing a sensation. An estimated 500,000 copies would be printed by the end of the war. Paine's arguments for separation from the Mother Country, for independence, now struck a chord. Reconciliation on terms the Americans could accept had become increasingly unlikely as Britain acted against the colonies and was sending thousands of troops to defeat them. Congress had no navy but agreed to license privateers to attack British shipping, put an embargo on trade with Britain and its Caribbean islands, and looked abroad to France and Holland for help. To the delight of Josiah Quincy and family, Samuel and John Adams, and many others, independence as the primary goal became increasingly likely. One by one the colonies fell into place, adopting constitutions and taking actions against residents who hesitated to take up arms against the Mother Country.

In addition to intimidation and spying on possible dissenters, as Congress moved to endorse independence, every colony would eventually impose an oath of allegiance on all male residents over a certain age. Massachusetts, one of the first, required an oath swearing to support the war for independence against Great Britain.[23] At first oaths were required of public officials as a condition of office. Later the oath was imposed on all men except for slaves. It was harder and harder to remain neutral under these circumstances. There were penalties for refusing to take the oath. Many men who took the oath must have remained ambivalent, believed the war unnecessary and doomed, or violated the oath by quietly helping the royalist side. Some simply sold goods to the British, who paid in hard currency instead of the nearly worthless money printed by the states. It is customarily reckoned only 20 percent of the population were activist on either side. If so, thousands must have sworn support for the war whose hearts were not in it, afraid even to share this with their own families. Their secret violations of a sacred but coerced oath died with them.

By the following March, as the British prepared to leave Boston, Congress passed a resolution to disarm all Tory residents. Delegates were instructed to transmit the resolution to their colonies for execution. When some troops raised for the Continental Army lacked proper firearms, it was pointed out that weapons would be forthcoming "by executing the Resolution of Congress." The resolution to disarm opponents was "to be kept as secret as the Nature of the Service will admit."[24] The "Nature of the Service" did not permit much secrecy, however, as the resolution for disarming disaffected persons was printed in the *Pennsylvania Gazette*. This was before the passage of the Declaration of Independence.

The relief Washington and his army felt as the British fleet sailed out of sight of Boston was short-lived. Washington's army was to face months of retreat and dismay. The commander had made a priority of taking

Canada to protect New England and New York. However, the ambitious campaign the previous fall to take Montreal and Quebec with an army of 900 men had ground to a screeching halt when its assault on the mighty fortress of Quebec failed in a blinding snowstorm. A miserable winter siege outside Quebec left the Americans with inadequate shelter and supplies, sick with cold and dying from smallpox. By spring they left Canadian soil, retreating to New York, back to the fort at Crown Point, south of Lake Champlain. General Gates, who was sent to shore up the defenses at the fort, arrived to find "the wretched remains of what was once a very respectable Body of Troops."[25] Smallpox "had taken so deep a root, that the Camp had more the appearance of a General Hospital than an Army form'd to Oppose the Invasion of a Successful & enterprising Enemy." The American army abandoned Crown Point and retreated farther south to Fort Ticonderoga, summoning Massachusetts militia to help hold the fort.

The full realization of what challenging the powerful British Empire entailed was brought home to patriots and their commander the summer of 1776.[26] However keen the men of the Continental Army were, they were undisciplined and inexperienced. The battle at Lexington and Concord, Bunker Hill, and the seizure of Fort Ticonderoga perhaps gave them false confidence. The British were tough professionals. The battle for New York City was to demonstrate the audacity of what they had undertaken. While Congress was drawing up a Declaration of Independence, the British navy was converging on New York City and its harbor, the best port in the colonies. Congress insisted American troops undertake the complicated defense of an island, Manhattan, against a formidable force of professionals and without the benefit of a navy. Washington meant to do that. He and his men nearly came to grief there.

The war had left Massachusetts, but some Massachusetts men left with it as part of Washington's army. It was Massachusetts men, John Glover's regiment of mariners from Marblehead, north of Boston, that saved the

Continental Army. They were a feisty group, those Marblehead men. They had gotten into scraps when the army was camped at Cambridge, and their mixed-race regiment (with their round jackets and fisherman's trousers) came into contact with a regiment of lanky Virginia riflemen. They traded insults, then blows, and soon hundreds of men joined the fight. Israel Trask, an eleven-year-old bystander, remembered how Washington and William Lee, a slave and constant companion to the commander, leaped onto their horses and galloped into the middle of the fray. Washington dismounted and "with an iron grip seized two tall, brawny, athletic, savage-looking riflemen by the throat, keeping them at arm's length, alternatively shaking and talking to them."[27] The other fighters stopped brawling and fled. But combat would change opinions, and those Virginia riflemen would owe their lives to the efforts of the mariners from Marblehead.

The British navy, carrying thousands of troops, had been gathering in the New York area all summer. First to arrive, on June 9, was General William Howe, whose fleet had evacuated Boston in March. They had set sail south from Halifax, bringing more than 9,000 men.[28] Three days later they seized Staten Island, which became a base of operation. From the east came Admiral Richard Howe, William's brother, commanding a fleet of 150 ships. They had set off from Britain in May and reached Staten Island on July 12. Richard Howe had hoped to arrange a negotiated settlement but, on his arrival, was handed a copy of the Declaration of Independence, signed while he was at sea. From the south, on August 1, came Major General Henry Clinton and General Charles Cornwallis with Commodore Parker's fleet. The combined force totaled some 45,000 British and Hessian soldiers and sailors, and 400 vessels.

The British assault on Long Island began on August 22, a scorching summer morning, as warships opened fire on Long Island beaches. The few Americans nearby fled inland as 15,000 British troops landed. The British plan was to trap the Continental Army between British armies advancing from the north and south. British warships bombarded Brooklyn Heights for four hours to keep the Americans busy while Clinton and Cornwallis led 10,000 men north around and behind American lines. The Americans were outflanked. Washington's raw militia troops panicked. At one point sixty British infantrymen routed two entire Connecticut brigades. Washington and generals Israel Putnam and Thomas Mifflin were seen caning and whipping their men to keep them from fleeing, although a Maryland and a Delaware regiment stood their ground. The slaughter was terrible. The Americans were not given the courtesies of war by enemies who held them in contempt.

The 9,000-man American army ended up stranded on a square mile of open ground on Long Island, with the sea behind them and the enemy in front, without shelter and famished, swept by a cold northeasterly gale. But the dreadful weather saved them, as a drenching rain prevented the British warships from coming up the East River. Washington got every boat he could find to evacuate his army to Manhattan. Two days after John Glover's Marblehead sailors reached New York, they went into action. Shrouded by a deep fog they rowed the entire army to Manhattan and safety. Among the last to leave, on the last boat, was their commander.

Two weeks later the British began their assault on Manhattan. In this crisis Washington's army was shrinking as many militiamen, their enlistments up, were heading home. Washington wrote Hancock, president of the Congress, "Our situation is truly distressing" and pleaded for a more permanent army. The British again began with a fierce bombardment followed by an amphibious landing. Again, the American militia fled in panic, and even the presence of their commander did not stop the rout. The artillery was saved by General Israel Putnam, "Old Put," who raced to Manhattan to help bring the men of his detachment and their artillery to safety. As the rout gained momentum one of Washington's aides grabbed the bridle of his horse and pulled him away before he was captured.

The British captured New York City, with its superb harbor and central location. For Washington and his remaining men, a year of defeats began as they were forced to retreat time and again, through New York then south across New Jersey to Pennsylvania. It was no longer a matter of victory; it was a matter of survival.

FIFTEEN

Strangers in a Strange New Land

We americans are plenty here and very cheap. Some of us at first coming are apt to think ourselves of importance but other people do not think so, and few if any of us are much consulted or enquired after.

— Thomas Hutchinson, London, February 1776 [1]

I see many faces I have been used to. America seems to be transplanted to London. St. James's Park wears an appearance not unlike the Exchange in Boston. . . . I long much to see my father. It is now more than eighteen months since I parted with him in a manner I regret.

— Samuel Quincy to his wife, London, January 1, 1777 [2]

Samuel joined the growing number of loyalists fleeing New England for old England. He was unusual in his high hopes that the exile would prove lucrative. For most of his fellow exiles, the need was for safety. Mob violence and the dangers and casualties of war were left 3,000 miles across the ocean. They and their families were safe. Although Samuel and the others who fled in 1775 and 1776 differed in their expectations and circumstances, they soon came to share many of the same problems and disappointments. And the knowledge that they were, at heart, Americans.

On their arrival Americans marveled at the size and prosperity of the Mother Country, with mile after mile of well-tilled countryside, villages and market towns surrounded by fine farmland, and good roads (by eighteenth century standards). These roads, some built by the Romans, were studded with taverns and inns. Then they reached London, a grand bustling river port and the seat of government. There were grimy slums in London, but also grand buildings and monuments, fashionable districts, theaters, and coffee houses. It was the place to be. But London was a very expensive place to live, at least to live in a tolerably decent style. Samuel Curwen, a judge from Salem who, like Samuel, fled from Massachusetts in 1775, wrote in dismay: "Those who bring property here may do well enough, but for those who expect reimbursement for losses, or a supply for present support, will find to their cost the hand of charity very cold; the latter may be kept from starving, and beyond that their hopes are vain."[3] The property of most refugees was back in America, where it was vulnerable to confiscation by the rebels.

Curwen's experience was different from Samuel's in many respects. At home in Salem, a busy seaport north of Boston, Curwen had suffered as the tempers of his neighbors became "more and more soured and malevolent against all moderate men, whom they see fit to reproach as enemies of their country. . . among whom I am unhappily (although unjustly) ranked." Being "unable longer to bear their undeserved reproaches and menaces hourly denounced against myself and others," he explained, "I think it a duty I owe myself to withdraw for a while from the storm which to my foreboding mind is approaching."[4] His wife, like Samuel's, refused to accompany him, but not because she didn't share his political views. Rather "her apprehensions of danger from an incensed soldiery, a people licentious and enthusiastically mad and broken loose from all the restraints of law or religion, being less terrible to her than a short passage on the ocean."[5] Still she encouraged him to leave. In the summer of 1775, he wrote, I "left my

late peaceful home (in my sixtieth year) in search of personal security and
those rights which by the laws of God I ought to have enjoyed undisturbed
there." He traveled first to Pennsylvania, hoping to find asylum among the
pacifist Quakers, but arrived just as military regiments were organizing
and parading, and the Second Continental Congress preparing to meet.
Feeling threatened he sailed for England.

Most Americans fled with no real sense of how they would live in
England. If the war were short and England prevailed, as seemed certain, then their absence would not be long and the expense manageable.
Some who had government offices in America, like Samuel Quincy and
Samuel Curwen, might expect to continue to receive a stipend. A very
few, like Samuel Quincy, expected to get a post or some lucrative business
opportunity. Indeed, John Adams credited the former governor of Massachusetts, Thomas Hutchinson, with having "seduced" his friend Samuel
to become a loyalist. Samuel was in good spirits. He may have found some
work, probably with the help of former governor Hutchinson, or had a
sufficient government stipend since he remained in London after many
absentees moved to less expensive towns like Bristol. In his letters home
he didn't complain about his finances. He occupied himself visiting friends
in Brompton, where there was a "whole Circle" of New Englanders, and
was part of a group of refugees living near elegant St. James's Park.[6] He
lived in the same building as the North Carolinian John Burgwin, and the
two became good friends. But if Samuel's hopes were pinned on help from
Thomas Hutchinson, they likely came to nothing. Hutchinson, who had
spent two hours conferring with the king on his arrival, wrote in dismay
in February 1776, "We Americans are plenty here and very cheap. Some
of us at first coming are apt to think ourselves important but other people
do not think so and few if any of us are consulted or enquired after."[7]

For most exiles finances were a serious and growing worry. Curwen
wrote frequently of his shrinking funds. At the end of December 1776,
he confided to Judge Sewell, who had left London for Exeter: "My little
bark is in imminent hazard of being stranded unless the wind shifts
quickly, or some friendly boat appears for its relief. In plain English, my

purse is nearly empty." Curwen moved to Bristol and counted eighteen other exiles in the town.[8] Jonathan Sewell, John Adams's old friend, had an income but feared living on it indefinitely, advising Edward Winslow in New York, "Unless a gentleman can get his Share of [the wealth] he has no business here." In London his stipend of "£600 per An. is but as a Drop in the Ocean,'" and a man living in England will find that sum "Is Nothing—less than Nothing & Vanity—& his contemplation of his own Comparative Littleness is Vexation of Spirit."[9] The Reverend Isaac Smith complained that in London he "truly cannot breathe the vital air without great expense," and since other exiles had more worthy claims for help he was determined to delay his own request "to the longest period, if it please the great Disposer of events to prolong my uneasy abode in this country of aliens for many days yet to come."[10] Americans who were prominent in their own country quickly found, to their chagrin, no comparable social niche in England. They did not correspond in status to the country gentry or wealthy city merchants, let alone the great nobles with their vast estates and fortunes. They didn't fit in.

New England refugees began to meet regularly at a coffee house on London's Threadneedle Street to socialize, commiserate, and share news of American and of British politics. Before he left London Curwen wrote, "There is an army of New Englanders here."[11] Less prosperous New England merchants, young attorneys, and government employees formed the New England Club. Most poorer loyalists were unable to afford exile and had to make their peace with the conditions in war-torn America and hopes for peace. If some got to London there is little surviving record of their experiences.[12] Highly anticipated letters from home, shared with fellow exiles, were often gloomy, complaining of hardships, money depreciated, people already tired of war, and moves by Congress and local governments against the absentees. All the more reason to believe there was "an almost certain prospect of annihilating the rebellion in America, in one year."[13] Then everyone who wanted to return could go home.

Samuel Quincy was not worried, at least not at first. He was confident the British would prevail. Shortly after the bloody Battle of Bunker Hill in June 1775, which cost the lives of half the British soldiers engaged, he wrote his brother-in-law Henry Hill that the costly victory had simply convinced the British government to send more ships and troops, every species of ammunition and warlike implements, and all kinds of supplies for the support of Boston, and listed various officers on their way to reinforce the army in America.[14] "I mention these things minutely," he added smugly, "to show you of how small importance are those flattering articles of intelligence which sound well upon paper and appear highly spirited and influential. These are facts, not of conjecture only, but visible and operative." If Henry believes the colonies must work out their salvation by trusting in their strength and in the Lord, Samuel sees it differently: "I view the dangerous and doubtful struggle with fear and trembling; I lament it with the most cordial affection for my native country and feel sensibly for my friends." Ultimately, he concludes, the outcome rests with "the God of armies." Samuel was not alone in his assessment, of course. No colony had ever won its independence. The British, with their vast resources and trained troops, seemed certain to overwhelm the feisty colonists with their bold talk of liberty.

There were other reasons for the financial difficulties the refugees experienced apart from the suddenness of their flight. Most had left their property behind. Furthermore, since they weren't sure how long they would be in Britain, training for another career did not seem worthwhile. One Massachusetts lawyer explained he could have been qualified to practice law but "I expected every year, to return to America, and well I knew, that [the qualification] . . . would not have added the smallest weight to my Character in America, and judg'd it to be totally impossible, to make myself known, and obtain business in England."[15] Even the rector of King's Chapel in Boston was told, when he asked for an appointment in England, "We cant think of your residing here, we want such men as you in America."[16] He concluded, perhaps uncharitably, that the English clergy looked upon the Americans "as coming to take the Bread out of their mouths."[17] He advised friends in America to remain there, for there were no provisions in England yet, nor were they likely to be able to get anything. When he was eventually offered the post of curate in Essex at £50 a year, he regarded it as an insult.[18] Still the refugees came. Parson Punderson escaped from his home in Norwich, Connecticut, rowing himself eighteen miles out to sea until he was picked up by a British vessel and put on board the *Rose*, a British man-of-war. Despite having made two abject confessions to the Sons of Liberty, he had been pursued, threatened with the loss of his eyes and with death before he made his escape.[19] However uncertain life in England was, at least it was safe.

How to pass the time while waiting on events? For Samuel and other exiles there were regular travels about England, visits to each other and to British friends, trips to the theater and to parks. By 1776 Curwen writes that for him these "harmless amusements" had already "[l]ost their novelty" and could "delight no more."[20] Many Americans were startled by the boisterous English lower class, who mingled noisily with their "betters" in the theaters and strolled public gardens along with pickpockets and prostitutes. Many absentees sought more sedate pastimes, delighting in strolling in St. James's Park.[21]

To be fair the English government was unprepared for the flood of loyal refugees they were receiving and had no policy to provide assistance. The first exiles to petition for help were four New England loyalists fleeing mobs in late 1774. In January and February of 1775, three of them were given small sums from the treasury. Then treasury payments stopped, and nothing was forthcoming for any absentees for the entire year.[22] As the numbers of exiles grew, the British government was urged to help them, or at least reimburse them for losses suffered for their loyalty. In February 1776 George Lord Germain, secretary of state for the colonies, distributed the modest total of £177 to "Persons who appeared to him to be particular Objects of the Attention of Government."[23] He got another £200 to defray further needs. In March 1776, when the British forces evacuated Boston, where many loyalists had sheltered, more loyalists fled to England. Germain described them as in a "deplorable situation," and at this point the Lords issued £5,000 for the benefit of the most deserving. In July Germain suggested the salaries of colonial officials be continued, pointing out "the

Honor of Government is pledged to make good [their salaries] to such of them as have adhered to their Allegiance and stood firm in support of the Constitution."[24] Those who were not government officials, and most were not, got funds haphazardly through the colonial office. At the end of the year, another £15,000 was allotted for their aid. By early 1777 the treasury finally set up a formal pension list, providing annual stipends to some 100 loyalists living in London. After that the treasury board allotted six days a year to consider American applications for pensions, three in summer, three in winter, and in 1777 drew on some £58,500 for the purpose.[25] When the war was eventually over, the commissioner of claims, John Wilmot, wrote with satisfaction: "Whatever may be said of this unfortunate war, either to account for, to justify, or to apologize for the conduct of either country, all the world has been unanimous in applauding the justice and the humanity of Great Britain . . . in compensating, with a Liberal hand, the Losses of those who suffered so much for their firm and faithful adherence."[26] However much the exiles complained about neglect and financial hardships, by the war's end Britain had awarded them some £3,033,091, or about $100 million in today's money.[27]

Life in exile without gainful employment could be depressing, and quite soon there were complaints about Britain and a longing for home. Thomas Hutchinson's "deepest wish" was to return to his home in Milton. "I can't help thinking," he mused, "that nature alone has done as much in some parts of America as nature and art together have done in England, and I should prefer even my humble cottage upon Milton Hill to the lofty palaces upon Richmond Hill, so that upon the whole I am more of a New England man than ever, and I will not despair of seeing my country and friends again, though I fear the time for it is farther off than I imagined."

By January 1, 1777, even Samuel Quincy was writing his wife, Hannah, with a less cocky confidence than he wrote her brother in 1775. He was distressed at the separation from his family in Massachusetts. "The continuance of our unhappy separation has something in it so unexpected, so unprecedented, so complicated with evil and misfortune, it has become almost too burdensome for my spirits, nor have I words that can reach its description."[28] He wrote of the "thousand varying objects, some of them affording amusement, and others admiration" and faces of those he knew in America now in London. Then he added, "I long much to see my father. It is now more than eighteen months since I parted with him in a manner I regret." Neither she nor Henry included any news of his family at Braintree.

On March 12, 1777, he replied to a letter from his wife. She asked, "whether I cannot bear contempt and reproach, rather than remain any longer separated from my family!" She urged that his countrymen "will not deprive me of life." He responded that he had never harbored such an idea, pointing out that "difference of opinion I have never known to be a capital offence, and were the truth and motives of my conduct justly scrutinized, I am persuaded they would not regard me as an enemy plotting their ruin." He insisted "I am conscious of the purity of my intentions." When he departed, he admitted, he did not expect "so hurried a succession of events" and had "an accommodation taken place, my tour would have been greatly advantageous, especially on the score of business; what it will be now, time must tell." Samuel worried about his father and family in Braintree: "I have not received a line nor heard from them since I left America." Nor, it seems, did he write to them but fretted about what they thought of him. "They ought not to think me regardless of them though I am silent; for, however, lightly they may look upon me, I yet remember them with pleasure."[29] He ended his letter, "God bless you all; live happy, and think I am as much so as my long absence from you will permit."

A week later he wrote her again, concerned about what was happening to his remaining American possessions. "I am not surprised much that, to the loss of property, I have already sustained, I am to suffer further depredations, and that those to whom I am under contract should avail themselves of this opportunity and endeavor to make what is left their own." "All I ask," he added, "is that my brother [Henry] and my other friends (if I have any) would think of me as they ought, and to be assured, that as far as they interpose their assistance to save me from suffering, they will not hereafter find me deficient in return."[30]

By October Samuel suggested that Hannah consider coming to England. "If things should not wear a more promising aspect at the opening of the next year, by all means summon resolution to cross the ocean." On the other hand, "if there is an appearance of accommodating this truly unnatural contest, it would be advisable for you to bear farther promise; as I mean to return to my native country whenever I may be permitted" adding the stipulation "there is a chance for my procuring a livelihood. But I do not say that I will not accept of an opening here, if any one should offer that I may think eligible." It is hard to know what Hannah was to make of this. Samuel was prepared to return home and reunite the family, but only if he could find a respectable post in America, otherwise he would be quite happy to remain abroad if some lucrative opportunity should turn up there. Even as it became ever less likely he would be able to return on terms sufficient to get a worthy job in Massachusetts, he was hoping to find a good position abroad. Poor Hannah. Although she continued to urge him to return home, the prospect of permanent separation from his wife and children does not seem to have distressed him.

The British military assumed the conquest of the American colonies would be an easy task. The American militia would be cowardly and easily intimidated. The arrogant British attitude toward Americans was deeply resented by those exiles finding shelter in England. They came to discover that they were Americans at heart and defensive about any demeaning of their countrymen. By the end of 1776 Curwen deeply resented this contemptuous attitude:

> It is my earnest wish the despised Americans may convince these conceited islanders, that without regular standing armies our continent can furnish brave soldiers and judicious and expert commanders, by some knock-down, irrefragable argument; for then, and not till then, may we expect generous or fair treatment. It piques my pride, I confess, to hear us called *'our colonies, our plantations,'* in such terms and with such airs as if our property and persons were absolutely theirs, like the

'villains' and their cottages in the old feudal system, so long since abolished, though the spirit or leaven is not totally gone, it seems.[31]

The British evacuation of Boston in March 1776 caused Curwen to angrily wish "this ill-judged, unnatural quarrel was ended, but I fear thousands of useful innocents must be sacrificed to the wickedness, pride and folly of unprincipled men." Still, he and the other absentees assumed the British army would be victorious and their stay in England would be short.

In October 1777, after the astonishing British surrender at Saratoga, and with it the realization the war with America would become a worldwide conflict, with Britain now in danger too, the demeanor and calculations of the exile community changed abruptly.

Home Fires

The Small Pox is ten times more terrible than Britons, Canadians and Indians together. This was the Cause of our precipitate Retreat from Quebec, this the Cause of our Disgraces at the Cedars.
—John Adams to Abigail Adams, June 26, 1776 [1]

THESE are the times that try men's souls. The summer soldier and the sunshine patriot will, in this crisis, shrink from the service of their country; but he that stands by it now, deserves the love and thanks of man and woman.
—Thomas Paine, *Crisis*, December 1776

Even in the midst of war and sickness Hannah Lincoln blossomed. She was forty in 1776 when the British left Boston. The three years living in her father's home after the death of her husband, Bela, had restored her to the lively and self-confident woman she had been before her disastrous marriage. From the beginning Bela had been an abusive and ungrateful husband. Tending to him in his last illness had taken its toll on her, as supporting any seriously ill family member would do. In his case, though, it was especially trying since he was a fretful and demanding patient. Now back home she helped her stepmother Ann raise sixteen-year-old

Elizabeth (Betsy), whose mother had died when she was a toddler, and Ann's own two little daughters, Nancy and Frances. She and Ann also looked after Hannah's father, Josiah. Josiah, despite describing himself as old and infirm, was busy helping the patriot cause. One painful aspect of family life was the defection of oldest son Samuel to England, but all correspondence between him and his family had ceased. As much as possible he was forgotten. Otherwise, it was a lively household in the roomy house overlooking Boston Harbor, and they were as happy a family as one could have under the circumstances, with periodic military alarms and fear of illness.

Speaking of illness, relief over the departure of the British soldiers from Boston in March 1776 was replaced by the fear of smallpox. The disease had been rampant in the city. One of the worst outbreaks in memory had occurred in 1774. In the crowded streets the disease had spread quickly, particularly striking the local population, as most of the British soldiers had been previously exposed and were immune. By the fall of 1775 it had spread to towns around Boston, its victims dying in droves.

The symptoms were a headache, backache, fever, and vomiting, then the fever would drop, but start again as the first sores appeared. As they spread over the body, the victim would endure excruciating pain. Once the pustules ran together the person would likely die. If they managed to recover before that occurred, the sores would be replaced by scars, often leaving pox marks. It took about a month for the illness to run its course, and the patient was contagious until the last scab dropped off. Some who survived were blinded. But if you survived, you would be immune thereafter.

It was a highly contagious disease and could be spread by simply inhaling droplets from the air around victims or touching them or their possessions, then touching your nose or mouth. The virus was carried through the air when floors in sickrooms were cleaned and clung to the bedclothes used by the sick. The incubation period was up to two weeks. The only way to prevent the deadly and painful disease was inoculation with smallpox virus. With inoculation you would get the disease but in a milder form. This approach was controversial. Special hospitals were set up to permit patients to be inoculated and then treated when they became ill. But some patients didn't remain quarantined during the two weeks before they became sick. There were riots in Salem and Marblehead in 1774 after such hospitals were set up for fear that those who had been inoculated would spread the disease to the general population. Wild mobs forced both hospitals to shut. Four Salem men who stole bedcovers from hospitals were tarred and feathered for fear the covers they took were contaminated.

While New York and New Jersey permitted doctors to inoculate patients with the virus and set up hospitals, New England banned inoculation except during the worst epidemics. In 1776 the ban was lifted, and doctors were able to operate in Boston. It was a fearful choice to get purposely infected with the disease, but considering the miserable and usually fatal impact of the disease itself, one worth making.[2]

In July Hannah and family and her friend Abigail Adams, with her children, were part of a group of seventeen who traveled from Braintree to Boston to get the inoculation. Dr. Thomas Bulfinch was their physician.[3] The group from Josiah's household included wife Ann, Hannah, and daughters Betsy and Nancy. They stayed near Abigail Adams and her four children in neighboring houses in Boston. "The Town and every House in it, are as full as they can hold" with people coming to get inoculated, Abigail wrote John. They had to bring their own bedding, and Abigail had a cow driven from Braintree and some hay to set up housekeeping while they recuperated from the disease.[4] She reported that her "little ones stood the operation Manfully," praying "God grant we may all go comfortably thro the Distemper, the phisick part is bad enough I know."

Hannah had a challenging time catching the weakened virus through innoculation. After three weeks in Boston Hannah had the inoculation repeated four times, but it did not take.[5] Others had the opposite reaction. Abigail Adams reported that Becky Peck, who was staying with the Adamses, "has it [smallpox] to such a degree as to be blind with one Eye, swell'd prodigiously." Abigail judged her "an object to look at; tho she is not Dr. Bulfinches patient." Abigail's own son John caught the disease "exa[c]tly as one would wish, enough to be well satisfied and yet not be troublesome."[6] Dr. Bulfinch's prescriptions for his inoculated patients sound very modern in their mix of activities and diet. He ordered them all to get as much fresh air as possible, and "when we cannot walk, we must ride, and if we can neither walk nor ride, we must be led." They slept with windows opened at night lying on carpet or straw beds, a mattress, or anything hard, and were not to have spirits, salt, or fats. They were to eat fruit and unseasoned vegetables.

Many people who didn't think they had the virus left and then got very sick. It was an uncertain business at best, and doctors did not understand why some people had not gotten it and others were terribly sick and died. Some 7,000 in the state were reckoned to have gotten the disease. Abigail thought it would be five weeks before the Braintree contingent all got through the illness. The inoculated Quincy and Adams households returned home to Braintree at last, sound and immune from a recurrence of the dread disease.

Military matters swirled around Hannah and the Quincy household that spring and summer, some joyous despite the general gloomy picture for Washington and his army. Immediate family members were involved as well, as many local men joined the militia. Josiah Senior, for his part, had been very busy helping defend the country with his suggestions and advice. He had insisted the previous summer that with enough gun powder and heavy cannon he would undertake to make prisoners of the British army in Boston and their fleet in the harbor. John Adams gave the older man credit for being absolutely correct on that strategy. It was powder and the cannon, hauled with such effort from Ticonderoga, that drove the British from Boston in March of 1776 and their ships from the harbor.[7]

Hannah's brother-in-law, Bela's younger brother Benjamin, became deeply involved in the fighting. Benjamin was a short, stocky man, very different in temperament from Bela. He was a man a sister-in-law could be proud of. He would eventually earn the rank of major general in Washington's army. Unlike Bela, who had been given a good education as a doctor, even traveling to Scotland for further training, Benjamin's formal education stopped at the primary level. His work was needed on the family farm and in their brewery. There he worked as a farmer until the age of forty. While Bela and Hannah had no children, Benjamin and his wife, Mary, had eleven. Despite his labor to support them all, he was active in public service in Hingham, at one point or another holding every one of the town's administrative posts. He served as the town's representative to the Massachusetts General Court and later to the Massachusetts provincial Congress. Benjamin joined the Suffolk County militia at the age of sixteen, the militia regiment Josiah had served in as colonel.

By 1775 Benjamin had risen to become a lieutenant colonel and commanding officer. He was a stellar administrator, though not so stellar a field commander. When war broke out, he recruited and arranged to equip and train thousands of local militia. A year later he was promoted to brigadier general of the militia. His early military engagements were not successful. The militia, particularly in its first battle encounters, was at a disadvantage against professional soldiers, and often lost their nerve. In October 1776, at Benjamin Lincoln's first battle, his men, part of the Massachusetts militia, were defeated at White Plains. Up against Hessians and British soldiers, they fled in panic with many killed and wounded or taken prisoner. Others simply fled home. Undeterred, Lincoln returned to recruiting.

Amid the illness and military setbacks, the greatest event of the summer of 1776 was the Declaration of Independence, issued by the Continental Congress on July 4 and approved unanimously by the thirteen colonies. In Massachusetts every town meeting was asked whether its representative to the colonial legislature should vote for independence. When a majority voted yes, they instructed the delegates to the Continental Congress to approve the historic measure. Josiah, impatient for the step, wrote to his friend Benjamin Franklin in April asking when a new government would be formally established. [8] Franklin and John Adams would be among the five members Congress selected to prepare the Declaration. Franklin's answer was thoughtful and perceptive:

"At present, that nothing seems wanting but that 'general consent.' The novelty of the thing deters some, the doubts of

success others, the vain hope of reconciliation, many. But our
enemies take continually every proper measure to remove these
obstacles, and their endeavours are attended with success, since
every day furnishes us with new causes of increasing enmity,
and new reasons for wishing an eternal separation; so that there
is a rapid increase of the formerly small party, who were for an
independent government."

Others agreed. Joseph Hewes, a member of the Continental Congress,
wrote to Samuel Johnston in March agreeing with Franklin's assessment
that Parliament was furnishing new causes of enmity. One example was the
new act of Parliament prohibiting all trade and commerce between Great
Britain and the colonies, making all American property seized at sea subject
to confiscation.[9] Hewes adds, "I see no prospect of a reconciliation" and "I
fear it will make the Breach between the two Countries so wide as never
more to be reconciled. . . . Nothing is left now but to fight it out." He was
sorry the Americans were not unanimous in their Councils and particularly bemoaned the fact that "we do not treat each other with that decency
and respect that was observed heretofore. Jealousies, ill natured observations, and recriminations take place of reason and Argument." Even John
Adams, working diligently for independence, admitted, "Independency is
a Hobgoblin of so frightful Mien, that it would throw a delicate Person
into fits to look it in the Face."[10] But Adams judged that all the hesitancy
about declaring independence had it not been "for a Misfortune, which
could not be foreseen, and perhaps could not have been prevented, I mean
to Prevalence of the small Pox among our Troops. . . . This fatal Pestilence
of the small Pox among our Troops . . . this fatal Pestilence completed our
Destruction—It is a Frown of Providence upon Us, which We ought to
lay to heart."[11]

At the same time, even before passage of the Declaration of Independence, Congress was doing its part to increase the division. It passed
a resolution recommending the "several Assemblies, Conventions and
Committees or Councils of Safety, of the United Colonies, immediately

to cause all Persons to be disarmed, within their respective Colonies, who are notoriously disaffected to the cause of America."

Congress finally moved to declare the independence of the United States. John Adams had been lobbying hard in the Congress to achieve that result for months and was on the five-man committee, with Ben Franklin and Thomas Jefferson, to draft the formal Declaration. It both proclaimed independence and listed the violations of the rights of Americans that propelled the separation. John announced the momentous decision to Abigail on July 3: "Yesterday the greatest Question was decided, which ever was debated in America, and a greater perhaps, never was or will be decided among Men. A Resolution was passed without one dissenting Colony 'that these united Colonies, are, and of right ought to be free and independent States, and as such, they have, and of Right ought to have full Power to make War, conclude Peace, establish Commerce and to do all the other Acts and things, which other States may rightfully do.'"[12] He fretted, however, that the people will have "unbounded Power" and an addiction to corruption and venality. He was also concerned that the rich were not suitably virtuous to preserve such a government.

Copies of the Declaration were printed and ordered sent to every colony's legislature and committees and to the commanding officers of the continental troops. It was to be read to the people in each state and to the army soldiers. John believed it would "cement the Union" and predicted the day of its passage (he thought it would be July 2 rather than July 4) "will be celebrated by succeeding generations as the great anniversary Festival. . . . the Day of Deliverance . . . solemnized with Pomp and Parade, Shews, Games, Sports, Guns, Bells, Bonfires, and Illuminations from one End of this continent to the other from this Time forward forever more."[13]

On July 18 Hannah Quincy, Abigail Adams, and family members who were in Boston at the time heard a rousing sermon and joined a large crowd converging on Kings Street to hear the reading of the Declaration of Independence.[14] Several cannon and troops under arms were gathered there. The Declaration was read from the balcony of the State House.

When the reading ended, the cry from the balcony was "God Save Our American States!" Then the crowd erupted with three cheers, bells rang, privateers in the harbor fired their guns, forts and batteries and the cannon were discharged, the soldiers followed firing their muskets, and "every face appeard joyfull."

The echoes of that cheering began to ring hollow in the months that followed. Washington's army and the accompanying state militia regiments suffered defeat after defeat and retreated across New York State into New Jersey. The original enthusiasm for the fight began to wane, and it became harder to find recruits. Militia units had enlistments of only a few months, and Washington found it difficult to maintain a fighting force when it was needed. States and Congress were shirking funding, not meeting their commitments, and the British posed a formidable challenge with their ample supplies and hard currency. The rough, if patriotic, recruits suffered against the expertise of professional soldiers and suffered again from the inability or unwillingness of Congress and the States to keep them properly furnished in food, equipment, and warm or at least adequate clothing. Hundreds who left home became casualties of battles, illness, or imprisonment. Many never returned. In December Thomas Paine, whose bestselling essay *Common Sense* had buoyed the independence movement, was writing in another pamphlet, *Crisis*, focused on the present as "times that try men's souls": "The summer soldier and the sunshine patriot will, in this crisis, shrink from the service of their country; but he that stands by it now, deserves the love and thanks of man and woman."

Then, at the very end of the year, when summer soldiers were everywhere and winter soldiers a dwindling number, a Christmas gift arrived. George Washington, given new powers of command by Congress but soon to lose many of the militia whose enlistments were up at year's end, secretly crossed the turbulent Delaware River on Christmas night. The army was rowed across by the Marblehead mariners who saved the army in Manhattan. It was a daring and risky business. Major James Wilkinson, who joined the crossing, remembered: "The force of the current, the sharpness of the frost, the darkness of the night, the ice . . . during the operation, and a high wind, rendered the passage of the river extremely difficult. [15] At dawn Washington's army surprised the still-celebrating Hessian regiment holding Trenton and achieved a grand and badly needed victory. Several days later they beat the British again in nearby Princeton. In short, the trying year ended well: the army had survived and there was still hope.

SEVENTEEN

An Unexpected Turning Point: 1777

We have confused accounts of a Battle at the Northward Last fryday, in which the Enemy were put to flight. God grant it may prove true. Vigorous Exertions now on all sides may prove of the most happy concequence and terminate this cruel War. I long for a decisive Battle—and for peace, an honourable peace. I hope the enemy are as much in our power as you fancy them.

—Abigail Adams to John Adams, September 21, 1777[1]

In January of 1777 a betting man would have had no doubt the British would win. They controlled New York City and Newport, Rhode Island, and threatened Philadelphia, causing the Congress to move to Baltimore, with serious threats in the South to Charleston and Savannah. The British had a great navy, well-trained troops, professional officers, and ample supplies. By contrast the Americans had a mix of troops, some who enlisted for the duration, others serving short terms in state militias, who often lacked experience and equipment.

Furthermore, Washington's men struggled with poor, unreliable supplies of food, arms, and clothing, while he was subject to constant second-guessing by a grudging Congress. Delegates were growing impatient with Washington's lack of success. John Adams was among those who thought General Horatio Gates would make a better commander. Congress also suffered from civilian distrust of the military, even military composed of their friends and fellow patriots. In short, it was all a hodgepodge that left their commander in chief distraught. Many Americans were thoroughly tired of the war, wondering aloud whether it would have been better to make concessions rather than risk everything on this unequal fight.

October, three years into the war, however, was to be the start of a dramatic turning point for patriots and absentees, for Hannah Lincoln and her absentee brother Samuel, and for Great Britain and her former colonies. But at the beginning of the year, no one could have predicted it.

The year began with Congress meeting in Baltimore rather than Philadelphia as the British threatened to attack that city. The commander in chief had a different concern. Washington was worried about keeping his little army free from smallpox. He decided in January he had no option but to take the considerable gamble of ordering the 3,000 to 4,000 troops in their winter camp in Valley Forge to be inoculated.[2] Should the British attack during these months, the army would be nearly helpless, but winter was a slow time for military campaigns. He couldn't take the chance that hundreds of his troops would become ill and die from the disease. There were other camp illnesses in those years, but smallpox was especially virulent and contagious. He arranged for group after group of the soldiers to be rotated through the process—inoculation, illness in the hospital, then recuperation. All new recruits that spring were ordered to be inoculated when they were still two to three days' march away from the army camp. Happily, the strategy paid off. By the end of May the American army was free of the disease. That June, when Washington led his troops out of their winter quarters for the new campaign season, his men were sound and in good spirits. They were also better trained, as the winter months were used to give them the professional training they sorely needed. Keeping them usefully occupied during those famously difficult months at Valley Forge was also an excellent strategy to keep morale up.

The British position was strong. Their campaign to take New York State by sending a fleet from Canada down Lake Champlain had failed a year earlier when Benedict Arnold built a small fleet to oppose them. Arnold's few ships were no match for the British ships and their experienced crews but delayed them long enough to prevent their taking Albany that year. The British commander retreated to Canada rather than spend the winter snowbound in upstate New York. They still held New York City, with its excellent harbor, and this New Year they planned another campaign from Canada with a stronger fleet and large force of soldiers and Indians. Their plan was well-known both in Britain and America. Washington's northern army spent much of late summer of 1777 preparing to stop that assault. General Gates, with a large force of troops and militia, was sent to defend New York State. In the fall the British took Philadelphia. Their control of the major American port cities made it seem certain they would have the ultimate triumph.

Back in March Congress had returned to Philadelphia, although the British were on their way to capture it. John Adams, exhausted from the heat there that summer, claimed the British were welcome to it. "This Town has been a dead Weight, upon Us—it would be a dead Weight also upon the Enemy." He found the summer heat unbearable: "The Weather here begins to be very hot. Poor Mortals pant and sweat, under the burning Skies. Faint and feeble as children, We seem as if We were dissolving away. Yet We live along."[3] The British would capture Philadelphia in September. Congress and the Pennsylvania government fled to Lancaster, Pennsylvania, while many of the city's citizens scattered inland, wherever they could find safety.

The American military seemed no match for the British. Still, Adams and others wondered: "What would Britain do, surrounded with formidable Powers in Europe just ready to strike her, if Howe's Army threatening Philadelphia should meet a Disaster? Where would she find another Army?" Four months later, after the surrender of a British army at Saratoga, that was the very question the British government and the American exiles there asked themselves.

Back home in Massachusetts in July, the courts were intent on prosecuting loyalists and lawbreakers. Some "Tories so calld," Abigail Adams wrote, were brought to Boston to be tried before justices Edmund Quincy, Col. Josiah's brother, and John Hill.[4] Edmund Quincy's own daughter Esther, who was married to Jonathan Sewell, was then in exile in England. Nevertheless, he was prepared to prosecute accused loyalists who remained in Massachusetts. The attorney for the so-called Tories pointed out, however, that Justice Quincy was not qualified to try them since he had not taken the oath of loyalty himself since the Declaration of Independence, and the recognizances were not signed. As a result, "they all marchd back again." The so-called Tories were rightly afraid of being imprisoned on board the guard ship. Seven others were condemned at the town of Bridgewater.

Even loyal old Josiah Quincy was embarrassed to find himself in trouble with the Massachusetts legislature. It was not because of any doubt about his patriotism, but because he refused to accept Massachusetts paper money in payment of debts owed to him. Patriotism can extend only so far. As the saying went the new money was "not worth a continental!"

There was good reason for Josiah's unwillingness to accept the questionable value of the new currency. In June the value of the American money plummeted. "Every thing here is extravagantly high," Abigail complained. In Braintree, "A Dollor now is not eaquel to what one Quarter was two years ago, and there is no sort of property which is not held in higher estimation than money."[5] The cost of labor to help on the local farms was also much higher. "I endeavour to live with as great frugality as possible," she added. She was not alone in that effort.

In the midst of the great and frightening events of revolution and war, private life and love went on. That summer of 1777 Hannah Lincoln was courted. She was a widow, forty years old, but a fine, intelligent, and kindly woman. Ebenezer Storer of Boston could not have been more different from Bela Lincoln, her late and not-much-lamented husband. Ebenezer was forty-seven that year, and a respected deacon at Boston's church in Brattle Square. He was known as a philanthropist, and the list of organizations that he worked for amply justifies that reputation. Like Hannah's brothers, Ebenezer graduated from Harvard College, earning bachelor's and master's degrees in 1750 and a complimentary degree from Yale University. A year later he married Elizabeth Green. The two had six children, four sons and two daughters. He joined his father as an apprentice in his warehouse, and the firm eventually became Ebenezer Storer & Son. Like the Quincys, he was active in public life. In Boston he served variously as warden, selectman, and an overseer of the poor. Ebenezer was also an intellectual and was a founder of the American Academy of Arts and Sciences, serving as its first treasurer. He must have been a talented handler of funds, because he also served for seventeen years as treasurer of the Society for Propagating the Gospel in North America. In July of 1777 he was recruited to serve as treasurer of Harvard College, whose funds were in a terrible mess. His task was to restore the college's finances to order after the former treasurer, John Hancock, had neglected his duties presumably because of his deep immersion in revolutionary affairs.

He was a wonderful match for Hannah, although the childless woman now found herself mother to six. Ebenezer's four oldest children, however, were in their twenties, leaving only the two youngest at home needing her care. She had helped her father and stepmother with their young daughters and being the good, sensible person she was, was well up to the task. Her close friend, Abigail, wrote in October of the number of marriages that had taken place, especially noting "our Friend Mrs L[incol]n of this Town to Deacon S[tore]r of Boston, an exceeding good match and much approved of."[6] It was a joyous change for Hannah as she moved to Boston to begin her new life, partnered with a kind and distinguished man.

The Battle of Saratoga took place in October. It was one of those rare decisive battles. The British attack from Canada on Albany, New York, which had been stalled in 1776, was once more attempted with a far more extensive force this time. It was part of a strategy to cut the New England states off from the mid-Atlantic states by taking New York. King George himself helped to plan it. There was an elaborate, three-pronged battle plan. An elaborate plan, however fine it looks on paper, is always a bit of a gamble, especially in an age when forces had difficulty keeping in touch and the planning was done 3,000 miles away. General John Burgoyne, "Gentleman Johnny" as he was affectionately known to his troops, was flamboyant and cocksure and had lobbied hard to get the position of commander. Burgoyne was to lead the main force, a large combined army of British and Hessian regulars, Canadians, and Indians, south from Canada along Lake Champlain to Albany. As a diversion a second army from Canada would go west up the St. Lawrence River to Lake Ontario, sweep south to the Mohawk River in central New York, then east to link up with the main army. Lastly General Howe, Britain's North American commander, based in New York City, would march his army up the Hudson to join Burgoyne in Albany. New York State would be conquered.

Things quickly went awry. Instead of waiting in New York City to march north and link up with Burgoyne, Howe went south to seize Philadelphia. Burgoyne was short of manpower to accomplish the second prong into central New York State and began to recruit Indians, who were brave but undisciplined and fought their own way, sowing terror. Burgoyne was carefully trying to bring them into line with British rules. They were instructed, for example, not to scalp innocent victims or wounded prisoners, although they could scalp the dead. The second prong of the assault managed to besiege Fort Stanwix in the Mohawk Valley, but the siege collapsed when the rumor that a huge American force was about to arrive caused the Indians to panic. They fled and afterward the rest of the troops lost heart and retreated. Burgoyne was left on his own with shrinking numbers and a lengthening supply line.

Burgoyne and his troops met staunch opposition from a well-positioned American army and militia blocking their path south. The Battle of Saratoga proceeded in two phases. In the second phase a brilliant and daring attack by General Benedict Arnold forced a breakthrough in British lines. With his army cut off from any possibility of reinforcement or retreat, Burgoyne surrendered. [7] Benjamin Lincoln was there commanding troops in the battle, but his men saw little action. He and Arnold were both wounded in the fighting and spent the next several months hospitalized in Albany, painfully and slowly recuperating. The American commander at Saratoga, General Gates, never set eyes on the battlefield while his men were fighting. Instead he stayed in his tent, which had no view of the battlefield. A messenger found him there debating the virtues of the revolution with a wounded British officer. Nevertheless, as the officer in charge, Gates was honored by Congress for the victory.

The victory at Saratoga was a stunning upset. The American army accepted the surrender of an entire British army. New York State was safe. The impressive victory persuaded France to openly support the colonists, who were giving their British competitors such trouble. Their expenses in sending aid, men, and ships to the task would help propel the French monarchy into bankruptcy and revolution not long after the American war ended. Once France allied with the colonists, the war became a world war between the two great colonial powers. Britain could no longer afford to focus its military might solely on America and began to consider negotiations. There was great relief and joy in America, while the American exiles in England were shocked and dismayed. Everything had become topsy-turvy.

EIGHTEEN

The Beginning
of the End

[T]hose sanctified hypocrites," those "damned fanatical, republican, New England, rebellious, ungenerous, ungrateful sons of bitches.
—Jonathan Sewell to Edward Winslow, a Massachusetts exile,
Bristol, England, September 20, 1778–January 4, 1779 [1]

I am more sick and more ashamed of my own Countrymen, than ever I was before. The Spleen, the Vapours, the Dismals, the Horrors, seem to have seized our whole State. More Wrath than Terror, has seized me. I am very mad. The gloomy Cowardice of the Times, is intolerable in N. England.
—John Adams to Abigail Adams, Philadelphia, April 26, 1777,
regarding slowness in sending recruits [2]

W e now know that Burgoyne's surrender at Saratoga was a turning point in the war. But that was not obvious to the exiles in England nor to those patriots at home, overjoyed at the victory but still facing further battles and hardships in America. Nor was it obvious to King George and his government. Opportunities for reconciliation slipped away, leaving anger, frustration, and fear in their wake. A war of attrition would continue.

War-weariness was taking its toll. By the dawn of 1778, many people had lost their enthusiasm for the conflict, and their once solicitous attitude toward friends and family who supported the enemy vanished. It was not really surprising. All the bloodshed, burnt villages, economic hardships, constant anxiety, and terrible treatment of prisoners of war did their work to destroy civility. Judge Edmund Quincy, Josiah Senior's brother, whose own daughter was in exile with her husband and his grandchildren, sat in judgment on local loyalists for their refusal to take the oath of allegiance to the state. Gouverneur Morris, a delegate to the Congress from Westchester, New York, was one of a very few in his family to support the American cause. He kept in contact with his two loyalist sisters, his mother, his brothers-in-law, and his half-brothers. Nevertheless, he prosecuted loyalists at home and urged public executions for them, believing terror would frighten or inspire them to fight for the American cause.[3] Edmund Randolph of Virginia, prominent member of the Congress, was of "contrary political principles" with his brother and his father, John, who went with the British governor of Virginia, Lord Dunmore, to England in 1775.[4] Patriots were also becoming furious at their more moderate neighbors for the loss of the ardor they once had for the struggle. When British troops raided the arsenal at Danbury, Connecticut, John Adams was disgusted at "the degenerated Country Men" who failed to oppose them and needed to be aroused from "that state of security and turpitude into which they seem to be sunk."[5]

Many farmers and merchants preferred dealing with the British, who paid in pounds sterling, to accepting the nearly worthless paper money the states were producing. Other Americans were simply profiteering from the war. George Washington did not mince words in writing to Joseph Reed of the Pennsylvania executive council referring to these profiteers as murderers of our cause, "the pests of society, and the greatest Enemys we have to the happiness of America." He added, "I would to God that one of the most atrocious of each State was hung in Gibbets upon a gallows five times as high as the one prepared by Haman. No punishment in my opinion is too great for the Man who can build his greatness on his Country's ruin."[6]

On November 20 King George opened the new term of Parliament with the customary speech from the throne. He was a proud, serious man and deeply and personally involved in the campaign to subdue the wayward Americans. It was more than a month after Burgoyne surrendered his army at Saratoga, but no word had reached him yet. He could celebrate the capture of Fort Ticonderoga and victory at the Battle of Brandywine. He was eager to announce to Parliament the conquest of America, but instead hoped for an important success to come, referring to "the obstinacy of the rebels" and hinting at "another campaign with an increased force."[7] The American exiles, like most Britons, were convinced Burgoyne's skill, energy, and seasoned troops would overwhelm the ragtag American army and militia, win the campaign, capture New York State, and draw the war to a satisfactory conclusion.[8]

News of the American victory at Saratoga traveled slowly. It reached Boston about a week after the battle, on Saturday October 25. There was great joy at the news and a service of thanksgiving and praise in Boston that Sunday to thank "the Supreem Being who hath so remarkably deliverd our Enemies into our Hands."[9] It took several more days before Congress learned of the victory. James Wilkinson, given the honor by General Gates of delivering the amazing news to Congress, traveled in a leisurely fashion, stopping to court a young woman on his way south.

Even in this perilous time Congress was still wary that one of their successful generals might copy Oliver Cromwell and take power. John Adams, who often criticized Washington for lack of success, thought one cause for thanksgiving was "that the Glory of turning the Tide of Arms, the victory at Saratoga, was not immediately due to the Commander-in-Chief nor to southern Troops." For all his eagerness for victory, he admitted he was afraid the idolatry and adulation of Washington would become so excessive "as to endanger our Liberties for what I know," adding, "Now We can allow a certain Citizen to be wise, virtuous, and good, without thinking him a Deity or a saviour."[10] It was an odd line Adams walked—upset at apathetic countrymen but fearful of his own brave and successful military officers fighting for victory. That old suspicion of a military threat to civilian government persuaded Congress to keep a watchful eye on its army and their officers even while the army lacked the basic necessities of blankets and shoes. Any lapse on the part of officers, any retreat or surrender, was met by Congress with the threat of a court-martial. Many officers sitting on these court-martials were survivors of their own court-martial. No wonder some of these brave men simply resigned and went home.

If news of the British surrender in upstate New York on October 17 took time to reach Congress in Pennsylvania, it took still longer to be carried across the Atlantic to the British people and American exiles. Not until December 16, two months after the event, did the British public learn of the disaster. It reached them by way of Quebec. "This day," Samuel Curwen wrote a friend from Exeter, "General Burgoyne's mortifying capitulation arrived in town. Nothing could be more disgraceful and humiliating, unless a submission to the victor's power without terms. The loss of the military chest estimated at seventy-five thousand pounds, the finest train of artillery ever sent out of this kingdom before; all the boasted acquisitions of the year's campaign gone at a blow, and Canada on the point of joining the grand American alliance."[11] That last was not correct, the Canadians were *not* about to join with the lower thirteen colonies. Curwen poured out his dismay to Reverend Isaac Smith: "Pray what resources, then, has Great Britain, without allies, able or willing to afford the needed help? . . . What measures can be adopted consistent with the honor and dignity of this late mighty empire—alas, how fallen!—that gave law but a few years ago to two of the most powerful, politic, and wealthy states in Europe, and thereby peace to almost all the world?"[12] Hutchinson wrote of the "universal dejection" among absentees. "Everybody in a gloom: most of us expect to lay our bones here."[13] For the exiles Britain had been the place of safety. Suddenly their sanctuary was itself in danger.

As an American, however, Samuel Curwen couldn't resist sneering at the arrogant Britons who had taunted the American rebels as a weak rabble, easily cowed:

"The account of General Burgoyne's surrender is confirmed,
and what think you of the Congress now? Of American
independence? Of laying the colonies at the ministers' feet?
Of Lord S.'s boast of passing through the continent from
one end to the other with five thousand British troops; and
with a handful of men keeping that extensive continent in
subjection? . . . Of the raw, undisciplined, beggarly rabble of
the northern colonies? . . . Of the humiliating surrender of a
British general . . . to the aforesaid rabble? [14]

British officers who had just returned from America declared the conquest of it "a vain expectation" even with a large additional force. [15] Nevertheless, there was popular enthusiasm in Britain for bringing the Americans
to heel. A recently arrived loyalist, Richard Howard, told Jonathan Sewell
some British gentlemen were convinced the rebellion would be crushed:

"a number of gentlemen of influence and property, who have
been lying on their oars to see which way the game would
finally go . . . are unanimously of opinion, that from the unexpected tyranny of the congress and their sub-devils, that almost
universal poverty and distress of the people, and the general
aversion to French connections, the quondam union of the
thirteen states is upon the point of dissolution, and that nothing
is wanting but a single effort to crush the rebellion, root and
branch . . . From all these appearances I augur well." [16]

While Britons disagreed on the likely outcome, most absentees were no
longer optimistic about a British victory.

Apart from the shock of it, the loss at Saratoga had a serious economic
impact on the absentees. Faced with a long-term stay in England, many
left London, scattering about the country for less expensive cities. Thomas
Hutchinson Junior wrote his brother Elisha that "the very few Americans
that are left in and about London wear pretty long faces. . . . it is now

become a rare thing to meet a Yankee even in the Park."[17] They tended to choose port cities on Britain's west coast that had extensive trading links with the colonies. Many Virginians moved to Glasgow, on the west coast of Scotland. That city's merchants had been carrying on an extensive trade in tobacco with the Virginians for many years.[18] New Yorkers favored Chester, also on the west coast, just north of the Welsh border. Many other exiles were already established in Bristol, a key west coast port city. All were some distance from the expensive southeast of England. Despite old commercial and social links, the Americans had little success blending into English society. They felt isolated and moved close to other Americans for comfort and society: "with out sum American Friends lives near you it is very difficult to form any society in this Country."[19] It was a tale experienced by refugees and immigrants in other times and places.

One exile who did not leave London was Samuel Quincy. Somehow, he managed to afford to remain in the capital, at least for the time being, still hoping for a promising opportunity to make money. If he had found some lucrative opportunity, he never mentioned it in his letters home, but he may have been receiving a stipend to reimburse him for the loss of his post as solicitor general in Massachusetts.

Attempting to live frugally was wise because, with the defeat at Saratoga, the lords of the treasury gradually became aware they might have to support increasing numbers of American refugees for some time, and the government needed to economize. In some cases treasury officials began to dole out a single grant in full payment.[20] The government had apparently been holding back on granting Americans appointments. It now began to look more favorably on that expedient. But these changes took place gradually and, in the meantime, a more frugal way of living seemed the wisest course for them all.

In May of 1778 Samuel learned of the Massachusetts Act, which precluded anyone returning who had left the state since the Battle of Lexington in April 1775 and had "joined the enemy."[21] His wife, Hannah, had not mentioned the act in her letters to him. As a lawyer he wondered what was meant by "joining the enemy." Was merely living in England but not fighting on her behalf joining the enemy? He was distraught. "The love of one's country and solicitude for its welfare are natural and laudable affections; to lose its good opinion is at once unhappy, and attended with many ill consequences" but "how much more unfortunate to be for ever excluded from it without offence!" He had never joined the enemy as far as assisting their cause, but simply left America. Furthermore, he noted a resolve of congress "that no absentee shall be permitted to take up his residence in any other colony without having been first received and admitted as a citizen of his own." This was another blow, since he had planned to go "southward," where he had "an advantageous offer of countenance and favor."[22] Samuel now bent all his energies to coming up with another plan, perhaps a post in another British dominion.

The king and his government probably knew for some time that France was secretly helping the rebels. It was to be expected. The British victory against France in the French and Indian War in 1763, with the loss of Canada, still smarted. What better way for France to get revenge than to help British colonists evict the British? Indeed, the French had been giving aid to the rebels, hoping the rebellious colonists would join an anti-British alliance with France and Spain. With the American victory at Saratoga, the American cause seemed viable, and France was likely to openly ally with the Americans. The formidable French navy and army and their colonial strength in the Caribbean would be substantial assets to the struggling American forces. Worse than French assistance, the French entry into the war would transform the British war against her North Atlantic colonies into a worldwide conflict between the two great colonial powers. It wasn't just the shocking loss of a British army that was the actual turning point. It was France's alliance with the colonists that changed the war. At the end of January, in a panic, King George warned his prime minister, Lord North, that "every letter from France adds to the appearance of a speedy declaration of war; should that even happen, I might perhaps be wise to strengthen the forces in Canada, the Floridas, and Nova Scotia; withdraw the rest from North America, and without loss of time employ them in attacking New Orleans and the French and Spanish West India possessions."[23] The king's desperate plan never went into effect. Instead, a variety of alternatives were hastily suggested, some by the political opposition, to add men to the forces in America and plan for a sea war. There were offers from cities and individuals of new regiments as well as general confusion and, for the first time in the war, uncertainty. With the threat of a war against France looming, the British withdrew from Philadelphia that spring and began consolidating their troops. The Royal Court still talked of destroying the rebellion, but when Lord Germain, the secretary for the colonies, informed Parliament of the startling news of Burgoyne's surrender, he pointed out "the impracticality of carrying on this war any longer."[24]

The Reverend Richard Price, a Welsh Presbyterian and a staunch defender of the American cause, had the same opinion in a sermon he preached in February:

> "There is a distant country, once united to this, where every inhabitant has in his house, as part of his furniture, a book on law and government, to enable him to understand his colonial rights; a musket to enable him to defend those rights; and a Bible to understand and practice religion. What can hurt such a country?"[25]

Timing, as they say, is everything, and thus far the sporadic attempts at negotiation to end the war had come to nothing. Negotiations are always tricky between warring sides. No one wants to negotiate at a disadvantage, and if confident of victory, why negotiate? But sometimes stopping the bloodshed and the devastation of a war and making concessions rather than losing all is worth the risk. Efforts at negotiations between the Americans and the royal government revealed fractures in the thinking of the leaders and supporters of each side. Sadly, opportunities to avoid full-scale war, particularly the Olive Branch Petition from the Continental Congress in the summer of 1775, were lost to pride and misperceptions. A second attempt was made by the Continental Congress in September 1776, and delegates met with Admiral Lord Richard Howe. The Howe brothers had been anxious to find some moderate solution to the conflict. But the Congress had declared independence in July of that year, and Howe and the American negotiators had limited authority to agree to terms. Again, failure.

Now, three years later, it was the British government's chance to halt the war and make peace with their former colonists, but they had to act quickly and generously. The king, his ministers, and members of Parliament wrestled through January and February, often debating late into the night, over the appropriate concessions to make to the Americans, who should be on the commission to negotiate, and what powers to give them.[26] They lived in expectation of a declaration of war from France when they were vulnerable, with the bulk of their army in North America. Lord North got Parliament to repeal the Tea Act and the Massachusetts Government Act, which had caused such furor.

The question was, what would the French do? That February the other shoe dropped. News of an official alliance between France and America was announced. Benjamin Franklin had spent many frustrating years in France to negotiate a treaty, but it was the American victory at Saratoga that made it happen. On February 6, 1778, they signed two treaties. The Franco-American Treaty of Amity and Commerce recognized the independence of the United States and established commercial relations between them. The second treaty, the 1778 Treaty of Alliance, was a military agreement, signed immediately thereafter as insurance, in case fighting with Britain erupted as a result of signing the commercial treaty. The military alliance promised the Americans the support of the French army, navy, and treasury. In exchange the United States guaranteed "from the present time and forever, against all other powers . . . the present Possessions of the Crown of France in America." France did promise not to increase French possessions anywhere in America. Spain and the Netherlands later joined the alliance against Britain. Britain had no allies.

How was Britain to survive a war against its old enemy France, and later Spain, with a substantial part of its fleet and troops in North America? Britain's forces were spread thin. Apart from India, Britain's troops were in North America: in New York, on the Delaware, in Florida, north in Quebec and Halifax, on the Great Lakes, in the West Indies at Jamaica, Grenada, St. Vincent, Tobago, Bermuda, the Bahamas, and the Mediterranean at Gibraltar and Minorca.[27]

How was the homeland to be protected? Hutchinson was "struck dumb."[28] There was panic among residents along England's south coast who feared a French invasion. American exiles had fled to Britain for safety, certain Britain would win the war and in the meantime they and their families would be safe. It seemed unthinkable that Britain itself would be in danger, that France might invade it. Now the unthinkable seemed possible.

The British government had a new concern, the fear that France, in return for recognizing American independence, was gaining power over the new American states. If Britain could not bring its American colonies back into obedience, they certainly did not want them to be under the control of France. To forestall that likelihood, the British ministry decided to offer substantial concessions to the rebels.[29]

The Carlisle Commission was named for its leader, the Earl of Carlisle. A fellow commissioner, George Johnstone, former governor of West Florida, felt Carlisle was too young for the role and "totally unacquainted with business." Richard Jackson had been appointed to the commission but refused to serve when he found the United States had already signed a Treaty of Alliance with France. All the commissioners learned of the American alliance with France in April before they set sail. What they did not know was that General Clinton had been ordered to evacuate Philadelphia, a sure sign of retrenchment, one likely to make the Americans less inclined to concede. Carlisle pleaded with Clinton to delay the retreat, but Clinton had his orders and acted on them. The plan as laid out would have granted the Americans the ability to act and govern independently but within the empire, rather like today's British Commonwealth of Nations. Had those terms been offered early in the war, they would probably have been happily accepted. But the French had recognized American independence, and the Commission was not authorized to recognize American sovereignty. It was all too late.

On June 13 the Carlisle Commission sent their proposals to Congress. Congress insisted Britain recognize American independence or all British forces be withdrawn before further discussion. Appeals to public sentiment by the commissioners, promising the end of bloodshed with virtually everything Americans had previously demanded, failed to move Congress. Since the commissioners were not authorized to recognize American independence, the discussion was at an end. However, it became public that the commissioners were authorized to offer bribes to members of Congress and military officers. Marquis de Lafayette, who played a stellar role in training the American soldiers, challenged Carlisle to a duel over some of his anti-French comments. In short, the Carlisle Commission was a failure.

The American alliance with France was a desperate act, of course. The French had long been the enemy not only of Britain but of her American colonies. The French and their Indian allies had streamed down from Canada to attack the New England villages and coastline. Nor were the French king and his government in favor of the rights of subjects and constitutional controls on government. But since, as the saying goes, "the enemy of my enemy is my friend," American diplomacy sought immediate advantage, hoping to avoid French control over their fate. It was a dangerous alliance for desperate times.

NINETEEN
Casualties

The continued series of untoward events on the side of Great Britain, in this unnatural contest between her and the colonies, has, I fear, given the coup de grace to her glory. The sun of Britain is past the meridian and declining fast to the west, and America is for ever emancipated from the legislative authority of this once potent empire; alas! No more so. The prophetic falling off of the best jewel from our king's crown when on his head at coronation, is now accomplished by the loss of America.
— Samuel Curwen to Mr. George Russell, Birmingham, from Sidmouth, England, July 13, 1778 [1]

But the loss of the colonies, the independence of America, her connexion with France their hereditary foe, could not yet be digested by the king, the ministry, or the nation; and the conciliatory proposals were noted to be carried forward on other principles than those of humanity or equity. The army and navy establishments were augmented; and the proud display of war, power, and conquest, was again to accompany the soft voice of peace and reunion.
— Mercy Otis Warren, *History of the Rise, Progress, and Termination of the American Revolution,* 1805 [2]

Curwen and posterity saw the alliance with France and loss of Burgoyne's army as the war's end. Sadly, it was only the beginning of the end. There were casualties of all sorts at home as the war dragged on for several years after the Saratoga battle. If American absentees were eking out a living in Britain, longing for home, there were British and German casualties in America hoping to return to their homelands. There were thousands of American loyalists who chose not to leave their homes and to take their chances with hostile neighbors and vindictive governments, while other residents simply tried to remain neutral, carefully picking their way between warring parties and armies.

Among the casualties were the British prisoners of war taken when Burgoyne surrendered at Saratoga. Large numbers of prisoners of war are a huge problem. Of course, it is preferable that they be prisoners rather than still fighting against you. But they must be guarded lest they break loose and threaten their captors. They must be housed, fed, and cared for in as humane a manner as possible until exchanged. When a war-torn nation is already having problems with shortages for its own army and its own people, this can be virtually impossible. In the 18th century there was a system of parole. Captured soldiers could be released on their promise not to engage in the fighting again until officially exchanged. The Saratoga Convention—Burgoyne insisted the treaty of surrender be called a convention—included this arrangement for Burgoyne's army. But that promise was never honored by the Continental Congress. Therein hangs a tale.

At Saratoga in October 1777, British troops suffered the shame of defeat when their commander, General Burgoyne, surrendered his army of 6,200 men. On a crisp, beautiful October morning in upstate New York, in accordance with the customary honors of war, the British troops marched out of their camp, drums beating. Regiment by regiment they laid their battle flags on the ground. To Lieutenant William Digby, one of the defeated, "the drums seemed to have lost their former inspiriting sounds, and though we beat the Grenadiers march, which not long before was so animating, yet then it seemed by its last feeble effort as if almost ashamed to be heard on such an occasion."[3]

Tears (though unmanly) forced their way, and if alone, I could have burst to give myself vent. I never shall forget the appearance of their troops on our marching past them; a dead silence universally reigned through their numerous columns, and even then they seemed struck with our situation and dare scarce lift up their eyes to view British troops in such a situation. I must say their decent behaviour during the time (to us so greatly fallen) merited the utmost approbation and praise.

This was just the beginning of the British soldiers' trials. The victorious American general Horatio Gates had offered moderate terms of surrender to Burgoyne, mindful that General Clinton still had an army in New York City and might march his men north to rescue Burgoyne's men. Article IV of the so-called Saratoga Convention allowed the British troops, many of them Hessians, to march to the nearest port and from there be ferried to Great Britain on their promise not to fight in North American again. So generous were the terms that Burgoyne actually boasted this was not a surrender.[4] Congress began to think that, too, and had second thoughts about permitting the troops to return to Britain, where they might be used elsewhere to free other troops to fight in America. Burgoyne was permitted to sail for England, but when Congress ordered him to provide a list of all his officers to ensure they would not return, he refused. Congress took advantage of his refusal to revoke the terms of the agreement, insisting on holding Burgoyne's army until the king himself ratified the Convention. They were sure he would refuse since it would be an acknowledgment of American independence. They were correct. As a result, no fleet came to the nearest port, or any port, to take them home.

The defeated army, accompanied by another army of camp followers, trudged the nearly two hundred miles to Cambridge, where, on a stormy November day, Hannah Winthrop saw the sad procession. She described the sight to her friend Mercy Warren: "I never had the least idea that the Creation produced such a sordid set of creatures in human figure—poor, dirty, emaciated men, great numbers of women, who seemed to be the beasts of burthen, having a bushel basket on their back, by which they were bent double—the contents seemed to be pots and kettles, various sorts of furniture—children peeping thro' gridirons and other utensils, some very young infants who were born on the road; the women [with] bare feet, cloathed in dirty rags."[5]

Hannah Winthrop noted that the privates were marched off to the hills and to surrounding towns. But they were not confined as she had expected. In the morning she found "an inundation of those disagreeable objects filling our streets! How mortifying is it—they [officers] in a manner demanding our houses and colleges for their genteel accommodations." This, she felt, was an unkindness to poor Cambridge, "almost ruined before this great army seemed to be let loose upon us." Indeed Harvard, "the first University in America," was "to be disbanded for their accommodation and we poor oppressed people seek an asylum in the woods against a piercing winter!" The Cambridge area was now expected to feed and provide for some 7,000 persons. Hannah fretted over the amount of wood they would require to keep them warm, when the cost of wood had risen and it was hard to get. "I never thought I could lie down to sleep surrounded by these enemies," she mused, "but we strangely become enured to those things which appear difficult when distant." For their part the prisoners were just as upset. Lieutenant Colonel Thomas Anburey found their situation "not only very unpleasant but dangerous, both to officers and soldiers," who were constantly getting into brawls with their militia guards.[6] He was especially humiliated by the ragtag militia army that guarded them, "an old man of sixty and a boy of sixteen; a black and an old decrepid man limping by his side; most of them wear great bushy wigs." How degrading for a professional officer to be the prisoner of such men.

Some 5,900 troops were put up in surrounding towns, where they remained for nearly a year while the negotiations about their fate dragged on. Despite the complaints about their presence, the common soldiers helped supply farm labor that, as Abigail Adams complained, was in short supply, and the families of British and German officers sent money to provide for their care. Hannah Quincy Storer's husband, Ebenezer Storer, working as treasurer at Harvard College, was kept busy as the college transitioned from a place of education to housing for British prisoners. In 1775, just after the Battle of Lexington and Concord, the college students had been dismissed to provide housing for the Continental Army. That army had departed in 1776. It is unclear how providing housing for the British prisoners impacted the college's already chaotic finances.

During their time in limbo the numbers of British prisoners shrank. About 1,300 of them had escaped on their journey to Massachusetts, others while working on local farms met women who helped them to blend in with the locals. Some Germans had found German-speaking villages to take them in. Other soldiers had abandoned the British army even before the Convention was signed. Peters, a member of the Queen's Loyal Rangers, although suffering from a bayonet wound and a foot grazed by a musket ball, fled north leading about 117 of the Rangers to Canada.[7] Lieutenant Simmons, a loyalist from New York who had left his wife and children to join Burgoyne's army, escaped with twenty-eight men. Traveling by boat and on foot, they all reached Canada safely. Some 680 other American loyalists also had joined Burgoyne's army.[8] They were helpful, but nowhere near the large numbers he had been assured would join him.

In November Congress decided the British prisoners had to leave New England. The Convention prisoners, now some 2,000 British, upward of 1,900 German, and roughly 300 women and children, were forced to leave Massachusetts in bitter wintry weather and trek the 700 miles to the Charlottesville, Virginia, of Thomas Jefferson. They arrived there in January 1779 to cold, snowy weather and were housed in the Albemarle Barracks until late in 1780. One of Congress's members, Col. John Harvey Sr., and his sons had offered some of his lands for this prisoner-of-war camp. Since the barracks were barely sufficient in construction, the officers were paroled to live elsewhere, some as far away as Staunton or Richmond Virginia, the latter some seventy miles distant. The camp was never adequately provisioned, and yet the prisoners did manage to make something of the site, as British prisoners have done in similar circumstances over the centuries, including building a theater. Hundreds also escaped, owing to the inadequate number of guards.

Oddly, their need for food and supplies boosted the local economy. Their families in Britain and Germany, as was customary at that time, sent money for their upkeep. Jefferson reckoned this hard currency increased the area's money supply by about $30,000 a week.[9]

Congress had promised supplies for the upkeep of American prisoners in British hands in New York and elsewhere but was sadly remiss. Elias Boudinot, charged with meeting that commitment, agreed in desperation to advance his own money if necessary to supply them.[10] Washington promised that if Boudinot was not reimbursed by Congress, he would pay half the cost himself. But the terrible story of prisoners of war on both sides is beyond the scope of this book. More American prisoners would die in British hands than in the fighting.

Burgoyne's troops were badly needed in Britain. In July of 1778 French and British fleets fought an indecisive battle one hundred miles northwest of the island of Ushant, at the mouth of the English Channel. The next year there was an attempted invasion of Britain, justifying the fears of residents and American exiles living along the English Channel.

The British prisoners were not the only casualties of the Saratoga battle. Hannah Quincy Storer's former brother-in-law, General Benjamin Lincoln, had led an army of 2,000 at Saratoga. His men saw no action during the battle, but in a skirmish the following day his lower right leg was hit by a musket ball. He was transported by boat to a large military hospital at Albany that housed wounded men of both armies. Lincoln spent four months recuperating there, along with Benedict Arnold, who also had suffered a terrible leg wound in the fighting. Benjamin's son Benjamin remained by his father's side at the hospital. Most of October's casualties had been discharged by December, but the day before Christmas, when Dr. James Brown, an army surgeon, visited the hospital, both Arnold and Lincoln were still there.[11] Dr. Brown found General Lincoln "in a fair way of recovery" behaving as "the patient Christian." This was a contrast with General Arnold, "for his wound, though less dangerous in the beginning than Lincoln's, is not in so fair a way of healing. He abused us for a set of ignorant pretenders." While the surgeons were not a "set of ignorant pretenders," they did not possess modern skills, and neither man's wound healed completely. Once Lincoln was finally back home in Hingham, he spent another five months hoping to recover the flexibility of his leg, with only limited success. His right leg was two inches shorter than his left, and the wound was susceptible to opening and infection. He had to wear a special boot and limped for the rest of his life. Arnold also had to learn to walk again and was left with a limp. Washington honored both generals with a gift of French epaulets and a sword knot.

On the other hand, Washington was anxious to have his best generals in the field as soon as possible, so despite Lincoln's serious leg injury he was asked to return to the army within the year. At least his first task did not involve battle. He was to preside over the court-martial of Major General Arthur St. Clair for abandoning Fort Ticonderoga. St. Clair was acquitted. In September of 1778, when the British began a campaign in the South, Lincoln was given command of the Southern department, assisted by Lafayette and "Light Horse Harry" Lee. This was a difficult and brutal battlefield for the patriots, with recalcitrant locals and unreliable militia. After their defeat at Saratoga the British military had decided on a Southern campaign. And for the first time they actively recruited American loyalists and integrated them into the British forces.[12] With Lincoln's leg still not healed, he was understandably anxious about the assignment. The long journey south was certain to be painful and risky, quite apart from the military challenges.

Although the Congress realized it would be difficult to recruit troops, members were insistent that Charleston be vigorously defended. In 1778, rushing to defend Charleston, Lincoln fell from his carriage in Virginia and reinjured his wounded leg. He reached Charleston in early December. When the British began marching north from Florida to Georgia, Lincoln assembled some 1,250 men to rescue Savannah. He was too late to prevent the British from capturing the city. Both armies then began a series of maneuvers and countermaneuvers. The British surprised Lincoln's men, who had been following them, and, in a skirmish at Brian Creek on March 3, delivered a serious blow to the Americans, killing more than 150 of

Lincoln's men and capturing another 173. Nearly half of the 800 who escaped deserted. In this one disaster Lincoln had lost a third of his force and Charleston had nearly fallen. Still, he carried on and was involved in the French-led siege of Savannah in October 1779 before retreating to Charleston.

Poor Lincoln was harshly criticized by the press. Although he convinced Congress to release him from his command, he was persuaded to remain. Only occasional reports of Lincoln's situation got back to his anxious wife and family in Hingham. How upsetting the harsh rebukes for military failures must have been to a reluctant warrior ready to fight, though suffering from a debilitating injury.

Charleston was a nightmare. In August 1779 Lincoln learned the French fleet under D'Estaing was coming to his aid. Unfortunately, the British were not the easy prey he thought they would be. And the French, though hampered by delays, would be the ones to deprive Lincoln of reinforcements. Lincoln was unable to get troops he needed for the city's defense because the leaders of South Carolina, a state with more enslaved Africans than white citizens, refused Congress's suggestion that they arm the slaves. They preferred surrendering to the British and began negotiations to permit the British army to pass through South Carolina.

A large amphibious British force from New York City headed for Charleston. Lincoln wanted to lead his army away before the city was completely encircled, but the leaders of Charleston insisted he remain. In the end the South Carolina politicians who had pleaded that Lincoln defend their capital decided they really did not want any further devastation and instructed him to surrender unconditionally to the British. The result was that, in May 1780, the biggest American army at the time, 5,000 continentals and militia, were taken prisoner and a large cache of badly needed American weapons and supplies fell to the British. It was a British triumph and a terrible blow to the Americans. Lincoln was allowed to return home to Hingham until exchanged, which he was in November 1780. He remained surrounded by friends and family all winter and into the spring of 1781. He had asked Washington to convene an investigation that would restore his reputation, but Washington refused on the grounds that many witnesses were still prisoners of the British. The humiliation of the surrender on top of other losses stung poor Lincoln and would not be redressed until the following summer.

Lincoln's sister-in-law, Hannah Lincoln Storer, now living in Boston with her husband, Ebenezer Storer, and his family, was supremely happy in her home life despite the tensions and alarms of war. Unlike her dear friend Abigail Adams, her husband was home, and she was not left managing a family farm and young children in his absence. True, Ebenezer was busy straightening out Harvard's chaotic finances, which the war's currency problems made worse. There was now the additional problem of finding accommodations for the officers of the British Convention Army, camped on their doorsteps. But she was spared the pain of separation and injuries suffered by friends and relatives and the arduous task many women shouldered of managing a farm or business in wartime. Not only was poor Abigail left to handle the Braintree farm and family the many months John was sitting in the Continental Congress, but John was then sent as a minister to France, necessitating more months alone. Stoic that she was, Abigail could not help complaining, "to my Dearest Friend that his painfull absence is not as formerly alleviated by the tender tokens of his Friendship, 3 very short Letters only have reached my Hands during 9 months absence. . . . I cannot charge myself with any deficiency in this particular as I have never let an opportunity slip without writing to you since we parted, tho you make no mention of having received a line from me; if they are become of so little importance as not to be worth noticeing with your own Hand, be so kind as to direct your Secretary."[13] She was somewhat comforted to learn that he had received few of her letters to him. In truth, while John claimed to have no time to write to her, he was constantly writing Congress of his progress to obtain help for the war effort.

Exile was tragic but staying home was difficult and dangerous. Those loyalists who remained in America despite the confiscatory laws and ostracism of their neighbors also suffered. In December 1779 Samuel Curwen

received a letter from William Pynchon, a friend in America, in response
to Curwen's regrets he didn't stay home:

> "in answer to my complaint of my banishment is truly piti-
> able; what he says will serve instead of a hundred instances to
> exhibit to your view a picture of the distressful situation of some
> of our friends, viz: 'If you knew half the inconveniences your
> continuance here would have occasioned, it would surely lessen
> your discontent; had you lost your business, all your debts, the
> fruits of many years' labor; been driven to sell your home and
> lands for payment of your debts and expenses; and thus reduced,
> you still would not freely nor safely walk the streets, by reason
> of party rage and malevolence and the uncontrolled rancor of
> some men.'" [14]

Curwen wrote his fellow exile, "This comforts me, and ought to console
you and every other sufferer."

It was even risky to stay home and remain neutral, especially if you were
prominent. The Shippen family of Philadelphia tried. They were one of the
wealthiest families in America. Edward Shippen was a judge as was his
father before him. In 1776, when the Pennsylvania Constitution was passed,
Edward Shippen lost his post as a vice admiral judge and his other offices,
putting the family in some financial distress. He was careful not to take a
public stand but was suspected of being a loyalist and put on parole. He and
his family were regarded as a risk to the cause and had to leave Philadelphia.
They moved to their country house. In August of 1777 he was freed from
parole and moved back to Philadelphia. John Adams and George Washington dined at his table, but so did British officials when British troops
captured the city. [15] Shippen tried but failed to keep the younger men in
the family from joining the respective armies. His daughter Elizabeth's
fiancé, Neddy Burd, who had studied law with him, fought in the American
army. Neddy was captured by the British in 1776 in the battle for Long
Island. He was held prisoner on one of the notorious British prison ships but

was eventually freed. Edward Shippen's own son, defying his father's strict orders, sneaked off with friends and joined the British army at Trenton. His timing was terrible. He reached Trenton just before Washington crossed the Delaware and captured it in December 1776. Young Edward was taken prisoner but personally freed by Washington at his father's urgent request. The senior Shippen never forgave his only son and stripped him of all financial power over the family's finances. His daughters enjoyed the parties of the British officers when they occupied Philadelphia. But when the British evacuated the city and the American army returned, the Shippens remained. Benedict Arnold, placed in command of the transfer to American control, courted Judge Shippen's beautiful youngest daughter, Peggy, and they were married. The Shippens have been labeled loyalists by historians, but they were really neutrals, careful to take no side.

Army physician James Thacher, passing with the army through about fifty miles of New York State called "neutral ground," characterized "the miserable inhabitants who remain" as "not much favored with the privileges which their neutrality ought to secure to them. They are continually exposed to the ravages and insults of infamous banditti, composed of royal refugees and Tories. The country is rich and fertile, and the farms appear to have been advantageously cultivated, but it now had the marks of a country in ruins. A large proportion of the proprietors having abandoned their farms, the few that remain find it impossible to harvest the produce."[16] Thacher adds that those inhabitants who were Tories joined friends in New York City and the Whigs retired into the interior. "Some of each side have taken up arms, and become the most cruel and deadly foes."[17] To be genuinely neutral was often to be a victim of both sides.

Two patriotic fathers, Josiah Quincy and his good friend Benjamin Franklin, experienced the pain of sons who turned against the cause for which their fathers were risking everything. The most public father-son divide was that of Benjamin Franklin and his son, William. While Josiah's loyalist son Samuel's exile and defection were known only to a relatively small group, Benjamin Franklin's split was far more public, as he was one of the outstanding leaders of the patriot cause while his only son, William, served as the loyalist governor of New Jersey from 1763 until 1776. Before the war they had worked together obtaining land grants, and Benjamin had lobbied to get his son a good post from the royal government. He had dedicated his autobiography, written before the war, to William. The disaffection between father and son was notorious and painful. They were unable to agree on the political questions between royalists and patriots. William was wholeheartedly dedicated to the Crown and was prepared to, and did, suffer for that cause. For the first six months of 1776, William was placed under house arrest. After the Declaration of Independence was passed, the Provincial Congress of New Jersey took him into custody. He was sent to Connecticut and imprisoned there for two years. While there he secretly sent intelligence to the loyalist party. When discovered William was put in solitary confinement for some eight months. In 1778 he was exchanged and moved to the royal stronghold of New York City. There he worked to organize troops to join the British side. When the war was over, William went into exile in Britain, where he spent the rest of his life.

The two patriotic fathers and old friends, Josiah and Benjamin, were both badly hurt by the actions of their sons but undeterred in their own efforts for the American cause. At least Josiah could take considerable comfort in the stellar reputation of his younger son, Josiah Junior, still dubbed "the Patriot." Franklin had no similar consolation. But Samuel Quincy, the absentee, was Josiah's only surviving son, just as William was Franklin's only son. Fortunately, Franklin's grandson, Temple, stayed close to his grandfather and worked as his secretary from the age of sixteen. The pain of Josiah and Benjamin in effectively losing their sons forever plumbs the depths of John Adams's reminder: "Posterity! You will never know, how much it cost the present Generation, to preserve your Freedom!"[18]

Happily, the end of the war was in sight. Yet unlike the end of a traditional war, the end of a civil war left many questions to be answered. How would peace affect those who lived through the conflict at home and abroad? Would divisions between neighbors and loved ones be healed? Would there be forgiveness? Would the absentees come home; would families be reunited? Or was it too late for reconciliation? Was there no way home?

TWENTY

Third Time Lucky: Yorktown and Peace

This year has not been a very glorious one to America. The unfortunate failure of their Expedition against Rhoad Island shagrined, mortified and disappointed to such a degree that they cannot yet mention it with patience, for they had every humane appearance of being crownd with Success and victory. Our Arms have rather been imployed in the defensive way. Our Enemies however have nothing to boast of since they have not gained one inch of territory more than they possessed a year ago and are at least Philadelphia out of pocket. What the winter may produce I know not. I wish it would give us peace but do not expect it.

—Abigail Adams to John Adams, December 13, 1778 [1]

At the very beginning of the war, in September 1775, John Adams warned against the dangers of alliances with foreign powers:

"If we united with either nation [Britain or France] in any future war, we must become too subordinate and dependent on the nation, and should be involved in all European wars . . . foreign powers would find means to corrupt our people, to influence our councils, and, in fine, we should be little better than puppets, danced on the wires of the cabinets of Europe."

Yet after nearly three years of fighting, an exhausted and desperate Continental Congress welcomed an alliance with France. Shouts of "Long Live the King of France! Long Live the Friendly European Powers!" boomed from the entire Continental Army drawn up on parade in May of 1778. [2] Washington had decreed a special "day of rejoicing" to celebrate the treaties of alliance with France. Each soldier had been issued a gill of rum, and, thus fortified, cheered as instructed for King Louis XVI. It was strange to be toasting the French king. They all realized he was a tyrannical monarch, leader of their ancient enemy, yet his help in their cause, anyone's help, actually, was a great relief. The French had a powerful army and strong navy. Britain's navy had been able to sail along the American coast at will and seize leading American port cities. The French fleet could take on and neutralize the British navy. So Americans were cheered by hopes that the French would provide the men, ships, and weapons they desperately needed to defeat the British.

But in the months that followed, French help had been disappointing. The first joint operation was a campaign to recapture Newport, Rhode Island. The city had been under British control since December 1776, when the British attacked it with a large fleet and an army of 7,000 troops. It was a key harbor, the only harbor in the Northern states that could be entered by large ships directly from the sea. With its loss, the government of Rhode Island had retreated to Providence as the British dug in.

The British hold on Newport was a thorn in the side of the Congress and its army, leaving the British fleet to prey on shipping. Washington hoped with the help of the French fleet, on its way across the Atlantic under the command of the Count D'Estaing, they could drive the British out of Newport at last. D'Estaing was an experienced general and admiral, with a reputation of being arrogant but, more importantly, brave. Actually, all the French officers must have seemed arrogant to the American army, who were a tough group of soldiers and militia, proud but not up to European standards of training or equipment. D'Estaing was a veteran. He had begun his military career in his teens; not unusual at the time. He had fought in the French and Indian War and was briefly a prisoner of the British. At forty-nine he looked every inch the French officer, slim, elegant, and completely in command.

Washington was charged with coordinating the Rhode Island campaign with D'Estaing but, for some reason, to Washington's surprise, D'Estaing refused to engage in a land battle, insisting on a naval battle against the British fleet.[3] Naval battles are tricky and weather-dependent. D'Estaing got his way. Admiral Richard Howe, commanding the British fleet based in New York, sailed to confront D'Estaing. Howe was delayed departing New York by contrary winds and arrived off Point Judith on August 9. Since d'Estaing's fleet outnumbered Howe's, the French admiral, fearful that Howe would be further reinforced and gain a numerical advantage, reboarded his French troops and sailed out to do battle with Howe the next day. As the two fleets prepared to fight, a fierce storm, presumably a hurricane, descended and raged for two days. Both fleets were scattered and severely damaged. The French fleet regrouped off Delaware. While Howe sailed back to New York City to repair and refit his ships, D'Estaing put in at Newport to inform the American commanding officer, Major General John Sullivan, that rather than securing Newport, the French fleet was off to Boston to repair its damaged vessels. Sullivan, a feisty Irishman who had tried Washington's patience more than once, was prepared to await D'Estaing's return. The French fleet was met at Boston by crowds angry at the French for abandoning the battle. General Sullivan naturally assumed D'Estaing and his fleet would return to Newport once the vessels had been repaired. When he discovered they were not coming back, he was furious. His militia was returning home as their enlistments expired. The British were bringing in reinforcements. Without French help he had no option but to retreat. A battle won was now lost. Unperturbed, D'Estaing sailed off to the warm waters of the Caribbean to protect the French Caribbean islands from the British fleet. Sullivan and General Nathaniel Greene sent an angry letter to the French admiral accusing him of betrayal. Washington

insisted the two officers mend fences and restore good relations. It was a
sober reminder for Americans that they were not the first priority for the
French, who had their own colonies to secure. Although the French had
been quietly shipping war materials to the Americans for some time before
signing that alliance treaty, they were always cautious, unsure whether
the American army would remain intact and keep fighting. France was
always ready, if necessary, to pull out and abandon their allies.

Congress was as angry as Sullivan about D'Estaing's retreat but, as
French aid was essential, members passed a resolution thanking D'Estaing
for his efforts and, tongue-in-cheek, praising his bravery and zeal. [4] John
Adams approved that approach, hoping "the unfortunate Events at Rhode
Island will produce no Heart Burnings, between our countrymen and the
Comte D'Estaing, who is allowed by all Europe to be a great and worthy
Officer, and by all that know him to be a zealous friend of America." [5]
Benjamin Franklin, American minister in France, and his friends joked
caustically that the French court should provide America with the names of
other gifted admirals. The entire alliance with the French was a desperate
measure. Machiavelli in *The Prince* had warned that an alliance with a
stronger power required caution. If you won with their help, your country
could fall under your ally's control. But it seemed worth the gamble to the
war-weary and needy American Congress.

French help the following year was equally disappointing. The British
had turned to a southern strategy, and the American aim was to drive the
British from Savannah. D'Estaing arrived in early September with twenty-
two ships of the line and eleven frigates to begin a siege of Savannah. The
British garrison, as protocol demanded, was called on to surrender. Playing
for time, the British commander stalled while a daring troop of British
soldiers sneaked into Savannah to reinforce the city. The Franco-America
campaign then opened with weeks of heavy bombardment. D'Estaing's
aim was to take Savannah by storm. However, there were critical mishaps
by the assaulting troops. A fierce defense confronted those attackers, who
managed to scale the ramparts. They were blasted by withering direct
fire and crossfire and suffered more than 800 casualties. The defending

British had only about 150.[6] D'Estaing was wounded twice in the battle and rescued by one of his officers. Once again, he abandoned a campaign, this one with far more serious casualties. On October 20 he sailed home to France, ordering his troops to return to their fleet and find their own way back. He arrived home on crutches.

However difficult these war years were for residents of New England worried about British control of Rhode Island and New York City, they were far worse for Americans living in the South. Loyalists from New England fled to Canada or England or took shelter in British-controlled American cities. The few black people in the North chose different approaches. Some free black people joined the Continental Army; some enslaved black people joined for the promise of freedom if they served three years. They fought side by side with the white soldiers, sharing their training and hardships.[7] A few Northern slaves escaped to join the British army on the promise of freedom. When the British turned to a Southern strategy, they urged Southern loyalists to join the fighting and welcomed enslaved black people who escaped to fight on their side or help with general duties. Some slaves believed it safer to remain where they were, however unpleasant, but in the growing chaos others simply slipped off into the countryside to face whatever dangers might await. The Southern back country became a cauldron of wandering marauders both white and black, in addition to loyalist and patriotic troops, resulting in vicious murder, plundering, and mayhem. Army surgeon James Thacher was shocked by the viciousness he witnessed in Virginia: "Not a day passes but there are more or less who fall a sacrifice to this savage disposition. . . . some thousands have fallen in this way in this quarter, and the evil rages with more violence than ever." He feared, "if a stop cannot be soon put to these massacres, the country will be depopulated in a few months more, as neither whig nor tory can live."[8]

Thus far the Franco-American military alliance was a disappointment to both sides. The French had thought Washington had twice the force that he did, while Washington hoped for a larger French force than he received.[9] But the third campaign with a new French force, another French fleet, and a new target was the charm.

The war may have moved south, but year after year New England men were required to reinforce the militia and the Continental Army for the new campaign season. Just as the planting season began, the army and militia needed recruits. The initial enthusiasm for militia and army service had long since evaporated. And no wonder. Military service was hard, it was poorly paid, and the American troops often left with inadequate boots and clothing, poor shelter, and little food. Congress called on each state to recruit a specific number of men, and each town in Massachusetts had a quota to fill. Both the state and the local communities now offered bounties to entice men to enlist. In June 1780 the Braintree town meeting, Quincys present, selected a committee to assist in procuring the men required.[10] "After a considerable debate," the records note, the town meeting voted to give each man one thousand dollars' bounty and half a bushel of corn for every day, from the time they marched to the time they were discharged or left the army, and half a bushel of corn for every twenty miles from home when they were discharged. The town also agreed to pay them forty shillings more, promised by the state in hard money. In addition, Braintree's General Joseph Palmer "generously gave into the hands of the moderator One Thousand & Eighty Dollars to be equally divided among the thirty-six men that shall first engage in the six months service as a Reinforcement to the Continental Army—for which the thanks of the Town was Voted him." Since the families of the recruits would be short-handed, the town agreed to supply them with corn, wood, or such other articles "as they stand in need off which is to be charge & Reducted from the wages of that person which is to be paid in Corn upon his Returning home." The town met again in early July to vote on an officer's pay for three months' service. It was unclear where that service was to be. Some service was nearby, in the Hudson highlands of New York. Other soldiers found themselves marching hundreds of miles south with Washington to Virginia. There would be many bushels of corn owed for that discharge.

In 1780 nearly 6,000 French soldiers landed in Rhode Island under the command of Jean-Baptiste de Rochambeau. Unlike his predecessors,

Rochambeau made a serious effort to develop a friendly working relationship with Washington. Washington was still eager to attack the British at New York, but the French had other ideas. The British had shifted to a Southern strategy, and in 1781 Rochambeau persuaded Washington that a quick march hundreds of miles south to Virginia would catch the force under Cornwallis at Yorktown. A large French fleet of 36 men-of-war, 32 smaller vessels, and 100 transports, with 9,000 soldiers and seamen was then in the Caribbean under the command of Admiral François-Joseph-Paul de Grasse. At Rochambeau's suggestion, Washington and Rochambeau wrote to de Grasse asking him to bring his fleet north to help in their campaign. He agreed. The plan was that the French fleet would arrive in time to cement the siege of General Cornwallis and his army at Yorktown and block any attempt by Clinton's fleet in New York to rescue Cornwallis. [11]

It wasn't until August 14 that Washington and Rochambeau got word from de Grasse that he would help, but time was of the essence. De Grasse could only sail as far north as Chesapeake Bay because of his other responsibilities and could only remain until October 15. That gave Washington and Rochambeau two months to bring the Continental and French armies 450 miles, as quickly as possible, to corner Cornwallis and prevent him from getting supplies and reinforcements. Great secrecy was needed. To trick Clinton into thinking Washington meant to attack New York, 3,000 men were left behind with orders to light campfires every night and collect boats for the supposed assault.

The two armies marched south in the oppressive August heat, often marching at night when it was cooler, day after exhausting day. The French and Americans took different routes due to lingering bitterness from a long history of French raids on New England and religious differences. Hannah's brother-in-law, General Benjamin Lincoln, and his men were part of the army along with other Massachusetts troops, most never having been so far from home before. They trudged through Pennsylvania, Delaware, Maryland, and finally Virginia, where, as in Massachusetts, late crops were being harvested but, in the case of Virginia, much land had been devastated.

Fortunately for the Americans the two British generals they faced, Clinton in New York and Cornwallis in the South, disliked and distrusted each other. Cornwallis favored an aggressive approach and considered Clinton timid. Not worrying about winning hearts and minds, Cornwallis roamed the southern countryside permitting his men to lay waste to farms and villages. They confiscated horses and freed enslaved people. These men and women were happy to be free but were left with little protection from their former masters and no way to earn a living in the chaotic countryside. Washington had dispatched General Greene to the South weeks earlier to keep Cornwallis and his army busy by striking here and there. Greene was careful to treat residents fairly and keep his men in check while keeping Cornwallis on the hop.

Clinton may not have been timid, but he was indecisive, although perhaps the result was the same. He couldn't make up his mind where he wanted to send Cornwallis and his army. He ordered him to New York, then to Philadelphia, again to New York, and finally advised him to stay in Virginia. Even while Washington and Rochambeau awaited a response from de Grasse, Cornwallis had set to work to fortify Yorktown, a town on the mouth of the York River, near Chesapeake Bay. He was confident the British fleet would come to his aid, if need be, but he didn't think it necessary. He and Clinton assumed Washington meant to strike New York, not Virginia. It turned out to be a fatal mistake.

When they were within a mile of Yorktown, the French and Americans immediately began to encircle the city. Rochambeau was a master at sieges (this was his fifteenth), and quickly deployed hundreds of cannon and thousands of troops to furiously pound Yorktown. British cannon returned fire. The ground shook. Whenever the British fell back from their trenches, French and American soldiers rushed forward to occupy them, drawing an ever-closer ring around the town walls. The fighting was ferocious. Inside the city rations were running out and smallpox was taking a dreadful toll. In a shocking move the British thrust the hundreds of black people who had been helping them in Yorktown out into no-man's-land, leaving them helpless between the two armies. Cornwallis tried to break out of the tightening noose, but a fierce thunderstorm drove his army back. The longed-for help from Clinton's fleet arrived too late and was driven off by de Grasse's ships. On October 17, with British cannon nearly silent amid an "almost incessant" American and French bombardment, Cornwallis sent a lone drummer out to parley. It was the anniversary of the great victory at Saratoga. Two days later it ended. At two o'clock in the afternoon on a bright, cool October day, the American army lined up on one side of the field, their French allies across from them, their lines extending nearly a mile. The British and Hessian troops solemnly marched out of Yorktown between the ranks of the allied armies. They were led not by Cornwallis, who claimed he had a cold, but his second in command, General Charles O'Hara, tears streaming down his portly face. Washington chose Lincoln for the honor of officiating for the allies. It was a gracious gesture to make amends for the indignity Lincoln had suffered at the surrender of Charleston, when the British had denied the surrendering Americans the honors of war. Washington now refused to permit the British the honors of war. Traditionally the vanquished would be permitted to march out with their regimental flags flying and playing one of their tunes, but since they had refused the honors of war to the American army surrendering at Charleston in May 1780, they were to receive only the "honors . . . as granted to the garrison of Charleston." The British troops were to "march out. . . with shouldered arms, colors cased [regimental flags laid on the ground], and drums beating a British or German march." They were then to lay down their arms and return to their encampment until dispatched to their destinations.

The ceremony completed, the allies and their conquered foes parted ways. Rochambeau returned to France, where he was handsomely honored by King Louis XVI. De Grasse sailed for the West Indies and Cornwallis for New York, British and Hessian prisoners were taken inland, and Washington and his men began the long march north to spend the winter in the Hudson Highlands. It was a great victory.

Word of the triumph at Yorktown was greeted with great joy, wonder, and relief. John Adams was in Europe on October 30, when his brother-in-law,

Richard Cranch, in Boston sent him two "hand-bills" announcing the extraordinary victory at Yorktown. "American affairs never wore a more agreeable Aspect than at present," he rejoiced and was eager to know "how this News will be relish'd at St. James's." On November 3, Cranch followed the news with another letter to "heartedly congratulate" Adams "on the great and important Event, the taking of Lord Cornwallis and his whole Army.[12]

Suddenly, apart from a few skirmishes, it was over, the fear and devastation, the uncertainty and violence. Suddenly the guns were silent. Thousands of lives had been lost in the American Revolution. Of the approximately 175,000 men who fought in the American army, navy, and militia, 25,674 died, some in battle, another 10,000 from disease in camp, and 8,500 more as prisoners in British hands. Thirty to forty percent of the casualties were continentals. There were many permanently empty seats at family tables. Other veterans returned home to poorer farms, lost livelihoods, and lonesome or uncomfortable welcomes. Whatever the relief and joy at being home, it was hard to readjust from the high drama of battle to the humdrum cares of daily life.

New England was fortunate. Its farms and villages were not as ravaged as the farms and towns of the mid-Atlantic and South. Still, there was much to be restored and if possible repaired, and many knotty national and personal issues were still to be settled. The chief question for so many families was whether their family divisions would be healed. Would the exiles be able to return? Would they want to come home? Would they be welcomed? Would the empty seats at the table, like those of military casualties, be permanent?

TWENTY-ONE

When the Guns
Went Silent

These unfortunate people were very difficultly placed—if they had joined the American party, they would have been Rebels to England, but when the war was over and they applied for the restitution of their estates, they were told they were Rebels to America.

    —Thomas Hutchinson Jr., to his brother, November 15, 1788 [1]

Whenever the loyalists are mentioned in a collective body, it is but just to make a reservation of some exceptions in favor of such as fled, from the terrors awakened in their bosoms by the convulsive sounds of war. These only wished to return to their native soil, to enjoy a quiet residence in the land which gave them birth. Persons of this description were to be found in every state in the union, after they were permitted by treaty to return. These were objects of commiseration rather than blame. They had lost their property, their friends, and their felicity . . .

    —Mercy Otis Warren, *History of the Rise, Progress, and Termination of the American Revolution,* vol. 2

T he war was officially over. After more than two years of negotiations, the final treaty was signed in Paris in October 1783. A month later

Washington and his war-weary veterans descended from the Hudson Highlands to New York City, where they witnessed the amazing sight of the British fleet sailing off to Canada carrying with them thousands of loyalists who had been sheltering in New York, and some 3,500 freed slaves. Through the darkening days of late November, Washington's men now headed home, anxious to arrive before the onset of the winter snows. In his farewell to them, Washington had prayed to the God of Armies that they, who had secured innumerable blessings for others, might find justice here and Heaven's favor hereafter.

Three days before Christmas, their general stood before the Continental Congress to resign his commission as commander in chief. Duty done, he mounted his horse and galloped home to spend Christmas at Mount Vernon with his family. Now peace could return.

Wars end with treaties and ideally civil harmony is restored, or perhaps never was truly disrupted, after a war far from home. In the end, there is an overwhelming desire to return to ordinary life, to the business of farming and marrying, raising children, going to church on Sundays as a family. But a civil war like the American Revolution is different. It is a war without an enemy, at least at first. With family and neighbors on opposite sides of the conflict, it is far harder, if not impossible, to restore the former harmony. The American Revolution was such a painfully divisive war. It was fought in the midst of villages and farms. Families and friends had gone separate ways, men were killed or maimed, homes and entire villages were burned, terrible atrocities committed, property confiscated and sold. It was home itself that was the casualty. Love and charity and time can often mend divisions. Other times anger and losses, harsh government measures, terrible deeds, and mob violence can not be forgiven nor forgotten, nor, for many people, can the desire for revenge. And so it turned out.

The peace negotiations dragged on for two years in what had become a world war, with Holland and Spain involved on behalf of America. Britain had no allies. There were many difficult issues to settle and if, in the end, they were not settled to everyone's liking, at some point common sense had to prevail. It was time to move on.

The peace discussions began in 1781. Benjamin Franklin, longtime American diplomat in Europe, accompanied by John Adams and John Jay, spent month after tedious month in Paris on the effort. Hannah Storer's stepson Charles served as secretary to Adams, as did John Quincy Adams, his own son. Representing a new, untested country was especially tricky, maintaining its independence without yielding too much to the British or the French. At the start, the British government was still reluctant to recognize the independence of the United States, and it took another parliamentary election, with a more conciliatory membership and different prime minister, to achieve that. In 1782 Lord Shelburne, the new British prime minister, thought it a good deal to have a solid trade alliance with America without the burden of having to defend the States. Both that idea and the fear that the Americans would fall under French control convinced the British to agree to more generous terms. The French grew tired of insisting on points to their advantage. Much French treasure that France could ill afford had been expended on the war. The Treaty of Paris was signed at the Hotel d'York in Paris on September 3, 1783, and ratified by Congress on January 14, 1784.

The treaty began with two crucial articles, recognition of American independence and setting American boundaries. The Quebec Act, which gave what is now the American Midwest to Canada, was repealed. It was to be American territory. The third article gave Americans the right to fish in the rich fishing grounds of the Grand Banks and other North Atlantic areas.

The most problematic article for loyalists was Article 5, permitting loyalists, particularly those who, like the absentees, "have not borne Arms against the said United States," to return home for twelve months "unmolested" to obtain the restitution of their estates, rights, and properties. Clearly the negotiators did the best they could to cobble together this compromise, but it relied on the goodwill of all parties, those who stayed home to defend the country and their state governments, and those who fled into exile and whose property was confiscated and sold by those governments. Congress was merely to "earnestly recommend" that states restore the confiscated estates and other property that belonged to "real British subjects." This referred to those to whose loyalty America made no claim, such as former royal governors who were British and those living in districts held by the British, but who had not borne arms against America.[2] Despite the request that Congress did "earnestly recommend" states restore confiscated property or give absentees the opportunity to do it, and reconsider and revise laws regarding these properties "so as to render the said Laws or Acts perfectly consistent not only with Justice and Equity but with that Spirit of conciliation which on the Return of the Blessings of Peace should universally prevail." Individual states were basically free to comply or not with these recommendations.

Like Article 5, Article 7 was to have major repercussions for loyalists, who had sheltered in British-controlled cities and owned large numbers of enslaved people. It was Henry Laurens's one contribution to the text of the treaty. Henry Laurens, former president of the Congress, was meant to join the American negotiators in Paris but was seized by the British on his way there and clapped in the Tower of London until exchanged for Cornwallis. While in prison he learned that his son John was killed in one of the minor skirmishes that continued a year after the Battle of Yorktown, a reminder of fighting that often occurs even after a war ends. Laurens's only contribution to the treaty was to add a line preventing the British from "carrying away any Negroes or other property" when they evacuated the country. That stipulation caused agony to many enslaved people sheltering with the British and affected where many loyalists decided to live. The treaty also required a general amnesty, agreeing there were to be no further property confiscations, and any current prosecution cases were to be halted. No one seemed happy with the arrangement.

The treaty left the British with the formidable task of evacuating not only some 30,000 troops from their former colonies but 27,000 loyalist refugees as well. Sir Guy Carlton, who replaced Clinton as commander in chief in America, was charged with this unenviable task. He had extensive administrative experience in Canada and, when he first landed in New York in May 1782, was assigned to serve as a peace commissioner to persuade the Americans to remain in the empire. By August, Carlton learned, to his dismay, that the Americans had been offered independence and his task was now to arrange to evacuate loyalists and British troops and property and do so in such a way as to "revive old affections and extinguish late jealousies."[3] People and property needed to be withdrawn from New York, Charleston, Savannah, and St. Augustine in East Florida. Loyalists were to be moved to "whatever other parts of America in His Majesty's possession they choose to settle." Carlton had fewer than fifty ships to accomplish the task. He dispatched orders to Savannah that troops and loyalists with their property were to prepare to depart within a day or two, and two weeks later a similar order was sent to Charleston's troops and loyalists.[4] Some 800 loyalists in Charleston were said to be living in "miserable huts" dependent on the British army for their survival. Carlton was careful to uphold British protection for former slaves who had fled to the British for freedom and insisted that those claiming ownership of them appear before a court to plead their case. He kept his word, and thousands of former slaves left with the British fleet.

For white loyalists in the South, an important factor was where they could take their slaves. Slavery had been illegal in Britain since the 1770s, and the Canadian climate was harsh. The British government was offering free land to loyalists in Nova Scotia, however, and its governor, John Parr, had offered to provide refugees with 400,000 boards to build new houses. Many Northern loyalists and free black people were happy to take that offer, although some of the latter later left for Sierra Leone's warmer climate. Many Southerners, however, chose to go to the Caribbean, especially Port Royal, Jamaica. Others went to East Florida.[5]

Loyalist absentees were unhappy with the treaty arrangements for them. On the British side Lord North and Richard Wilbraham-Bootle, an independent MP, felt the government had abandoned the loyalists to their enemies.[6] Most loyalists certainly felt abandoned, while patriots thought the loyalists were to be treated too leniently. They feared hundreds of loyalists returning to get their property back. The banishment and confiscation acts were still in place but would be overridden. Abigail Adams wrote to

John, still in Paris, that the treaty arrangement "raised the old spirit against the Tories to such a height that it would be at the risk of their [the loyalists] lives should they venture here."[7] A cousin, Zabdiel Adams, was more charitable, pointing out that the British had "virtually acknowledged their faults" and it was the duty of the Americans to forgive them, "if not forget."[8] But the loyalists could not be forgiven. Curwen, reading newspapers from the states that summer, feared "the rising spirit of Americans against the refugees, in their towns and assemblies. . . . I find there remain but slender grounds of hope for success in attempting the recovery of debts or estates, a general shipwreck is seemingly intended of all absentees' property—the towns in their instructions to the representatives making it a point to prevent the return of them, and consequent confiscation of all their property, notwithstanding the provision of the fifth preliminary article."[9] What was to be done?[10]

Absentees now had to decide whether to take their chances and go home or remain in exile for the rest of their lives. Inflexible, intolerant state governments had made their return difficult and dangerous. It was also time for family and friends at home to decide whether they would welcome back loved ones who had fled. Exiles shared much correspondence and advice with each other and with those at home.

The fate of Thomas Hutchinson, former governor of Massachusetts, was especially tragic. He had been recalled by the Crown in 1774, having become toxic to residents for his rigidity and dutiful devotion to the British government. That government felt his undiplomatic approach brought on the Tea Party. His forty years of public service was of no consequence once his willingness to ensure American obedience to the Mother Country was exposed. He was too unpopular to be allowed to return to his beloved Massachusetts. Hutchinson's home and farm in Milton, with its view of the Blue Hills, was one of his greatest joys. His diary during his exile has been described as "a profoundly pathetic record of a man broken-hearted by his expatriation."[11] Hutchinson Street in Boston was renamed, and the town of Hutchinson in central Massachusetts changed its name rather than bear the name of "one who had acted the part of a traitor and parricide."

His sons, daughters, and their families, some twenty-five people, were dependent on him. He was relieved he could at least provide a home for them. His dearest wish though, he wrote in 1779, was "to lay my bones in my native soil." That was not to be. Writing again he admitted, "The prospect of returning to America and laying my bones in the land of my forefathers for four generations . . . is less than it has ever been." He died of a stroke not long after and was buried next to his dear daughter Peggy in the ancient church of Croydon Minster, just south of London.

Things didn't turn out as Samuel Quincy had expected when he left his wife and family for England in 1775. Unlike most exiles, he hadn't abandoned home and family because he had been attacked for his views or threatened by a mob. On the contrary, he was something of a hero in Massachusetts for prosecuting the soldiers involved in the Boston Massacre. Unlike those seeking safety, Samuel, a prominent and talented attorney, believed excellent business opportunities would come his way in Britain. He had supported Thomas Hutchinson, despite the controversial governor's loyalist views, in Massachusetts. Hutchinson may have assured Samuel of such opportunities, or at least Samuel's family and friends thought he had. But if true, when Hutchinson's own high hopes were dashed, Samuel's were as well.

No opportunities arose for Samuel. Having publicly supported Hutchinson and left for England, he was one of those specifically singled out by the Massachusetts Banishment Act of 1778. The following year, when a confiscation act to seize the property of absentees passed, his substantial estate was confiscated and sold at auction. For such a proud man the scorn and hostility toward him and these public humiliations were painful.

His letters to his family and friends track his fading hopes for business opportunities and reluctance to come home. In October 1777, before the results of the Saratoga victory were known, he wrote to his wife, "If things should not wear a more promising aspect at the opening of the next year, by all means summon resolution to cross the ocean. But if there is an appearance of accommodating this truly unnatural contest, it would be advisable for you to bear farther promise; as I mean to return to my native country whenever I may be permitted, and there is a chance for my procuring a livelihood. But I do not say that I will not accept of an opening here, if any one should offer that I may think eligible."[12] The British government had not offered absentees posts until the war was over. The expensive alternative was to keep giving the exiles pensions, and many were anxious to accept positions.

In the spring of 1778 Samuel noted the change in military circumstances and Britain's conciliatory offer to the states, which he hoped would reconcile the Americans: "I have lived to see the beginning, and thus far the progress of this cruel convulsion; my prayer is that I may live to see the end of it."[13] Near the end of his letter, Samuel confessed that while his first letters from friends congratulated him on "being out of the way," circumstances had changed: "I am indeed a poor man; but even a poor man has resources of comfort that cannot be torn from him. . . . I will therefore still endeavor to bear my calamities with firmness, and to feel for others." He sent grateful thanks to those, like his brother-in-law, Henry Hill, "who have befriended my family." "Whether it ever will be in my power to recompense them I know not, but no endeavor of mine shall be wanted to effect it."[14]

In May 1778, having been banished from Massachusetts, Samuel wrote of his disappointment that Congress was considering a resolution that an absentee could not reside in any other colony without having been first admitted as a citizen of his own.[15] He had hoped to move to the South, where he had "a very advantageous offer," but this new requirement had dashed that idea.[16] A year later Samuel wrote of his plan to establish a residence in some other part of the continent or in the West Indies and was especially interested in Antigua, where several friends and kin had settled. Antigua was unlike the Southern states, where acquiring business opportunities was uncertain, "public commotion yet continued," and he had neither property nor connections. On the other hand, "to stay longer in England absent from my friends and family, with a bare subsistence, inactive, without prospects, and useless to myself and the world, was death to me!" However, bare his subsistence, unlike many absentees, he was still living in London. Thankfully, through the influence of "some gentlemen," he obtained the post of "Comptroller of the customs at the Port of Parham in Antigua." He meant to embark for Antigua with the next convoy, aiming "to join the profits of business in the line of my profession to the emoluments of office." He muses, "I grow old too fast to think of waiting for the moving of the waters, and have therefore cast my bread upon them, thus in hopes that at last, after many days, I may find it."

As he typically did in letters home, he asked that his heartfelt wishes be sent to his father who, during his four years in exile, he had not written to once. It was his "intention to have written to him," he explained, "but the subjects on which I want to treat are too personally interesting for the casualties of the present day," adding, "he may rest assured it is my greatest unhappiness to be thus denied the pleasing task of lightening his misfortunes and soothing the evening of his days." If Samuel outlived Josiah Senior, he pledged to promote his father's posterity. Rather cold comfort for Josiah and the rest of the Braintree family, these claims of devotion.

Samuel wrote to his brother-in-law from London, pleased Henry meant to give his son a classical education. He was still upset that his books had been seized, which he found "more mortifying to me than any other stroke. If they are not yet out of your power," he asked Henry, "save them for me at all events."

By February 1782 Samuel was established in Antigua. Hannah, his long-suffering wife, had summoned the fortitude, as he put it, and perhaps forgiveness, to travel to Antigua to be with her husband. If he had suffered humiliations, so had Hannah, abandoned by her husband, losing their affluent lifestyle, and spending the war years living in Cambridge with her three children, dependent on the generosity of her brother and his family. Her pleas that Samuel return home were unavailing. He made endless excuses. She seemed unable to prevent the seizure of their property. Their long-postponed reunion finally occurred in 1782 when he was in Antigua. We do not know how warm and forgiving it was after their long separation. It was to be brief. Hannah died not long after arriving in Antigua. Some years later Samuel met and married Mary Ann Chadwell, widow of the Honorable Abraham Chadwell.

Three years afterward, responding to a plea from his son Samuel
Quincy Jr., Samuel remained as proud and unrelenting as ever. He would not
return "at the expense of my liberty; nor will I ever visit that country where
I first drew my breath, but upon such terms as I have always lived in it; and
such as I have still a right to claim from those who possess it,—the character of a gentleman." [17] He then urged his son to seek the post in the town
of Roxbury hinted at by Judge Increase Sumner and pursue a career as a
legislator and an advocate. In another letter in 1789, four years later, he
refused to return to Massachusetts until the act of 1779 against Crown
officers as traitors was repealed and some accommodation made with those
who had financial demands against him. [18] "If you ever wish your father to
repose under your roof, you will take some pains to examine the list, and
make the trial." He admitted he was not well and needed bracing air. Not
long after this letter Samuel and his wife set sail to England seeking that
bracing air in hopes it would restore his health. He died within sight of
the English coast. Samuel was buried on Bristol Hill. All three of Josiah's
sons died at sea. Samuel's widow turned back to the West Indies, heartbroken. On the voyage her ship was struck by a severe storm. She died on
the journey. Both of Samuel's sons became attorneys like their father and
left Cambridge. One moved to Lenox, a town one hundred miles away,
on the western border of Massachusetts. The second left for Romney, New
Hampshire, some hundred miles due north from Boston. Clearly, they both
felt their opportunities in life would be helped by getting far away from
the sorrows of their childhood.

Like the son of his old friend Josiah Quincy, Benjamin Franklin's son,
William, never came home. Both father and son were deeply involved
in their respective causes. Unlike Samuel, who was merely an absentee,
William Franklin was an active loyalist, royalist governor of New Jersey,
rallying loyalists in America, and after he left for England continuing from
abroad. He was handsomely compensated by the British treasury for lost
property and granted a brigadier's half-pay pension of £800 per year. [19] For
his part during the treaty negotiations, his father, Benjamin Franklin, had
been insistent that no compensation or amnesty be permitted for loyalists

who had gone into exile. There were sporadic attempts at reconciliation later. William wrote his father in 1784, receiving a letter a month later agreeing: "We will endeavor, as you propose mutually to forget what has happened relating to it, as well as we can."[20] They saw each other one last time a year later when Benjamin was in England on his return from France. The aim was to sort out remaining legal issues. Benjamin asked William to convey the land he owned in New York and New Jersey to his own son, Temple, whom Benjamin dearly loved and who had served as Benjamin's secretary, to repay a debt William owed his father. William did as asked, leaving the property to Temple in his will. In Benjamin's will he left William only some land in Nova Scotia that William already possessed, pointing out that had Britain won the war he would have had no property at all to leave.[21]

John Adams's dear friend, Jonathan Sewell, was another exile trying to decide what to do. He and his family had fled to England after a mob stormed their Cambridge home. Jonathan and John met in London years later, both convinced his friend was looking unhappy and careworn. There was ample reason Sewell looked careworn, as his funds were minimal and future uncertain. Like Samuel Quincy, Sewell had been offered a post, in his case in Canada, serving as a justice on a vice-admiralty court in Halifax, Nova Scotia. His wife, Esther Quincy, longed for home and family. Although she tried not to add to her husband's problems, it was difficult to hide.[22] He grew angry at her and became morose, worried for the future of his two sons. His appeal to the British treasury for recompence for the substantial loss of property he had suffered was upsetting in itself and took a long time to resolve. In Canada he was to continue to receive his stipend on proof of being alive and planned to go to Nova Scotia in the autumn or spring. However, the British government was considering abolishing the Halifax court on which he was supposed to sit and still owed him back pay. There were months-long delays made worse by the fact that the matter lay between the Treasury Department and the Admiralty, neither bothering to address his case. Frustrated, Sewell sent his son Jack to Canada alone. He then suffered from a deep depression. In November 1785 he shut himself in his bedroom and did not come out for eighteen months.[23] When the British bureaucracy finally addressed his case, he was nearly penniless. More months passed without any final answer. In the spring of 1787, four years after the end of the war, Sewell finally left Bristol for London with his whole family, and from there they set off to Canada. It was while he was in London that Sewell and Adams, the two old friends, met again. It was a warm reunion. Sewell recognized John Adams's "heart formed for friendship and susceptible to its finest feelings."[24] On the other hand, perhaps from envy, he felt Adams unqualified to do well in the courts of Europe, despite his other abilities, and concluded "he has none of the essential *arts* or *ornaments* which constitute a courtier." It was true Adams was no courtier. Adams, for his part, believed Sewell had become a morose and melancholy man who lived for his sons.

Sewell liked the cities of Saint John and Halifax, where the court sat. But the British government felt that the vice-admiralty court, which had never heard a case, should be closed. Still Sewell's appeals for the money owed him eventually helped restore his finances, and he was a wealthy man again, able to build a fine house in St. John. Nevertheless, he continued to brood over his ill fortune as he saw it. His friend Edward Winslow confided to Sewell's son Jack, "your worthy Father . . . is mad at a rascally World because they have not done Justice to his merit."[25] Sewell's depression set in again and took a toll on him with a steady stream of ailments. His wife Esther, whom he deeply resented, became his constant nurse, virtually imprisoned in their home to care for him. She wrote to her brother-in-law, John Hancock, that Sewell was confined to his bed. Increasingly ill and frail, he died peacefully in the fall of 1796. His old friend John Adams believed he had died of a broken heart.[26]

Some absentees did come home. One of those chancing his return was Samuel Curwen, who had so often berated the governors of Massachusetts and the fanaticism of the crowd. Yet he was assured repeatedly he would be welcomed home by many friends. And, of course, his wife had remained in Salem, unwilling to chance her fate to the ocean crossing. On his birthday in 1779 he wrote John Timmins from Exeter upset that he was not able to pursue something worthy: "Without something in pursuit, rightly or wrongly estimated worthy, life is insipid;—a connection with my fellow men, constant employment, and a much less sum would render me more pleased with the world and myself, than the supplies I receive whilst I dream the blank of life along, unknowing and unknown."[27] A list of the refugees banished from Massachusetts included only four out of the thirteen from Salem. After "a warm debate" in the Massachusetts assembly to decide whether his name should be inserted in the exclusion bill, a small majority won in his favor.[28] He was a cautious man and, rather than being comforted by this, feared being singled out by this reprieve, which "may operate disadvantageously here, being dependent on the bounty of the court." Four years later he was still weighing what to do. Writing John Timmins in Wolverhampton, from London, he noted that reading American newspapers that reached England he found "but slender grounds of hope for success in attempting the recovery of debts or estates; a general shipwreck is seemingly intended of all Absentees' property." He wrote his long-patient wife Abigail, "If it was not for your sake, or that you would follow my fortune or accompany my fate, I should not hesitate for a moment taking up my future abode . . . somewhere out of the limits of the republican government." He was thinking of Canada or some other English settlement if a final expulsion were concluded.[29]

A month later some principal merchants and citizens of Salem were encouraging him to return, "which instance of moderation" he viewed "as an honor to the town and respectful to myself," but he worried if the "popular dislike rise against me" he should be reduced to losing the British stipend" the very modest sum of £100 a year. Being further encouraged by friends in Salem to return, he decided to set out for home in the autumn.

He arrived at Long Wharf in Boston on September 25, 1784, "after an absence of nine years and five months," an absence "occasioned by a lamented civil war, excited by ambitious, selfish men here and in England, to the disgrace, dishonor, distress, and disparagement of these extensive territories."[30] What of his long-postponed arrival home? Curwen writes, "not a man, woman, or child, but expressed a satisfaction at seeing me, and welcomed me back."[31] He writes to another absentee, Captain Michael Coombs of Marblehead, still in London, to congratulate him that his wharf and warehouse remain his property and is full of praise for Coombs's wife: "Nor do I think one to be met with who has better acquitted herself in the late trying times. By her resolution she has preserved the household furniture from confiscation and waste, and your account-books from inspection, though menaced and flattered by the state agents." Curwen found his own affairs "deranged" and thought it unlikely his house could be saved. It was. Still, he claimed in a letter to Sewell in Bristol in November that he was completely ruined and planned to retreat to Nova Scotia. He ended his letter to Captain Coombs, "The triumphant here look down with contempt on the vanquished; their little minds are not equal to the astonishing success of their feeble arms. God bless the worthy and blast the villainous of every party."

The plans for Nova Scotia, perhaps considered in a time of panic, were never needed. Curwen remained in Salem. Replying to a former Harvard classmate in 1795, ten years after his return, he ends on the happy note that those like both of them, having been frequently confined by illness, "are continued to a comparatively long life, and rendered capable of more enjoyment than in the days of youth and middle age, of which number I profess myself to be one."[32] Samuel Curwen died at his home in Salem in April of 1802.

There were other exiles who returned home after the war, despite banishment and confiscation acts. Isaac Smith, son of prosperous Boston merchant Isaac Smith and his wife, Elizabeth Storer Smith (also aunt and uncle of Abigail Adams), was a confirmed loyalist. He completed two degrees at Harvard and was appointed a tutor there. On the crucial day of April 19, 1775, when Lord Percy marched through Cambridge to reinforce the British troops at Lexington and Concord, Isaac showed the officer which road to take to Lexington. For this he was scorned by the local people, and in May sailed to England with other loyalists. He spent several years abroad. In 1778 he was ordained a pastor of a dissenting church in Devonshire. He returned to America in the spring of 1784 and was promptly appointed by Harvard as a librarian and hired to give classes in Latin. Smith was later elected preceptor of Dummer Academy, in the village of Byfield, where one student described him as "a man of singular purity, gentleness, and piety." In 1809 he moved to Boston, where he was appointed chaplain of the Boston almshouse. His loyalist past did not seem to have harmed his career.

While individual loyalists went home to a warm welcome, or at least a quiet return, far more remained in exile permanently. Some 30,000 loyalists from New York and Savannah left America for Nova Scotia and New Brunswick. The villages and towns in Eastern Canada still bear the names and resting places of these American emigrants who chose to live under the British monarchy or had little other option. James H. Stark, author of *Loyalists of Massachusetts*, notes that Massachusetts had banished many members of its old historic families: Hutchinson, Quincy, Winthrop, Saltonstall, the Sewells and Winslows. For most of them Canada was to be their home. The rules for return to Massachusetts, New York, and other states had made it especially difficult to use Article 5 to come back home. And unless loyalists could be accepted in their home states, they could not move to another state. A new home in the British Empire was the answer, and loyalists were offered free land in British North America. On the other hand, historians have estimated that between 15 and 20 percent of the white population of the colonies were discretely loyal to the Crown. And while most active loyalists left, a large majority of loyalists preferred to remain in the United States as citizens. [33]

Those back home in Massachusetts who survived the pain and uncertainty of the war reestablished their normal or "new normal" routines and lived to see great transitions. There were some happy reunions and empty seats at the family table that would never be filled, and families permanently divided. But it was a relief to get back to ordinary life knowing the war was over.

The Braintree town meeting members continued to meet regularly to discuss the town business and, in these final years of the war and beginning of peace, were busy with the imposition of taxes and payments for men who

had answered the call to join the Continental Army. In 1783, at the close of
the war, the town meeting returned to concerns about repairing the roads,
tax collection, and now what many deemed lax religious practice on the
Sabbath, since the state legislature moved to tolerate "secular concerns or
Servile Labour to be carried on six hours of the same to the great distur-
bance of every sober and Consciencious Person in this State." The Braintree
meeting approved a report expressing dismay at this new laxity, as they saw
it, "when we are just emerging from the horrors of a most barbarous and
unparraled war curtail a part of the fourth Commandment" [34]

With the war's end residents found neighbor John Adams, a country
lawyer from Braintree, had become a prominent Massachusetts statesman
and a national leader. Adams sat in the Congress before and during the
war, helped draft the Declaration of Independence, and traveled to Europe
to help Franklin and John Jay negotiate the peace treaty. When the Massachusetts legislature drafted a constitution for the state in 1778, the cities and
towns of the commonwealth voted it down. John Adams drafted another
constitution, and in 1780 it was approved. It opened with the declaration
that all men are born free and equal. This statement was eventually used
in the highest Massachusetts court to outlaw slavery in the state. For Abigail and the Adams family, however proud they were of John Adams, his
absence from home for years at a time left Abigail to manage the family
farm and raise their children on her own, although sons John Quincy and
Charles did accompany their father when he was a diplomat in Europe.
When Washington was elected the nation's first president, Adams would
serve as his vice president for two terms and was then elected president in
his own right. He and Abigail were the first presidential couple to live
in the executive mansion in Washington, a long way from Braintree.

Hannah Quincy Storer's brother-in-law, Benjamin Lincoln, also rose to
national prominence, serving with distinction in the Continental Army and
becoming a brigadier general. He was one of the few men to be present at
the three major surrenders of the war, Saratoga, Charleston—where he surrendered his army—and Yorktown, where he had the honor of the British
surrendering to him. While he was at Yorktown, Congress appointed

him the first secretary of war. Lincoln remained in that position for three years. His administrative duties suited his talents better than battlefield command. He couldn't have been more different than his older brother Bela, who was Hannah's late and vicious husband. Benjamin Lincoln wasn't the shrewdest officer, but he was congenial, popular, and pleasant. He left the position of secretary of war at the end of the war in 1783 and returned home to Hingham, to his farm, wife, and many children. In the election that year for governor of Massachusetts, Braintree favored Lincoln by a wide margin over John Hancock.[35] Always somewhat stout, over the years Lincoln grew heavy, still limping, with one leg shorter than the other, from his injury at Saratoga. While he did not win the election for governor, he was chosen for other public responsibilities. In 1789 he was made collector of the Port of Boston, no longer the dangerous job it had been before the war. He held the post for nearly twenty years. He was also appointed a commissioner to negotiate with the Creek Indians, and in 1793 a commissioner to make peace with the western Indigenous groups. Benjamin Lincoln lived a long, fulfilling, and worthy life, living to see the ratification of the federal constitution and Bill of Rights, and dying in 1810 at the age of seventy-nine.

Josiah Quincy Senior lived to see the signing of the peace treaty and victory for American independence. He was renowned for being fond of hunting and fishing. One cold wintery day he sat on a cake of ice watching for wild ducks. The exposure was too much for him, and he died after a short illness on March 3, 1784, at the age of seventy-five.[36] Having outlived his three sons, he left all his property to his twelve-year-old grandson, Josiah III, Josiah Junior's only surviving child. The estate included several hundred acres and his house. Josiah III would justify his grandfather's faith in him with a distinguished career. He would write a memoir of the life of the father he never knew. In time he would become the president of Harvard University, a member of Congress, and mayor of Boston. Sadly, Josiah Senior left nothing to Samuel's two sons, orphans in 1784, although they had lived in Cambridge throughout the war and been raised by their mother, Hannah, and their uncle, both staunch patriots.[37] Both young men would move miles from Eastern Massachusetts to start their careers.

Hannah Quincy Lincoln Storer lived as happily ever after as anyone could, married to Ebenezer Storer, a talented and good man. He was involved in many charitable and learned organizations. He was a founder of the American Academy for Arts and Sciences, he was a charter member of the Society for Propagating the Gospel among the Indians of North America, and he served as warden and selectman of Boston, Overseer of the Poor, member of the Society for Encouraging Trade and Commerce, and other worthy groups. She could not have asked for a better husband or a finer family. In short, he was as kind and worthy a man as her late husband, Bela Lincoln, had been a mean and ungrateful one. After thirty happy years with Hannah, Ebenezer died in 1807.

Hannah would live nearly twenty years longer. She lived a long and amazing life, full of joy, pain, loss, and ultimately happiness. She lived to see John Adams, the husband of her dear friend Abigail, become president of the United States, and to see their son, John Quincy Adams, follow in his father's footsteps to the presidency. What a proud legacy. Hannah died in 1826 at the grand age of ninety.

So the generation that experienced that war without an enemy passed away. Those patriots living at home left to succeeding generations of Americans a new land with new freedoms and new challenges, and the memory of the divisions that tore apart families gradually faded but would remain embedded in the story of the founding of the country. Thousands of loyalists who never returned went to Canada or elsewhere in the British Empire to begin the process of creating a new home in a new country.

Acknowlegments

A work of many years, as this has been, depends on the help, friendship, and encouragement of a great many people. It is a real pleasure to thank those who enabled me to bring this book to completion.
First, thanks are especially due to my literary agent, Katherine Flynn of
Kneerim and Williams, who was excited about the topic of divided family
loyalties during the American Revolution and helped me develop the idea.
Jessica Case of Pegasus Books has been enthusiastic and patient, an expert
at transforming manuscripts into handsome books. She is always a pleasure to work with and always ready to help. The comments and questions
of friends and colleagues provided more encouragement and inspiration
than they ever realized. Among my colleagues at Scalia Law School,
George Mason University, I would like to thank Frank Buckley for his
probing questions and suggestions, Robert Cottrol, Josh Blackman, Bob
Dowlut, Helen Alvare, Eric Claeys, Nelson Lund, and Jeremy Rabkin
for their friendship and interest and Robby George and the fellows of
the Princeton James Madison program. Special thanks go to Scalia Law
School for research funds and to Deborah Keene, head librarian, and her
staff for searching for and finding often obscure sources.

Every historian stands on the shoulders of others and, in my case, particularly given the constraints of the Covid lockdowns, I especially valued
the key collections of letters, town records, and diaries in print and others

now online, among the former the Adams family correspondence, Samuel Curwen's journal and letters, Josiah Quincy's memoirs of his father's life, Thomas Hutchinson's history of Massachusetts Bay, the records of the Braintree town meetings, and the transcript of the Boston massacre trials. There are excellent modern books that probe the lives of loyalists by Maya Jansonoff, Mary Beth Norton, and Holger Hoock as well as those of patriots Samuel Adams, Joseph Warren, Benjamin Franklin and son William, and Nina Sakovitch's work on patriot families in the years leading up to the revolution. My footnotes make clear all those to whom I am indebted.

Finally, my friends and family are to be thanked for inquiring politely over the years about what I was working on and how the work was going, and then listening to far more than they had anticipated. Those related to, and living with an historian, are to be commended for their fortitude. My greatest debt is to my children, Mark, Arienne, and George and daughters-in-law Mary Liz and Katharine, my sister Ellen, and above all my dear husband, Michael, my best friend and constant companion and supporter. Puppy Darby helped in his own way by getting me outdoors to remind myself that there was a world to enjoy and explore. How fortunate I am to have been surrounded by their love and support.

Notes

Preface

1   John Adams to Abigail Adams, April 26, 1777, L. H. Butterfield, ed., *The Adams Papers*, series 2, *Adams Family Correspondence*, vol. 2 (Cambridge, Mass.: Harvard University Press, 1963), 224.

Introduction

1   Mary Beth Norton, *The British-Americans: The Loyalist Exiles in England, 1774–1789* (Boston: Little, Brown, 1972), 96.

2   George Atkinson Ward, *Journal and Letters of Samuel Curwen* (New York, 1842), 4.

3   Samuel Curwen to Judge Sewell, London, from Exeter, January 19, 1777, ibid., 96.

4   Samuel Eliot Morison, *The Oxford History of the American People: Prehistory*, vol. 1 (New York: Oxford University Press, 1972), 289.

One: Over the Sea: The Family Divided

1   *Adams Family Correspondence*, series 2, *The Adams Papers*, ed. L. H. Butterfield (Cambridge, Mass.: Harvard University Press, 1963), 190.

2   Nina Sankovitch, *American Rebels: How the Hancock, Adams, and Quincy Families Fanned the Flames of Revolution* (New York: St. Martin's Press, 2020), 215.

3   Ibid., 267.

4   Ibid., 273.

Two: Beginnings

1   Charter, Massachusetts Bay Colony, 1629, giving the Massachusetts Bay
           Company the right to govern the colony. Charles I would come to grief in the
           war against his Parliament over his expansion of royal prerogative and was
           executed in 1649.

2   The King's Privy Council had the right to veto any colonial laws it judged
           "repugnant to the laws of England."

3   "To the Kings most Excellent Majesty, The humble supplication of the
           Generall Court of the Massachusetts Colony in New England," Jack P.
           Greene, ed., *Great Britain and the American Colonies, 1606–1763* (Columbia:
           University of South Carolina Press, 1970), 64.

4   Greene, *Great Britain and the American Colonies,* 65.

5   Leonard Levy, *Origins of the Bill of Rights* (New Haven, Conn.: Yale
           University Press, 1999), 57–58. James II had made this change, which brought
           the New England and mid-Atlantic colonies under strict royal control. When
           James was deposed in the Glorious Revolution of 1688–89 and William and
           Mary became king and queen, the hated Dominion was abolished, and new
           charters issued for the colonies again guaranteeing them their rights.

6   Ibid., 58.

7   Ibid.

8   Ibid., 59. The Privy Council vetoed these acts, but beginning in 1710, under
           Queen Anne, the writ began to be extended to the colonies.

9   William S. Pattee, *A History of Old Braintree and Quincy,* (Quincy, 1878;
           facsimile, Legare Street Press, 2022), 612.

10   See Samuel Austin Bates, ed., *Records of the Town of Braintree, 1640–1793*
           (Randolph, Mass.: 1886), 371.

11   Ibid., 1ff.

12   Eliza Susan Quincy, "Josiah Quincy, Senior," *The Pennsylvania Magazine
           of History and Biography,* April 1, 1879, 183. The Massachusetts assembly
           paid for a tribute to be inscribed on a monument over his grave and gave
           his heirs one thousand acres of land in the new town of Lenox, in Western
           Massachusetts.

13   Ibid., 182.

14   Ibid., 183.

15   For the account of the *Bethel* see ibid.

16   Ibid., 184.

17   See Bates, *Records of the Town of Braintree,* 472–82.

18   Ibid., for example 250, 259, 327, 329, 332, 333, 334, 336, 362, 377, 381.

19   Quincy, "Josiah Quincy, Senior," 185.

20   For this account see Joyce Lee Malcolm, *The Tragedy of Benedict Arnold* (New
           York: Pegasus, 2018), 32–40.

Three: Fathers and Children

1   Josiah Quincy, *Memoir of the Life of Josiah Quincy, Jun. of Massachusetts: By His Son* (Boston: Cummings & Hilliard Co., 1825), 7.

2   Ibid., 5.

3   Pattee, *A History of Old Braintree and Quincy*, 589.

4   Sankovitch, *American Rebels*, 42.

5   Ibid., 43.

6   "Letter to Richard Cranch about Orlinda, October–December 1758, https://founders.archives.gov/documents/Adams/02-01-02-0010-0001-0003.

7   J. L. Bell, "Dr. Lincoln and His Lady," Boston 1775, October 23, 2020, https://boston1775.blogspot.com/2020/10/dr-lincoln-and-his-lady.html.

8   See L. H. Butterfield, ed., *The Adams Papers, Diary and Autobiography of John Adams,* vol. 1 (Cambridge, Mass.: Belknap Press, 1961), 176–177.

9   See John Adams cited in "Oxenbridge Thacher: Unsung Revolutionary," Revolutionary War and Beyond, https://www.revolutionary-war-and-beyond.com/oxenbridge-thacher.html.

Four: Men of Moderation

1   See Stanley Edward Ayling, *George III* (New York: Knopf, 1972), 54; John Brooke, *King George III* (London: Constable Books, 1972), 49; Christopher Hibbert, *George III: A Personal History* (New York: Basic Books, 1999), 31.

2   It took a letter at least three months, sent from London to New York, to receive an answer. It has been claimed that until 1760 the colonists possessed greater political freedom than perhaps any other people on Earth, and assuredly far more than Spanish or French subjects.

3   An American taxpayer paid a maximum of sixpence a year, an English taxpayer an average of fifty times as much. See John Cannon and Ralph Griffiths, *The Oxford Illustrated History of the British Monarchy* (Oxford, UK: Oxford University Press, 1998), 505.

4   For the list of taxes imposed on British subjects see www.parliament.uk.

5   Albert W. Alschuler and Andrew G. Deiss, "A Brief History of the Criminal Jury in the United States," *University of Chicago Law Review*, vol. 61, no. 1, 867, 874.

6   See Joseph H. Smith, "An Independent Judiciary: The Colonial Background," *University of Pennsylvania Law Review*, vol. 124 (1976), 1104.

Five: The Quincys and the First Trials

1   L. H. Butterfield, ed., *The Adams Papers*, vol. 1 (January 16, 1770), 349.

2   Mark Plus, *Samuel Adams: Father of the American Revolution* (New York: St. Martin's Press, 2006), 35.

3   *Quincy's Massachusetts Bay Reports, 1761–1777* (Boston, 1865), 557, n. 4
       cited in Akhil Reed Amar, "Fourth Amendment First Principles," *Harvard
       Law Review*, vol. 107 (1994), 757, 777. And see Governor William Shirley
       cited in Stephen Botein, *Early American Law and Society* (New York: Knopf,
       1983), 57.

4   Levy, *Origins of the Bill of Rights*, 151.

5   For information on Oxenbridge Thatcher see Clifford Putney, "Oxenbridge
       Thacher: Boston Lawyer, Early Patriot," *Historical Journal of Massachusetts*,
       vol. 32, no. 1 (Winter 2004).

6   *Dr. Bonham's Case, 8 Coke's Reports*, 114, Court of Common Pleas, 1610.

7   Coke wrote in *Dr. Bonham's Case*, "in many cases the common law will
       controul Acts of Parliament, and sometimes adjudge them to be utterly
       void: for when an Act of Parliament is against common right and reason, or
       repugnant, or impossible to be performed, the common law will controul it,
       and adjudge such Act to be void."

8   See transcript http://www.bartleby.com/268/8/9.html. By the 18th century
       the original articles in the Magna Carta had been stretched and interpreted to
       embrace an expanded list of individual rights, no less passionately held for all
       that.

9   See Otis's essay, "The Rights of the British Colonists Asserted and Proved."

10   See 30 Geo. II, c. 25(1757), 2 Gen. III, c. 20 (1761), 4. Geo. III, c. 17 (1763).
       The quotation is from the act of 1761.

11   Bates, *Records of the Town of Braintree*, 378.

12   Ibid.

13   Samuel A. Forman, *Dr. Joseph Warren: The Boston Tea Party, Bunker Hill, and
       the Birth of American Liberty*, (Gretna, La.: Pelican, 2012), 99.

14   See George H. Nash III, "From Radicalism to Revolution: The Political
       Career of Josiah Quincy, Jr.," *Proceedings of the American Antiquarian Society*
       (1969), 254.

15   James Otis, "Of the Political and Civil Rights of the British Colonists,"
       (Boston, 1764). Subsequent quotations are from this source as well.

Six: The Stamp Act and the Sons of Liberty

1   In 1768 Pitt fell prey to episodes of mental illness and resigned his post.

2   Edmund Morgan, *The Birth of the Republic, 1763–89* (Chicago: University of
       Chicago Press, 1956) 19.

3   Carol Berkin, *Jonathan Sewall: Odyssey of an American Loyalist* (New York:
       Columbia University Press, 1974), 35–36.

4   Theodore Draper, *A Struggle for Power: The American Revolution* (New York:
       Vintage, 1996), 219.

5   The Virginia Resolves, see Journal, Virginia House of Burgesses, cited in
Robert Middlekauf, *The Glorious Cause: The American Revolution, 1763–1789*
(New York: Oxford University Press, 2007), 83.

6   See Mark Puls, *Samuel Adams: Father of the American Revolution* (New York:
St. Martin's Press, 2006), 51–53.

7   Ibid., 52, n. 18.

8   See James H. Stark, *The Loyalists of Massachusetts: And the Other Side of the
American Revolution* (Boston: W.B. Clarke, 1910), 40.

9   Mercy Otis Warren, *History of the Rise, Progress and Termination of the
American Revolution*, 2 vols., ed. Lester H. Cohen (Boston: Manning &
Loring, 1805; facsimile, Indianapolis, 1994), vol. 1, 19.

10   Stark, *Loyalists*, 41–42.

11   Puls, *Samuel Adams*, 53.

12   Ibid.

13   George Nash III, "From Radicalism to Revolution." 255.

14   Puls, *Samuel Adams*, 53.

15   Nash, "From Radicalism to Revolution." 255, 257.

16   Gary B. Nash, *The Unknown American Revolution: The Unruly Birth of
Democracy and the Struggle to Create America* (New York: Penguin, 2006), 53.

17   Bates, *Records of the Town of Braintree*, 404.

Seven: Personal and Public Trials 1768 and 1769

1   Sankovitch writes that Edmund died in a shipwreck off Bermuda but
provides no source. All contemporary sources point to a death at sea in
the West Indies. The list of Bermuda shipwrecks does not include any
in 1768. Sankovitch, *American Rebels*, 100. She also claims he was ill
with consumption, i.e., tuberculosis, rather than pulmonary disease. But
tuberculosis is highly contagious, unlike pulmonary disease.

2   Samuel Quincy, "A Monody," (Boston, 1768). The Library of Congress has
several copies of this work.

3   Hyperion was one of the most powerful Titans in Greek mythology.

4   See Puls, *Samuel Adams*, 68.

5   Acts passed by Parliament in 1703, 1705, 1740, and 1779 authorized
impressment.

6   For this account I have depended upon *The Legal Papers of John Adams*, vol. 2,
eds. Kinvin Wroth and Hiller B. Zobel (Cambridge, Mass.: Belknap Press,
1965), Rex v. Corbet.

7   An act of Henry VIII (28 Hen. 8, c. 15, 1536), specified a jury trial before a
special admiralty court in England. Act of William III (11 & 12 Will. 3, c.7,
1700) ordered that trials in the colonies ought to be without a jury. An Act of

George I (4 Geo. 1, c. 11, 1717) reversed this and restored the right to a jury trial.

8   John Adams to Jedidiah Morse, January 20, 1816, 10 John Adams, *Works* 204, 209–210.

9   Ibid. Adams wrote "Panton and Corbet ought not to have been forgotten. Preston and his soldiers ought to have been forgotten sooner."

Eight: The Soldiers' Trial: Brother Against Brother

1   Cited in Samuel A. Forman, *Dr. Joseph Warren* (Pelican, 1952), 157.

2   William Blackstone, *Commentaries on the Laws of England*, 4 vols. (London, 1765–1769), vol. 1, 395.

3   Ibid., 1:395, 400.

4   Douglas O. Linder, "Famous Trials: The Boston Massacre Trials: An Account," https://www.famous-trials.com/massacre.

5   Frederic Kidder, *History of the Boston Massacre, March 5, 1770* (Albany, N.Y., 1870), 4–5.

6   There are claims that the sentry had been rude to an apprentice who claimed an officer had not paid his master for dressing his hair. It is unclear whether this is true or not or whether the apprentice later committed perjury.

7   Ibid., 85.

8   Linder, "Boston Massacre."

9   Ibid., 82–83.

10   Ibid., 83.

11   Ibid., 84.

12   Ibid., 86.

13   Clifford Olsen, "250th Anniversary of the Boston Massacre from the Viewpoint of the Colonies," *Sons of the American Revolution Magazine*, vol. 114, no. 3 (Winter 2019–2020), 16–17.

14   Quincy, *Memoir of the Life of Josiah Quincy*, 30–31.

15   Ibid., 33.

16   David McCullough, *John Adams* (New York: Simon & Schuster, 2001), 66.

17   Ibid., 34–35.

18   Josiah Quincy to Josiah Quincy, Jun., Boston, Braintree, March 22, 1770, 34–35.

19   Josiah Quincy to Josiah Quincy, Jun., Braintree, Boston, March 26, 1770, 36–37.

20   Ibid. Capitalization as in the original.

21   J. W. Fortescue, *A History of the British Army*, vol. 3, 39.

22   It is not known whether there were any notes taken of Captain Preston's trial, but a shorthand writer was employed to take notes of the trial of the soldiers, which were subsequently published. The information above is therefore from the trial of the soldiers. See Quincy, *Memoir*, 38.

23   Linder, "Boston Massacre."

24   Ibid.

25   The following account is from the trial of the soldiers. See Kidder, *History of the Boston Massacre*, 122 ff.

26   Ibid., 127.

27   Ibid., 127–128.

28   Quincy, *Memoir*, 39.

29   Ibid., 42.

30   Ibid., 43.

31   Ibid., 44–45.

32   Ibid., 48.

33   Linder, "Boston Massacre," deposition of Preston, https://www.famous-trials .com/massacre/210-evidence.

34   Ibid.

35   "Minutes of Robert Treat Paine's argument," by unidentified note-taker, October 29, 1770, Boston Massacre, Massachusetts Historical Society Collections Online.

36   *The Boston Gazette and Country Journal*, no. 813, (November 5, 1770), 2.

37   Quincy, *Memoir*, 50–51.

38   Ibid., 44.

39   Ibid., 63–64.

40   Samuel's Quincy's Argument for the Crown: November 29, 1770, Founders Online.

41   Letter Samuel Quincy to Robert Treat Paine, December 16, 1770, Boston Massacre, Massachusetts Historical Society Collections online, https ://www.masshist.org/database/2729?ft=Boston%20Massacre&from=/features /massacre/trials&noalt=1&pid=34.

Nine: Battling the Doldrums

1   Berkin, *Jonathan Sewall*, 83–84.

2   L. H. Butterfield, ed., *The Adams Papers*, series 2, *Adams Family Correspondence*, vol. 1, 75; Forman, *Dr. Joseph Warren*, 159.

3   Puls, *Samuel Adams*, 113.

4   Ibid.

5   Ibid.

6   Sankovitch, *American Rebels*, 67, 152, 175.

7   Ibid., 68.

8   Quincy, *Memoir of the Life of Josiah Quincy*, 66–67.

9   Ibid., 67.

10   Ibid., 70–71.

11   Ibid., 72; Forman, *Warren*, 99–100.

12   Forman, *Warren*, 99–100.

13   Quincy, *Memoir*, 74. *Memoir* contains much of Josiah's travel journal, and the
        following details are taken from it.

14   Ibid., 74–75.

15   Ibid., 91–94.

16   Ibid., 95.

17   Ibid., 102.

18   Ibid., 114.

19   Ibid., 114–115.

20   Ibid., 120, 121.

21   Ibid., 124.

22   Ibid., 128.

23   Ibid., 125.

24   Ibid., 126–127.

25   Ibid., 129–130.

26   Ibid., 134–135.

27   Ibid., 138.

28   Ibid., 41.

29   Ibid., 145–147.

Ten: No Tempest in a Teapot

1   See Forman, *Dr. Joseph Warren*, 167.

2   Samuel Austin Bates, ed., *Records of the Town of Braintree, 1640–1793*
        (Braintree, Mass., 1886), 439–440.

3   Joyce Lee Malcolm, *Peter's War: A New England Slave Boy and the American
        Revolution* (New Haven, Conn.: Yale University Press, 2009), 35.

4   Ibid., 36.

5   Ibid.

6   The damage to Hutchinson's house has been estimated to have been nearly
        $400,000 in today's money.

7   The Declaratory Act passed in 1766, just after Parliament repealed the Stamp
        Act, asserted that Parliament had the right to make laws for the colonies in all
        cases whatsoever.

8   Who sent the private letters to Franklin remains a mystery more than 200
        years later, however Samuel Adams's biographer, Mark Puls, claims they came
        from Thomas Whatley, a treasury official. See Puls, *Samuel Adams*, 133.

9   Edmund Morgan, *Benjamin Franklin* (New Haven, Conn.: Yale University
        Press, 2003), 187.

10   Esmond Wright, *Franklin of Philadelphia* (Cambridge, Mass.: Belknap Press,
        1988), 225.

11   B. Franklin to the *London Chronicle*, printed in the *Chronicle*, December 23–25, 1773.

12   Thomas Hutchinson, October 4, 1768, Copy of Letters, Boston, 1773.

13   Hutchinson, January 20, 1769, Copy of Letters, Boston. Italics not in the original.

14   Bernard Bailyn, *The Ordeal of Thomas Hutchinson* (Cambridge, Mass.: Belknap Press, 1974), 228.

15   James Stark, *The Loyalists of Massachusetts* (Boston, Mass.: W.B. Clarke, 1910), 164–165.

16   George R. T. Hewes, "A Retrospect of the Boston Tea-party," 1834. Hewes was the last survivor of the tea party.

17   L. H. Butterfield, ed., *The Adams Papers, Diary and Autobiography of John Adams* (Cambridge, Mass.: Belknap Press, 1961) vol. 2 (December 18, 1773), 4. Adams Papers, MHS; *Boston Gazette*, December 27, 1773, MHS.

18   Ibid.

19   Josiah Quincy Jr., writing as "Marchmont Nedham," December 20, 1773.

20   *Quincy's Massachusetts Bay Reports, 1761–1777* (Boston, 1865), 557 n. 4; see Governor William Shirley cited in Botein, *Early American Law and Society*, 57; Alschuler and Deiss, "A Brief History of the Criminal Jury in the United States," 867, 874.

21   Joseph H. Smith, "An Independent Judiciary: The Colonial Background," *University of Pennsylvania Law Review*, vol. 124 (1976), 1104.

22   The Revenue Act, June 29, 1767.

23   Stark, *The Loyalists of Massachusetts*, 188.

24   John Adams, diary entry, March 4, 1773, and March 2, 1774, *Autobiography of John Adams*, Founders Online.

25   Ibid.

26   Ibid., 188–189.

27   It was John Adams's idea to bring articles of impeachment against the judges, and he schooled the Sons of Liberty and others in the procedure as used in the English Parliament. See John Adams, diary entry, March 4, 1773, and March 2, 1774, *Autobiography*, Founders Online.

Eleven: Divisions Hit Home

1   Puls, *Samuel Adams*, 147.

2   Bates, *Records of the Town of Braintree*, 442.

3   Ibid., 446.

4   Ibid., 447.

5   Puls, *Samuel Adams*, 152.

6   Josiah Quincy Junior, "Observations on the Act of Parliament commonly
        called the Boston Port-Bill; with Thoughts on Civil Society and Standing
        Armies," May 14, 1774, 225–226.

7   Samuel Quincy to Josiah Quincy Jr., Boston, June 1, 1774; Josiah Quincy,
        Memoir of Life of Josiah Quincy (Boston, 1825), 161–162.

8   Many American families can sympathize with this approach to maintaining
        family harmony.

9   L. H. Butterfield, ed. *The Adams Papers*, series 2, *Adams Family Correspondence*,
        vol. 1 (Cambridge, Mass.: Harvard University Press, 1963), 152.

10   See "A speech intended to have been spoken on the bill for altering the charter
        of the colony of Massachusetts-Bay," by the Rev. Jonathan Shipley, Lord
        Bishop of St. Asaph. See Evans Early American Imprint Collection.

11   The Administration of Justice Act, May 20, 1774.

12   Puls, *Samuel Adams*, 166.

13   John Alden, *General Gage in America* (Westport, Conn.: Greenwood Press,
        1948), 15.

14   Andrew Jackson O'Shaughnessy, *The Men Who Lost America* (New Haven,
        Conn.: Yale University Press, 2013), 22.

15   Stark, *Loyalists of Massachusetts*, 125–126.

16   Ibid., 168–169.

17   Ibid., 169–170.

18   Puls, *Samuel Adams*, 157.

19   Ibid., 161.

20   Richard Ketchum, *Decisive Day: The Battle of Bunker Hill*. (New York:
        Doubleday, 1974) 18.

21   Forman, *Dr. Joseph Warren*, 209.

22   Quincy, *Memoir of the Life of Josiah Quincy*, 176–177.

23   Bob Rupert, "Josiah Quincy, Jr.," *Journal of the American Revolution* (June 4,
        2019), 6–7.

24   Quincy, *Memoirs of Josiah Quincy*, 182–183.

25   Ibid., 183.

Twelve: Partings: Two Ocean Voyages and a Death

1   Abigail Adams to Mercy Otis Warren, L. H. Butterfield, ed., *The Adams
        Papers*: *Adams Family Correspondence*, series 2, vol. 1, 183.

2   O'Shaughnessy, *The Men Who Lost America*, 23.

3   Ibid.

4   Ibid., 24.

5   John Adams to Abigail, July 1774; George H. Nash III, "From Radicalism
        to Revolution: The Political Career of Josiah Quincy, Jr.," Proceedings of the
        American Antiquarian Society (1969), 253–254.

6   John Adams to Josiah Quincy, Jun, September 18, 1774, Philadelphia;
         Quincy, *Memoir of the Life of Josiah Quincy*, 179.

7   Nash writes of Josiah's negotiations in England, "he wavered at times almost
         daily, between independence and reconciliation, between war and 'peaceful'
         coercion." Nash, "From Radicalism to Revolution," 254.

8   Ibid., 264, 266.

9   Ibid., 267.

10   Ibid., 269.

11   Ibid., 271–272.

12   Ibid., 272.

13   Ibid.

14   Ibid., 274.

15   Ibid., 281.

16   Quincy, *Memoirs*, 317.

17   Ibid., 337 ff.

18   Nash, "From Radicalism to Revolution," 281–282.

19   There is some confusion in the sources whether he set sail on March 4 or
         March 16. Whichever date is accurate, he was at sea for more than five
         weeks.

20   Quincy, *Josiah Quincy*, at sea, April 21, 1775, *Memoir*, 346–347.

21   Nash, "From Radicalism to Revolution," 284.

22   Stark, *The Loyalists of Massachusetts*, 455.

23   Berkin, *Jonathan Sewall*, 142.

24   Ibid., 143.

25   Holger Hoock, *Scars of Independence* (New York: Crown, 2017), 31.

26   O'Shaughnessy, *The Men Who Lost America*, 84.

27   Ibid.

28   Malcolm, *Peter's War*, 46.

29   Ibid.

30   For a detailed account of the Battle of Lexington and Concord see Malcolm,
         Peter's War, 59–73.

31   See Pauline Maier, *American Scripture: Making the Declaration of Independence*
         (New York: Knopf, 1997), 3.

32   Circular letter to Massachusetts towns from the Committee of Safety,
         Massachusetts Provincial Congress, April 20, 1775.

33   Josiah Quincy to Thomas Bromfield Esq., London, March 16, 1775; Quincy,
         Memoir, 343.

34   Ibid., 345.

35   Ibid., 347–348.

36   Sankovitch, *American Rebels*, 273.

37   Quincy, *Memoirs*, 353.

Thirteen: Parting Ways

1   Abigail Adams to Mercy Otis Warren, L. H. Butterfield, ed., *The Adams Papers*, series 2, *Adams Family Correspondence*, vol. 1, 190.

2   John Adams to Abigail Adams, Hartford, May 2, 1775, ibid., 191.

3   Abigail Adams to John Adams, May 24, Braintree, 1775, ibid., 204. The doctor was her uncle, Dr. Cotton Tufts. Bridgewater was about seventeen miles from Weymouth.

4   Ibid., 205.

5   Berkin, *Jonathan Sewall*, 107.

6   Ibid., 108.

7   Ibid.

8   Sankovitch, *American Rebels*, 153.

9   Samuel Quincy to Josiah Quincy, Jr., Boston, June 1, 1774, Quincy, *Memoir of Life of Josiah Quincy*, 161–162.

10   Ibid., 109.

11   Sankovitch, *American Rebels*, 200.

12   Ibid.

13   Ibid., 202.

14   Ibid., 202, 206. Samuel's letter to Josiah, Jr. was dated June 1, 1774.

15   The letters from Josiah Senior and Hannah are dated May 11, 1775.

16   Hannah Quincy Lincoln to Samuel Quincy, Braintree, May 11, 1775, Ward, *Journal and Letters of Samuel Curwen*, 562–564.

17   Samuel Quincy to Henry Hill, Esq., Boston, May 13, 1775, ibid., 564. When their father left, Hannah was thirteen, Samuel Junior eleven, and Thomas nine.

18   Sankovitch, *American Rebels*, 282.

19   For a detailed description of the battle see Malcolm, *Peter's War*, 84–86.

20   Samuel Quincy, London, July 25, 1775, *Journal and Letters of Samuel Curwen*, 565. Lord North was prime minister, Dartmouth, secretary of state for the colonies.

21   Samuel Quincy to Henry Hill, August 18, 1775, ibid., 565–566. Emphasis added.

22   Samuel Quincy to Hannah Hill Quincy, September 5, 1775; Sankovitch, *American Rebels*, 313.

23   John Adams to Abigail Adams, April 14, 1776, ibid., 323.

24   Abigail Adams to John Adams, March 31, 1776, ibid., 322–323.

25   Edmund Quincy to Dolly Quincy Lincoln, August 4, 1775, ibid., 294.

26   Caesar Rodney to Thomas Rodney, Philadelphia, May 11, 1775, Edmund Cody Burnett, *Letters of Members of the Continental Congress* (Washington, 1921), 90, n. 2.

27   Ibid., Silas Deane to Mrs. Deane, 90.

28   Malcolm, *Peter's War*, 78–79.

29   Malcolm, *The Tragedy of Benedict Arnold*, 81.

30   Malcolm, *Peter's War*, 97.

31   Ibid., 97.

Fourteen: The Horsemen of the Apocalypse Arrive

1   Warren, *History of the Rise, Progress and Termination of the American Revolution*, vol. 1, 95.

2   Abigail Adams to John Adams, November 27, 1775, L. H. Butterfield, ed., *Adams Papers: Adams Family Correspondence*, series 2, vol. 1, 329.

3   Malcolm, *Peter's War*, 106.

4   Abigail Adams to John Adams, September 1775, *Adams Family Correspondence*, 277.

5   Same to same, February 1776, ibid., 350–351.

6   Abigail Adams to John Adams, October 25, 1775, ibid., 313.

7   For information on slavery in Massachusetts see Malcolm, *Peter's War*, 3–24.

8   Bates, *Records of the Town of Braintree*, 464, 465, 469, 473.

9   John Adams to Moses Gill, Philadelphia, June 10, 1775, Edmund Cody Burnett, ed., *Letters of Members of the Continental Congress*, vol. 1, (Washington, 1921), 118. Gill was chairman of the committee of supplies, Cambridge, Massachusetts.

10   Delegates from Georgia were the exception.

11   O'Shaughnessy, *The Men Who Lost America*, 25.

12   Eliza Susan Quincy, "Josiah Quincy, Senior," *The Pennsylvania Magazine of History and Biography*, vol. 3, no. 2 (1879), 186.

13   O'Shaughnessy, *The Men Who Lost America*, 86.

14   Ibid.

15   Malcolm, *Peter's War*, 106.

16   Washington to Josiah Quincy, November 4, 1775; Quincy, *Memoir of the Life of Josiah Quincy*, 483–484.

17   Malcolm, *Peter's War*, 107.

18   Stark, *The Loyalists of Massachusetts*, 58.

19   This agreement to associate is the language used by Congress in its resolution of March 1776. See Oliver Wolcott to Lyman, *Letters of Members of the Continental Congress*, 397.

20   Hoock, *Scars of Independence*, 34.

21   Ibid., 38–39.

22   President of Congress to New York Convention, Philadelphia, October 9, 1775, Edmund Cody Burnett, ed., *Letters of Members of the Continental Congress* (Washington, 1921), vol. 1, 222.

23   John D. Sinks, "Oaths of Allegiance During the American Revolution," Sons of the American Revolution, May 8, 2021.

24   *Letters of Members of the Continental Congress*, March 15, 1776, Philadelphia, 390–391 and 391 n 6.

25   Malcolm, *Peter's War*, 121–122.

26   Ibid., 102.

27   Young Israel Trask would recount the incident in old age when he applied for a pension. Ibid., 134–136.

28   Malcolm, *Peter's War*, 134–136ff.

Fifteen: Strangers in a Strange New Land

1   Norton, *British-Americans*, 48–49.

2   Ward, *Journal and Letters of Samuel Curwen*, 567–568.

3   Writing in 1776, Norton, *British-Americans*, 42.

4   Ward, *Journal of Samuel Curwen*, 4.

5   Ibid., 4.

6   Norton, *British-Americans*, 66.

7   Sankovitch, *American Rebels*, 300–301.

8   Norton, *British-Americans*, 101.

9   Berkin, *Jonathan Sewall*, 119.

10   Rev. Isaac Smith, Exeter, to Curwen, London, June 6, 1776, Ward, *Curwen*, 57–58.

11   Stark, *The Loyalists of Massachusetts*, 249.

12   Norton, *British-Americans*, 78.

13   Ibid., 168.

14   Ward, *Curwen*, 567.

15   Cited in Norton, *British-Americans*, 52.

16   Ibid., 51.

17   Ibid., 51.

18   Ibid., 52.

19   Ward, *Journal of Samuel Curwen*, 40.

20   Ibid., 122.

21   Norton, *British-Americans*, 67.

22   For this information on the refugees, I am indebted to Mary Beth Norton's work on them. Norton, *British-Americans*, 52ff.

23   Ibid., 53.

24   Ibid.

25   Ibid., 55–56.

26   Maya Jasanoff, *Liberty's Exiles: American Loyalists in the Revolutionary War* (New York: Harper Press, 2011), 143.

27   Ibid., 138.

28   Samuel Quincy to wife, London, January 1, 1777, Ward, *Curwen*, 567.

29   Ibid., 567–568.

30   Samuel Quincy to wife, London, March 20, 1777, ibid., 568.

31   Ward, *Samuel Curwen*, 90.

Sixteen: Home Fires

1   John Adams to Abigail Adams, June 26, 1776, L. H. Butterfield, ed., *The Adams Papers*, series 2, *Adams Family Correspondence*, vol. 2, 23.

2   For details on the smallpox outbreak and innoculations see Elizabeth Fenn, *Pox Americana: The Great Small Pox Epidemic of 1775–82* (New York: Hill & Wang, 2001).

3   Abigail Adams to John Adams, Boston, July 13, 1776, ibid., 45.

4   There is confusion in the assumption that the first inoculation was in 1796 and that the Americans stopped using that technique in 1772. The Fenn book is a reliable source.

5   Same to same, Boston, July 29, 1776, 65–66.

6   Ibid., 66.

7   John Adams to Cotton Tufts, Philadelphia, June 30, 1776, ibid., 26.

8   Benjamin Franklin to Josiah Quincy, Saratoga, April 15, 1776, Edmund Cody Burnett, ed., *Letters of Members of the Continental Congress*, vol. 1 (Washington, 1921), 422.

9   Joseph Hewes to Samuel Johnston, Philadelphia, March 20, 1776, ibid., 401.

10   John Adams to Horatio Gates, Philadelphia, March 23, 1776, ibid., 405–406.

11   John Adams to Abigail Adams, Philadelphia, July 3, 1776, *Adams Family Correspondence.*, vol. 2, 30.

12   Same to same, July 3, 1776, ibid., 27–28.

13   Ibid., 30.

14   See Abigail Adams to John Adams, July 21, 1776, ibid., 56.

15   James Wilkinson, *Memoirs of My Own Times*, 3 vols. (Philadelphia, 1816, repr. 1973), vol. 1, 128. And see David Hackett Fischer, *Washington's Crossing* (Oxford, UK: Oxford University Press, 2004).

Seventeen: An Unexpected Turning Point: 1777

1   Abigail Adams to John Adams, Sept. 21, 1777, L. H. Butterfield, ed., *The Adams Papers*, series 2, *Adams Family Correspondence*, 347. First battle at Bemis Heights, Freeman's Farm, Sept. 19, 1777.

2   For information on Washington's inoculation of his army see Malcolm, *Peter's War*, 163–164. On the smallpox epidemic see Elizabeth Fenn's groundbreaking book, *Pax Americana*.

3   John Adams to Abigail Adams, Philadelphia, June 29, 1777, *Adams Family Correspondence*, vol. 2, 270–271.

4   Abigail Adams to John Adams, July 2, 1777, ibid., 273.

5   Same to Same, June 1, 1777, ibid., 251.

6   Abigail Adams to John Adams, Braintree, October 22, 1777, ibid., 356.
7   For a fuller account of the Battle of Saratoga see Malcolm, *The Tragedy of Benedict Arnold*, 216–225.

Eighteen: The Beginning of the End

1   Jonathan Sewell to Edward Winslow, September 20, 1778–January 4, 1779, Berkin, *Jonathan Sewall*, 125.
2   John Adams to Abigail Adams, Philadelphia, April 16, 1777, L. H. Butterfield, ed., *The Adams Papers*, series 2, *Adams Family Correspondence*, vol. 2, 224.
3   Hoock, *Scars of Independence*, 31.
4   Samuel Curwen, January 20, 1780, Ward, *Journal and Letters of the Late Samuel Curwen*, 232.
5   John Adams to Abigail Adams, April 30, 1777, *Adams Family Correspondence*, vol. 2, 228–229.
6   George Washington to Joseph Reed, December 12, 1778, Henry Steele Commager and Richard B. Morris, *The Spirit of Seventy-Six* (Indianapolis: Bobbs-Merrill, 1958), 804.
7   W. Bodham Donne, ed., *The Correspondence of King George the Third and Lord North, from 1768 to 1783* (London, 1867), vol. 2, 89.
8   Ibid., 96.
9   Abigail Adams to John Adams, Boston, October 25, 1777, *Adams Family Correspondence*, vol. 2, 358.
10   John Adams to Abigail Adams, Yorktown, October 28, 1777, ibid., 361.
11   Ward, *Curwen, Journal and Letters*, December 14, 1777, Exeter, 160.
12   Curwen to Rev. Isaac Smith, January 17, 1778, ibid., 164.
13   Norton, *British-Americans*, 95.
14   Samuel Curwen to Rev. Isaac Smith, Exeter, England, January 17, 1778, *Curwen, Journal and Letters*, 163.
15   Ibid., 167.
16   Martin Howard was a loyalist recently arrived in England from Rhode Island. Berkin, *Jonathan Sewall*, December 1778, 127.
17   Norton, *British-Americans*, 97–98.
18   In 1772 tobacco accounted for 80 percent of all Scottish imports from North America. See Jacob M. Rice, "The Rise of Glasgow in the Chesapeake Tobacco Trade, 1707–1775" *The William and Mary Quarterly*, vol. 11, no. 2, Scotland and America (April 1954), 179–199, 1.
19   Norton, *British-Americans*, 98.
20   Ibid., 111.
21   Samuel Quincy to wife, London, May 31, 1778, Ward, *Curwen, Journal and Letters*, 571–572.

22   Ibid., 572.

23   King George to Lord North, January 31, 1778, Donne, *Correspondence of King George*, vol. 2, 125–126.

24   Samuel Curwen to Rev. Isaac Smith, Exeter, January 17, 1778, *Curwen, Journal and Letters*, 165.

25   Curwin, *Curwen, Journal and Letters*, 192.

26   Donne, *Correspondence of King George*, vol. 2, 109–148.

27   J. W. Fortescue, *A History of the British Army*, 13 vols. (1899–1930), vol. III, 251.

28   Norton, *British-Americans*, 155–156.

29   Ibid.

Nineteen: Casualties

1   At King George III's 1761 coronation a large jewel fell from his crown. The incident was interpreted as a bad omen. Samuel Curwen to Mr. George Russell, Birmingham, Sidmouth, July 13, 1778, Ward, *Journal and Letters of the Late Samuel Curwen*, 197.

2   Warren, *History of the Rise, Progress and Termination of the American Revolution*, vol. 1, 257.

3   Journal of Lieutenant William Digby of the Shropshire Regiment, October 17, 1777, Henry Steele Commager and Richard B. Morris, *The Spirit of Seventy-Six*, 605.

4   Ibid., 866. They were expecting to march to Rhode Island to meet their fleet.

5   Hannah Winthrop to Mercy Warren, Cambridge, November 11, 1777, ibid., 867–868.

6   Lieutenant Colonel Thomas Anburey, December 7, 1777, ibid., 868.

7   Thomas B. Allen, *Tories: Fighting for the King in America's First Civil War* (New York: HarperCollins, 2010), 233.

8   Ibid., 234.

9   Philander Chase, "Years of Hardships and Revelations: The Convention Army at the Albemarle Barracks, 1779–1781," *The Magazine of Albemarle County History* (Charlottesville, Virginia, 1983), 41. When the British army was in Virginia, the army was marched north to Frederick, Maryland. Apart from some offers of exchanges, the soldiers were held until 1783, when the war ended and they were sent home at last.

10   Edmund C. Burnett, ed., *Letters of Members of the Continental Congress*, vol. 3 (Washington, 1926), 356–357.

11   Malcolm, *The Tragedy of Benedict Arnold*, 5.

12   By the end of 1778 there were nearly 7,500 provincials with the British army. See John Ferling, *Almost a Miracle: The American Victory in the War of Independence* (New York: Oxford University Press, 2007), 416.

13   Abigail Adams to John Adams, Braintree, 12–23, November 1778, L. H.
        Butterfield, ed., *Adams Papers, Adams Family Correspondence*, vol. 3, 118–119.

14   Curwen to Dr. Charles Russell, Antigua, Bristol, December 23, 1779, Samuel
        Curwen, *Journal and Letters of Samuel Curwen*, 227–228.

15   See Malcolm, *The Tragedy of Benedict Arnold*, 246–248.

16   James Thacher, *Eyewitness to the American Revolution* (New York:
        Longmeadow, 1994), 237–238.

17   Ibid., 238.

18   John Adams to Abigail Adams, April 26, 1777, Butterfield, *Adams Family
        Correspondence*, 224.

Twenty: Third Time Lucky: Yorktown and Peace

1   Abigail Adams to John Adams, December 13, 1778, L. H. Butterfield, ed.,
        Adams Papers, Adams Family Correspondence, vol. 3, 135–136.

2   See Malcolm, *Peter's War*, 164.

3   Ibid., 187.

4   Ibid., 188.

5   John Adams to Abigail Adams, Passy, November 6, 1778, *Adams Family
        Correspondence*, vol. 3, 116.

6   Commager, Henry Steele. *The Spirit of Seventy-Six*, 1090.

7   See Malcolm, *Peter's War*.

8   Thacher, *Eyewitness to the American Revolution*, 237–238.

9   Ron Chernow, *Washington: A Life* (New York: Penguin, 2010), 348–349.

10   Bates, *Records of the Town of Braintree*, 511.

11   Cotton Tufts to John Adams, Boston, October 29, 1781, *Adams Family
        Correspondence*, vol. 4, 239.

12   Richard Cranch to John Adams, Boston, November 3, 1781, ibid., 239–240.

Twenty-One: When the Guns Went Silent

1   Thomas Hutchinson to his brother, November 15, 1788, Stark, *The Loyalists of
        Massachusetts*, 176.

2   See Hoock, *Scars of Independence*, 362.

3   Maya Jasanoff, *Liberty's Exiles: American Loyalists in the Revolutionary War*
        (New York, 2011), 63ff.

4   Ibid., 67.

5   Ibid., 77, 87, 173, 254–255.

6   Ibid., 362–363.

7   Ibid., 363–364.

8   Ibid., 364.

9   Curwen to Mr. John Timmins, Wolverhampton, London, August 9, 1783,
        and August 6, 1783, Ward, *Journal and Letters of Samuel Curwen*, 385.

10   For their part the British refused to relinquish some of their forts in the
      Northwest Territory, while the Americans continued to confiscate property of
      citizens loyal to the Crown during the war.

11   Stark, *Loyalists of Massachusetts*, 171, 172.

12   Curwen, *Journal and Letters*, 568–569.

13   Ibid., London, April 19, 1778, 569.

14   Ibid., 571.

15   Stark, *Loyalists of Massachusetts*, 371–372.

16   Ibid., May 31, 1778, 371–372.

17   Ibid., June 10, 1785, 374.

18   Ibid., June 1, 1789, 375.

19   W. S. Randall, *American National Biography* (2000).

20   Benjamin Franklin, *Autobiography, Poor Richard and Later Writings*, (New
      York: Library of America, 2005), 356–358.

21   See Benjamin Franklin, *Last Will and Testament*, MS.

22   Berkin, *Jonathan Sewall*, 134ff.

23   Ibid., 140.

24   Ibid., 142.

25   Ibid., 150.

26   Ibid., 143.

27   To Mr. John Timmins, London, January 17, 1779, Curwen, *Journal and
      Letters*, 213.

28   February 20, 1779, ibid., 215.

29   Ibid., Curwen to Mrs. Abigail Curwen, Salem, from London, October 30,
      1783, 391–392, 397.

30   Ibid., 415.

31   Ibid., 416.

32   Ibid, to Noah Clap, from Salem, February 18, 1795, 418–419.

33   See Robert M. Calhoon, "Loyalism and Neutrality" in Jack P. Green and J.
      R. Pole, eds., *The Blackwell Encyclopedia of the American Revolution* (Malden,
      Mass.: Wiley Blackwell, 1991), 235; Robert Middlekauff, *The Glorious Cause:
      The American Revolution, 1763–1789* (New York: Oxford University Press,
      1982), 563–564; Jasanoff, *Liberty's Exiles*, 357.

34   Bates, *Records of the Town of Braintree*, 541.

35   Ibid., 540.

36   Stark, *Loyalists of Massachusetts*, 367.

37   Sankovitch, *American Rebels*, 348.

Index